The Conscience of the Game

BASEBALL'S COMMISSIONERS FROM
LANDIS TO SELIG   **BY LARRY MOFFI**

University of Nebraska Press
Lincoln and London

Part of chapter 2 originally appeared as "The
Winter Meetings, the King of Baseball, and
the Conscience of the Game," in *Baseball
and American Culture: Across the Diamond*,
ed. Edward J. Rielly, 249–58 (New York: The
Haworth Press).

Part of chapter 6 originally appeared as
"Baseball's Other Peculiar Institution," *The
Independent Scholar* 38, no. 1 (2004): 7–8.
Published by the National Coalition of
Independent Scholars, Berkeley, California.

Library of Congress Cataloging-in-Publication Data

Moffi, Larry.
The conscience of the game: baseball's
commissioners from Landis to Selig / Larry
Moffi.
    p.   cm.
ISBN-13: 978-0-8032-8322-0 (pbk.: alk. paper)
ISBN-10: 0-8032-8322-9 (pbk.: alk. paper)
1. Major League Baseball (Organization). Office
of the Commissioner—History. 2. Baseball
commissioners—United States—History.
3. Baseball—United States—Management.
4. Baseball—United States—History. I. Title.
GV875.A1M64 2006   796.357'64068—dc22
2006010479

Set in Scala by Bob Reitz.
Designed by A. Shahan.

to new generations: **Ethan Joseph Pomainville** and **Jamie Parr**

I profess in the sincerity of my heart that I have not the least personal interest in endeavoring to promote this necessary work, having no other motive than the public good of my country . . .

> **Jonathan Swift,** "A Modest Proposal," 1729

Contents

Acknowledgments

I am most grateful to the following people who generously agreed to personal interviews: Commissioner of Baseball Bud Selig and former commissioners Bowie Kuhn, Peter Ueberroth, and Fay Vincent; as well as Tal Smith, Roland Hemond, Cal McLish, Cliff Kachline, Bob Smith, Sal Artiaga, Bob Lurie, David Osinsky, Milt Bolling, Dan Wilson, Mike Moore, Stan Brand, the late Mickey Owen, Marty Marion, William Marshall, and Senator Mike Dewine.

In addition, I owe a debt of thanks to the Library of Congress and to the University of Kentucky for making available the papers and/or audiotapes of Branch Rickey and A. B. "Happy" Chandler, respectively. Also I am indebted to the authors of the following books and to the various newspapers I consulted, some more frequently than others: Ford Frick's *Games, Asterisks, and People*; Happy Chandler's *Heroes, Plain Folks, and Skunks*; David Pietrusza's *Judge and Jury*; J. G. Taylor Spink's *Judge Landis and Twenty-Five Years of Baseball*; Fay Vincent's *The Last Commissioner*; Bowie Kuhn's *Hardball*; Peter Ueberroth's *Made in America*; William Marshall's *Baseball's Pivotal Era, 1945–1951*; Jerome Holtzman's *The Commissioners*; Eliot Asinov's *Eight Men Out*; Robert Creamer's *Stengel*; John Helyar's *Lords of the Realm*; Connie Mack's *My 66 Years in the Big Leagues*; Bill Veeck's *Veeck as in Wreck*; Bob Costas's *Fair Ball*; Joe Morgan's *Long Balls, No Strikes*; William Cohen Finkelman's *Baseball and the American Legal Mind*; Robert F. Burk's *Much More than a Game*; William B. Mead's *The Explosive Sixties* and *Baseball Goes to War*; Andrew Zimbalist's *Baseball and Billions*; Marvin Miller's *A Whole Different Ball Game*; G. Edward White's *Creating the National Pastime*; Red Barber's *1947, The Year All Hell Broke Loose* and *Rhubarb in the Catbird Seat*; Gerald Eskenazi's *The Lip, A Biography of Leo Durocher*; Jules Tygiel's *Baseball's Great Experiment*; Harold

Parrott's *The Lords of Baseball*; Ira Berkow's *Red, The Life & Times of a Great American Writer—A Biography of Red Smith*; Doug Pappas and his extensive "Business of Baseball" essays from baseballprospectus.com; and the *Chicago Tribune, New York Herald, New York Times, Sporting News, Chicago Defender, Washington Post, Atlanta Journal and Constitution, Pittsburgh Courier*, and *Sports Illustrated*.

I am deeply indebted to many good people for their encouragement and support during my research and writing: to Paul Zimmer for putting the bug in my brain; to Richard Hart Moffi, Brandi Adams, and Mark Zollo, for their research assistance; and to Rick Zollo for remaining in my corner lo these many months. I am also grateful for the advice and assistance of Rich Levin, Phil Hochberg, Marty Appel, Eric Smith, Gary Gillette, Jonathan Kronstadt, Shep Ranbom, and Bob Hinck.

Finally, to my wife Jacquelyn for your uncommon support, your good common sense, and your great sense of humor: You're the best!

A Note to the Reader

This book covers the scope of the office of the commissioner of baseball, from 1920 to the present, though not chronologically. Nor is it exhaustive in covering the administrations of the nine commissioners to date. That was never my intent. It is a book about the office itself and one fan's relationship to that office. Specifically, it is one fan's journey across the often unforgiving and frequently mysterious terrain known as "the best interests of the game." It enters gullies and caves and nooks and crannies I never knew existed. Though it is informed by history—of the game and of the office and of the nine men who served the game of baseball in that office—it is definitively *not* a history. I trust the book itself to answer not so much *how* and *why* the office has evolved over the years but *where* we go from here with the office of the commissioner of baseball, a position I hold to be essential to the health of the game of baseball.

Except where indicated, directly or in context, quotations are from personal interviews, the majority of which were conducted from 2002 to 2005. Throughout the book I make clear distinction between major league baseball and Major League Baseball, and that difference is greater than typographical, a fact that will soon become clear if it isn't already.

Despite all odds, I consider this an optimistic book.

The Conscience of the Game

Prologue

Those were great days, but they're gone. > **Fay Vincent,** eighth commissioner of baseball

In 1997, when Paul Zimmer, then director of the University of Iowa Press, called to say he wanted to publish another baseball book of mine, I asked him, "What should I write about?"

"That's up to you," he said.

The next thing I knew we were talking about commissioners of baseball—Landis, Kuhn, Selig, and company—and the distance the office had traveled in almost eighty years. At the time, no one had written a book about the office, the nine men who'd served, and the office's influence on the game. The project struck each of us as a worthy undertaking, something that might have historical value while also appealing to core baseball fans, in other words Paul and me. Not for a moment did it occur to either of us that writing a history was out of my league.

I began my research that summer at the Library of Congress, attempting to build some historical perspective by reading back issues of the *Sporting News* and scanning the Branch Rickey papers, which the library houses. In late July I drove to Lexington, Kentucky, where I spent five days, from nine in the morning until closing, storming the University of Kentucky's Oral History Collection, specifically the A. B. "Happy" Chandler papers and tapes, and talking about the Chandler years with William Marshall, who oversees the library's special collections.

Meeting William Marshall, in a roundabout way, shaped this book. Minutes after shaking hands with him, I knew I would never write a history. The author of *Baseball's Pivotal Era, 1945–1951*, Mar-

1

shall talked about baseball during the Chandler years as only the most accomplished historians can: he turned everything into a story filled with suspense. Great stories! Great stories, and never enough. So with Marshall's "who-said-what-to-whom" details of those five eventful years as appetizer, I read and listened to and photocopied as much as I possibly could over the next forty hours. The drive home was glorious. Playing and replaying the hours of tapes that Marshall generously lent me, I kept turning the car onto the shoulder of the interstate so I could take notes, rewind the tape and copy down someone's exact wording, or simply remind myself: more driving, less listening.

Marshall had interviewed some of the most memorable people in baseball history: Chandler, of course, as well as Bowie Kuhn, Red Barber, Bob Feller, Leon Day, Bill Veeck, Ted Williams, Ralph Kiner, Gabe Paul, Larry Doby, and so many others. The collection also contained the voices and lives of folks who remain little more than asterisks in baseball history, players like Danny Gardella, a hybrid of Moe Berg, Joe Hill, and an archangel, who in 1949 sued baseball for reinstatement following his flight to and return from the Mexican League; or pitcher Rip Sewell who in 1946 herded his Pittsburgh Pirates teammates back onto the field like so many misguided ducklings rather than have them—shudder!—strike and form a union. I took the drive home at the most leisurely pace allowable by the highway patrols of three states, my head reeling with the voices and stories of another of baseball's great eras. Then, with the highway no longer running beneath me, reality struck. No sooner had I pulled up to my house than it occurred to me I had no idea what to do with this mountain of information I'd been gathering. Without a historian's nature, specifically Marshall's, the notion of me serving history was as likely as me hitting Roger Clemens. But I couldn't keep the voices and the stories out of my head. I needed a plan.

Without a plan, the research continued.

Then, in 1998, Jerome Holtzman published *The Commissioners*, a book that runs from Judge to Bud. Though there is much to take from *The Commissioners*—it's still the only book covering the nine administrations, and Holtzman's insider's view of the game gives the book an edge of authority—the work is an overview and is not as historically satisfying as, say, Marshall's or David Pietruza's biography of Landis, *Judge and Jury*. Holtzman, I'm sure, would agree. I felt a sense of relief and took some delight in the fact that Holtzman, the man who invented baseball's "save" statistic, had gotten me off the hook. That, conditioned as well by Paul's early retirement from publishing, was enough to relieve me of my blind ambitions. I felt strangely vindicated.

If the idea for a book was gone, the subject remained.

Baseball had been growing increasingly ugly since 1994, as ugly as Commissioner Landis pronouncing judgment over "the Chicago 8." The cancellation of the balance of that '94 season, including league playoffs and the World Series, by the acting commissioner, Milwaukee Brewers owner Bud Selig, likely was the death knell for the Montreal Expos, whose major-league-best record that season might have rejuvenated the franchise within its Francophone market.

"What's wrong with baseball?" was the question everyone continued to ask, four then five then six seasons after the strike year. Having already done a fair amount of research, I was smart enough to know I didn't have the answer and stubborn enough to think I could figure it out.

Commissioner of baseball. The title rattled my brain like a bad song that wouldn't quit ruining the day. (By now I had eliminated a strictly biographical treatment as well as the historical approach.) As a kid, I had learned so much from baseball. I learned math by figuring out batting averages, won-loss percentages, earned run averages. I learned about probabilities. I learned about language, the "sacrifice bunt" and the "error of omission." I learned chronology. Why was it so difficult now learning what I needed to learn? Were the bickering and name-calling and dollar-waving and union-busting threats just signs of the times or were they symptoms of an illness that actually threatened the game? Was there any hope at all that the commissioner would—or even could—act in good conscience ever again?

Conscience. Maybe that's what I was after. I began to think of the office of the commissioner of baseball as the conscience of the game. Not the man in office as conscience, but the office itself as the embodiment of conscience. Does the office carry with it certain responsibilities—to the game and its future, to the fans and to future fans—irrespective of, yet without disrespecting, the rights of labor, management, and the public (hell, of umpires and agents too and the very internationalization of the game!)? If yes, could the office withstand some serious retooling in order to accommodate the myriad—often drastic—changes that the game has withstood since Judge Kenesaw Mountain Landis etched his audacious law into stone eighty-five years ago?

Those were the questions. I believe I have found some valid answers.

It is probably utterly unjust that, as a bumbling nonhistorian, I have been the recipient of history's blind generosity, the beneficiary of fortuitous timing and what turns out to be some very memorable history. During the ten months following the 2001 World Series—which, of course, was preceded by a historic act of war against this country—and culminating in baseball's collective bargaining agreement of 2002, Congress held three significant hearings regarding baseball's (a) civic commitments and responsibilities, (b) legal restraints and obligations, and (c) ethics. Each hearing brought to light issues that spoke to the essence of the conscience of the office and its relationship to players, to business, and to fans. In its long and storied relationship with the United States Congress, never had major league baseball been called on to account for itself on the fundamental precepts of the office of commissioner, certainly never in so brief a time span. At a time when major league baseball's corporate alter ego, Major League Baseball, Inc., had seemingly relegated the office of commissioner to life support, conscience again seemed attainable.

As much as Bill Marshall's skill as a historian gave me serious pause regarding how I would go about this book, the congressional hearings of 2001, of 2002, and eventually those of 2005 served as a scaffold for its structure. Ultimately, I can say this: I have been more fortunate than I had any right to expect back on that July afternoon when I returned home from Kentucky. I was given a title, handed an argument, and discovered—both in myself and in the office of the commissioner of baseball—a restored sense of hope for the possibilities of the office and of the conscience that fans require of it.

Like any self-respecting fan of the game, I consider myself something of a "virtual commissioner." Bowie Kuhn once said that "every American boy dreams of being commissioner," which might have been true in a former time. (When I was a kid, my impossible dreams were equally succinct: to play major league baseball, to manage major league baseball, and to fly.) But I do have a warm spot in my adult heart for the sentiment of that same former commissioner, whose own fan-of-the-game apprenticeship included hanging numbers on the scoreboard in Washington's Griffith Stadium as a kid.

I think my own affection has to do, at least in part, with opinions and second-guessing. Opinions are so much a part of baseball. There's a lot of dead time in a baseball game, a lot of dead time to ponder futile questions. For fans like myself, opinions are about all we've got, and no one's point of view is voiced more strongly than the passionate fan whose skills fall light-years short of his love of the game. But there's more to being virtual commissioner than passion and cheap opinions. It's really a matter of birthright. In the wake of the "Black Sox" scandal of 1919 when eight members of the Chicago White Sox were banned from organized baseball for life, the creation of the office of commissioner of baseball was major league baseball's assurance to its growing population of fans that the game was legitimate. In short, ownership wanted those turnstiles turning. In a brilliant, if benighted, public relations gesture of good faith, the owners ceded authority over the game to a federal judge. Judge Kenesaw Mountain Landis saw to it that owners and players were as honorable as money and the times allowed. For nearly twenty-five years players and owners alike served what Landis determined to be the best interests of baseball. And he did it for us, the fans, just as major league baseball's sixteen owners had asked of him.

Justice on behalf of the game's public was not the exclusive achievement of Landis. Over the years, most baseball fans would agree, the game's best interests have been fairly well tended to by its commissioners. Happy Chandler, who succeeded Landis, saw to it that a small oversight on the part of the Judge, that black ballplayers were kept from playing organized baseball with their white counterparts, was rectified. Even some of the commissioners' more bone-headed decisions—Ford Frick's ruling designed to diminish Roger Maris's home run record, Fay Vincent's attempt at National League realignment, among others—were rendered in the belief that, on behalf of the fans, the best interests of the game were being served. In time we would even witness one of our own, the ultimate fan-at-heart, Bart Giamatti, anointed commissioner. Oh, but he did us proud, if only briefly.

What I love about being virtual commissioner is how kingly I feel, how confident I am of my imperious pronouncements. Still, though I'm only virtual I do worry. Not about the designated hitter or whether the mound should be raised another few inches. Oh, I have my gripes and a wish list I see no reason to part with: I would love to have watched a young Bernie Williams patrol the old outfield of Yankee Stadium; I wish someone would turn the music down between each half inning. But these are small luxury taxes on a game that, other than the recent epidemic of millionaire ballplayers, hasn't changed a whole lot in more than one hundred years. There is an inherent, undeniable value to an institution that has lasted as long—while sustaining a remarkably high caliber of play—as major league baseball has. As a then Washington Nationals outfielder observed the day after the first congressional hearing on steroid use in baseball in 2005, "The game will withstand this. Like it always has. It always weathers the test of time."

I worry about what happens above and behind the field of play. And though not a worrier, I found that I'd been worrying an awful lot. About the backlash of the game's rotten business affairs, which threaten not just the game on the field but the entire support structure of the past eighty-five years, a system that, with some conscientious fine-tuning could float us for another century or so. About the effect of the recent steroids scandal on the integrity of the game and its legacy. I worry that no one's minding the store. I worry that by naming Bud Selig, one of their own, commissioner of baseball—and then extending his contract—baseball's owners not only have usurped the impartial authority of the office but have destroyed its very integrity, its conscience. I worry that, after ten years of operation under an owner, the office may already be beyond repair, that whatever soul Fay Vincent left to the office has been shredded and reconfigured as that capitalized monster, Major League Baseball, Inc.

My questions are fundamental. Can a commissioner ever affect the conscience of the office in this era of players' rights? Does baseball need an overseer? Is the position even appropriate? Ever since Bud Selig was named acting, then permanent, commissioner, I had been hearing that the commissioner of baseball serves only ownership. This was a historic turn of events, owners designating one of their own to oversee the game. There was no more pretense to neutrality in the office, as Bowie Kuhn would remind me. Still, as hard as I looked, there was nothing truly new in the job description for the position, and much of what Commissioner Selig has publicly pronounced has been in the spirit of Landis's "best interest" credo.

What if, I kept asking myself, the commissioner chose to act independently? And the more I thought about it the more that seemed like the only viable solution to what ails the game. Couldn't many of baseball's problems be solved by an independent commissioner in whom both sides—players and ownership—had equal confidence? I was beginning to get a feel for what the late Robert

Hayden wrote in a remarkable poem of youth's knowledge of parental love, entitled "Those Winter Sundays," which ends:

> What did I know, what did I know
> of love's austere and lonely offices?

"Love's austere and lonely" office? The demands of conscience? Maybe I was simply dumbstruck by its absence.

Within a week of the 2001 World Series, when Commissioner Selig redefined contraction by announcing that Major League Baseball favored the elimination of two of its thirty ball clubs, the method to my madness began to reveal itself to me. What do we mean when we say, "the best interests of the game?" Whose best interests? As a kid, I would have answered, with great authority, "The fans! Who else but the fans?" And I would have been right. Don't the fans, who are responsible for making owners and players and umpires and MLB Inc. lawyers and the union reps and agents happy, have a voice in matters? Of course, we do! Our voice is the commissioner's! Eureka!

Ah, the mind, the repository of lost causes. No sooner had I memorized contraction then the term was pulled from the glossary. Baseball had been summoned to Capitol Hill, where the commissioner and others would testify before the House Committee on the Judiciary. Over the next seven months the Senate would conduct two hearings of its own, one on baseball's antitrust exemption, the other concerning the use of steroids by ballplayers. I have nothing but providence to thank for those hearings, and those that followed through 2005, which served as a context in which to do my work. I arranged interviews with former commissioners Kuhn, Ueberroth, and Vincent and with Commissioner Selig himself. I began to talk with people who had spent lifetimes in or around baseball. I began contacting Players Association team representatives, but needed to go no further than Mariners catcher Dan Wilson. I decided I would talk only with people who I knew loved baseball more than they loved their own self-interests or the ideology of their profession. Hence, I didn't speak with Marvin Miller, though I did repeatedly attempt to interview Players Association leaders Donald Fehr and Eugene Orza, with no luck. Through the summer of 2002 their counterparts on the management side of the fence also declined. Seems there was a gag order in place, and anyone who broke the silence faced a million-dollar fine. (All I wanted was an opinion or two.) When the umpires turned me down, I called it quits—I'm not half the man Michael Moore is.

But the more I pursued my new line of thinking, this sense of the "conscience of office," the more convinced I became that the crisis of conscience that has beset the office since 1992, accompanied by the seeming indifference of both labor and management to the game's best interests, must be addressed and that unless the powers that be in baseball (owners and players) restore the integrity of the office, the future of the game itself looks bleak. I found myself trying to formulate a sensible and cogent argument in favor of the efficacy of the office's independent authority—even today, when such thinking rubs hard against the grain of both labor and management. It would be one fan's plea to major league baseball—owners and players—to restore the authority of the office of the commissioner of baseball as independent arbiter of the game's best interests. At the very least, as Senator Mike DeWine would later suggest to me, taxpayers, too, have a stake in all of this.

Most baseball fans know the history of the game better than, say, dental hygienists know the history of dentistry. It's a fair guess that the brain of the average baseball fan swills on numbers and arcane information. What baseball and its fans don't need right now is a history of the office of the commissioner of baseball. But there remains an argument to be made here. And it's important to address it and hear out all sides, clearly and calmly, before the corporation that affectionately goes by the name Major League Baseball, Inc., swallows the office entirely, along with every last remnant of conscience.

Appearing at a congressional hearing is quite an opportunity to exercise one's conscience. My brother testified before the Senate once on behalf of residents of Vermont whose annual income qualified them for heating fuel assistance from the state agency he oversaw. He was remarkably eloquent as he rose to his moment, and he made that moment count. Not many of us ever have such an opportunity. Now, my brother is not the commissioner of baseball. Nor does he head the players union. But he took his stand upon the same stage as those men who, regardless of how accustomed they are to appearing in public, will seize the opportunity to brandish their integrity.

The six congressional hearings on baseball, between December 2001 and May 2005, offered an immediate focus for me. Attending each hearing I discovered certain concerns and concepts that resonate, not just on both sides of Capitol Hill, but from Landis to Chandler to Frick to Eckert to Kuhn to Ueberroth to Giamatti to Vincent to Selig—that's 1 through 9 if you're scoring at home, and the wildest triple-play rundown in history. Caught in the middle, I discovered three aspects of the game that make baseball (beyond its history) unique among professional sports: the original concept of the "best interests of the game"; the reserve clause and the antitrust exemption; and the minor leagues and the nascent international game. Given these unique conditions—unique among professional sports in this country—it seemed to me that an equally unique governing structure, an independent commissioner, merits being kept in place. In discussing these issues, I hope I have offered a sense of possibility, which follows a vital thread of history, for how the office of the commissioner of baseball can serve future generations.

Unbeknownst to me when I began this journey, I've learned that it's virtually impossible to think about the office of the commissioner of baseball without using as a continuum a combination of the administrations of commissioners Selig and Landis: Landis's for the resolute sense of ethics he put in place and consistently honored; Selig's for the larger perspective by which law and civic rights define the operation of the game today. More than anything else, however, what I discovered was the breadth and complexity of that "austere and lonely" office of the commissioner of baseball. (Landis made it austere, Chandler left it lonely—and it's been mostly lonely ever since.) Every commissioner from Happy Chandler to Bud Selig has suffered, to one degree or another, from not being Kenesaw Mountain Landis. And with the exception of Landis and Bart Giamatti, both of whom died in office, every commissioner exited, if not wounded or vilified, then certainly under appreciated. I appreciate them more now—including Commissioner Selig—even when I might disagree.

1. Baseball's Peculiar Institution, part 1

DECEMBER 6, 2001

Re House Resolution 3288 "To amend the antitrust laws applicable to the elimination or relocation of major league baseball franchises."

Commissioner of Baseball Bud Selig is as earnest as a car salesman or a Cubs fan—at one time he was both. His voice carries his message in that unmistakable nasal twang of the upper Midwest. Occasionally he leans forward, his fit and wiry torso seeming to hover, birdlike, in thin air above the microphone as he stage-whispers a conclusive something or other with a dramatic flourish of hands that, though totally unconscious, could easily be misconstrued as being timed for effect, especially considering the gravity of his subject matter today: whether Major League Baseball, Inc., can unilaterally dissolve a franchise irrespective of the will of the team's community, its fans, or its players. All of whom are protected, Congress has determined, by an antitrust exemption—the Antitrust Exemption of all antitrust exemptions—granted more than eighty years ago.

As rule riddled as baseball is, as mythologized as it has become in true history and lore, nothing—not the infield fly rule nor the suicide squeeze—is as open to interpretation and simultaneously indisputable as baseball's antitrust exemption, which for generations has determined that baseball, at least at the major league level, is more sport than business. It grants baseball a status unknown by all other professional sports. Today, the exemption serves once again as congressional carte blanche to call on the carpet Major League Baseball, Inc., in the body of Commissioner Selig, an easy target.

So, for the moment, indeed the remainder of the day here in

Room 2141 of the Rayburn House Office Building, Commissioner Selig will personify the institutional memory of major league baseball. Almost no one in the game today knows it better. (As a leader of a Milwaukee citizen's committee to stop the Braves from moving to Atlanta in 1964, Selig came to know, if not then to appreciate, on the floor of a Milwaukee courtroom, a young lawyer named Bowie Kuhn, who represented the National League in the Braves suit.) Owner of the Milwaukee Brewers from 1970 until he sold the team in 2004, Bud Selig's time inside the game covers the administrations of seven of the nine commissioners of baseball, including his own. Indeed, Selig has been eyewitness of and frequent participant in what—excepting Jackie Robinson's breaking the color barrier in 1947 and the very creation of the commissioner's office in 1920—is baseball's most evolutionary era.

In point of fact, Alan H. Selig is baseball's ninth commissioner and the man so many fans have learned to love to hate. Just a month ago, two days after a World Series that will be remembered as one of the greatest in history—both for the drama on the field and for the balm those seven games provided after the terrorists' attacks of September 11—the commissioner announced that baseball's owners would "contract" two of the game's thirty teams. The likely candidates, the Montreal Expos and the Minnesota Twins, could face extinction by the opening of spring training. According to the commissioner, the owners' financial troubles are so pervasive that baseball's "current renaissance could be destroyed."

Of course, what remains unspoken, if not unknown, is that the team Mr. Selig bought as the Seattle Pilots and moved to Milwaukee just days before the opening of the 1970 season was, in fact, a bankrupt franchise. Back then, it was a thankful Bowie Kuhn, as commissioner not counsel, who gave his blessings to that transfer of ownership. Taking some pride in staying the first dissolution of a franchise in major league baseball history, Kuhn turned over the keys to the man who would eventually become baseball's only owner-commissioner and who today will defend the euthanasia of at least two major league baseball franchises. But the great distinction between Kuhn's position more than three decades ago and that of Commissioner Selig today is that Kuhn never assumed the powers that today's commissioner and Major League Baseball, Inc., have. Back then there was no such thing as MLB, Inc., simply a lower-case definition—major league baseball—which, as antiquated as this sounds today, embodied both owners and players. And, despite all of his authority, the commissioner of baseball was but a guardian.

I can't speak for the media in attendance, the lawyers, or the corporate phalanx from MLB, Inc., but I'm convinced that the most kindly of fans still want to believe that Commissioner Selig will reveal some telling financial figures to justify ownership's decision to contract, not because we think teams should be eliminated but because we want to see some integrity restored to the office he occupies, some independence from the corporate behemoth that governs too much of the major league game today.

It's easy to willfully suspend disbelief and look to the commissioner to project himself as a man of conviction. That has always been the primary function of the office. I find myself thinking: If you'd never heard him in person before, regardless of where he stands on whatever issue, here is a man, you would conclude, whose heart is in the right place. Finally, though, even I have to admit that the commissioner's performance is like watching World Series replays and hoping against hope for reversals that can never be: that Bill Buckner will trap that demonic ground ball; that Kirk Gibson's long drive will fall just short of Dodger Stadium's right field wall.

This is not the first time baseball has been called to the mount to testify concerning the unprecedented antitrust exemption that the Supreme Court extended to it two years after Kenesaw Mountain Landis invented the office of commissioner. In 1958, for instance, in one of the most memorable testimonies in congressional history, Casey Stengel, addressing Estes Kefauver's Senate subcommittee, ran on for a good three-quarters of an hour in his inimitable Stengelese, an impromptu shtick that delighted everyone in attendance.

Early on, Kefauver told Stengel: "Mr. Stengel, I am not sure that I made my question clear."

To which Casey replied: "Yes, sir. Well, that's all right. I'm not sure I'm going to answer yours perfectly either."

"It was greeted as a great comic performance," wrote Robert Creamer in his biography of the legendary Yankees manager.

Commissioner Selig could use a Stengel in his corner, but there is no joy this morning on Capitol Hill. In fact, it's beginning to feel a lot like Mudville.

Most congressional hearings on baseball consist of a fair amount of grandstanding by a handful of committee members, a few loud pronouncements, and maybe a warning or two as cautionary hand-slapping. Truth be known, Congress would prefer a Stengel monologue to what the commissioner has to say. Besides, it's a good bet that most members of Congress—most baseball fans, for that matter—have no idea *how* the lifting of the antitrust exemption would affect the game.

But this morning's gathering is anything but a pro forma affair. The rank-and-file loyal opposition flanking the commissioner consists of Minnesota governor Jesse (née "The Body") Ventura, Minnesota Twins president Jerry Bell, and Steven Fehr, outside counsel for the Major League Baseball Players Association (MLBPA). Of the four, only the commissioner is in the hot seat.

Fehr explains the conspicuous absence of his brother by saying he is "sorry that Don Fehr, the executive director of the union . . . cannot be here today. He is at the players' annual executive board meeting being held near Dallas. . . . In any year, this is the most important week for someone who holds his job, and in a bargaining year that is even truer. [He] would be eager to testify in the future if you so wish."

I think he means for us to presume that the union leader's absence has nothing to do with the commissioner's presence. Which is nonsense. The union has nothing to gain by getting into a public scrum with the commissioner—it's like flipping Don Zimmer, a no-win for Pedro Martinez. (Besides, we are about to hear *written* testimony by the union's executive director that is damning enough.) Why would a union leader as savvy as brother Donald want to spare his opposition the pressure it has brought on itself by making himself a public target? He wouldn't.

In short order, the attention to politeness customary at the openings of most hearings gives way to a sense of purpose that baseball has never before encountered in a congressional hearing. Though no one actually states it, at issue is nothing less than the conscience of the game as embodied by the office of the commissioner of baseball. The tone of the testimony and the Q&A about antitrust, the heated arguments over relocation and contraction, and the allusions to conflicting bottom lines of profit and loss . . . each is a firm reminder of the extent to which the conscience of office has been compromised. Much to the dismay of many people who argue otherwise, the problem has less to do with the conscience of the man himself than with the ownership mentality that drives decisions these days.

The shorthand version of HR 3288 is the "Fairness in Antitrust in National Sports Act of 2001." The FANS Act. A catchy—and politically savvy, fan-generous, vote-gathering—acronym. But there is nothing generous about the committee's intent.

"For years the most feared phrase in the English language has been, 'I am from the government and I am here to help,'" begins James Sensenbrenner, House Judiciary Committee chair and Republican representative from the commissioner's home state of Wisconsin.

"In 1922, the judicial branch of government was there to help major league baseball. In a unique decision, the United States Supreme Court held that baseball was not a business and thus not subject to the antitrust laws. With minor modification, baseball's antitrust exemption has survived to this day. It is an exemption enjoyed by none of the other major league sports. Seventy-nine years ago major league baseball consisted of sixteen teams clustered in the Northeast and Midwest. Players were paid what was generously described as a pittance. Ballparks were privately owned, and genuine fan loyalty was built upon stars playing with the same team for most of their careers.

"Today thirty teams play in major cities throughout the country. . . . Players receive astronomical salaries, the newer parks [are] largely built with taxpayers' money, and free agency sends the stars from one team to another almost before they can warm their places in the dugout. The major argument for using taxpayers' funds to build new stadiums has been the economic boom brought to a community by having a major league baseball team.

"At this hearing we will receive testimony that baseball is in dire financial straits and that the antitrust exemption should remain. One of the many questions which baseball must answer is why so many teams are in financial peril with the protection of special legal status? . . . Perhaps the help given to baseball by the Supreme Court in 1922 really has not been so helpful after all.

"And another question to be answered by baseball is how a sport which grosses over $3 billion a year is still not a business when the presence of a team obviously stimulates business throughout the lucky communities.

"For years baseball has told Congress that it can heal itself, and it obviously has not done so, even though this year baseball has had record attendance and the best World Series in history. The numbers do not add up. Success on the field and at the box office should bring success to the bottom line. So maybe the Supreme Court's help . . . has outlived its usefulness, and the market should be allowed to work in baseball like it has in other major sports."

If enacted, the FANS Act would allow cities to invoke antitrust laws to challenge attempts by Major League Baseball to relocate or eliminate a franchise. As Sensenbrenner's long-drawn eloquence implies, neither the commissioner of baseball nor his fellow owners are, in the words of the late Bart Giamatti, baseball's seventh commissioner, re one Pete Rose, "superior to the game."

And now the courts are involved. Two weeks ago, Minnesota district court judge Harry Seymour Crump ruled that the Twins, under any ownership, are contractually obligated to play the 2002 season in the Metrodome, that God-awful bubble that serves as their home ballpark, which is precisely where Governor Ventura and Jerry Bell insist they belong. The frighteningly ironic precedent to Judge Crump's decision, however, is that forty years ago Selig, the owner of a paltry number of shares in the Braves, failed in his public campaign to keep that team in Milwaukee. This fact is never brought to light during today's hearing, but surely this apparent betrayal of the passion that initially drew him into the game weighs upon the commissioner's mind. At least I hope it does.

Michigan Democrat John Conyers, the bill's cosponsor, is characteristically more fervent and sarcastic than his colleague in expressing his own unhappiness with the national pastime. "I guess there may be somebody in America that really believes that baseball is not a business, but . . . just a sport," he begins. "And you may recall that in 1994, Congressman Mike Synar had thought . . . that the time had come to forget the partial exemptions, and every time the people in baseball screw up, that we take away a little piece of their exemption.

"So I come here very interested in what I have heard to be some tremendous accounting theories that the commissioner will put forward about how tough things are. And, God knows, I support the underdog, economically or on the field. I mean . . . that is the American way of doing business. Let's root for the little guys in baseball, like the owners that are hemorrhaging. . . . [T]his is a tough situation that brings us here. . . . [W]e are still . . . reacting to the Curt Flood episode in baseball history, and we remember that the owners got together—some say collusion, but I don't use those kind of legal terms—among themselves to reduce free agent salaries and were forced to pay a record $280 million in damages."

I'm struck by Conyers's usage, typical of members of the committee, of the term *baseball*. At the very least it seems a merciful gesture on their part, a gracious reminder that given their druthers—and unless the ownership side of the game refuses to discontinue shooting itself in both feet—Congress would prefer to continue to view the game as more sport than business, despite legal issues that all sides use at one time or another to suggest otherwise. But midway through the hearing, as the commissioner begins to muddy so many of the core issues about which he is questioned, the term refers less to major league baseball, the pinnacle of the game itself, than to Major League Baseball, Inc., that legal entity that binds the owners of baseball's major league teams as a corporation.

Congress's affection for the game is palpable. Even the harshest committee critic probably favors giving the game the benefit of the doubt, preferring to think of major league baseball in throwback Elysian terms: a more universal composition of owners, players, and umpires, that is, the highest level of professional baseball attainable anywhere in the world. Though I remain convinced that the commissioner understands that nuance, I am equally sure that the corporation of Major League Baseball has utterly no use for such warm and fuzzy distinctions, a position that surely takes a toll on the commissioner in his attempt to live up to the standards that the conscience of office demands.

"The record in minority hiring makes me wonder if the term 'affirmative action' has ever entered into the considerations of . . . these meetings," Conyers continues. In his rambling style, he invokes the sins of the fathers on Commissioner Selig and his brethren, though the commissioner does not deserve the barb. "And we remember what happened to your predecessor, Mr. Commissioner, when he thought that he could dare put the public interests ahead of anybody else's . . . [a]nd . . . the Minnesota Twins episode, which we won't go into now. This is going to be pretty interesting."

So much for understatement.

For the next three hours, including a news conference, the commissioner of baseball offers up highly questionable financial figures, sidesteps entire questions, and pays mere lip service to the principle of "the best interests of the game." By the hearing's conclusion he has alienated the entire panel, having long ago lost his audience of curious and hopeful fans, maybe even a reporter or two.

"There are clubs that generate so little in local revenue now that they have no chance of achieving long-term competitive and financial stability," the commissioner pleads. But his persistent allusions to his prized and (in his mind) definitive "Independent . . . Blue Ribbon Panel on Baseball Economics" of July 2000 have begun to sound like the defenseless whines of a child caught with his hand in the cookie jar. Besides, how curious is it that, as Chairman Sensenbrenner notes, one member of that doomsday quartet, Senator George Mitchell, is a member of "a partnership that is bidding between $300 and $400 million for slightly more than 50 percent of the Boston Red Sox?"

The Blue Ribbon Commission report is itself a fascinating compendium of statistical hogwash that would drive the most passionate of sabermetricians loony. Nearly 60 pages of the 107-page document (including 27 pages of updated material added to elucidate the commissioner's argument today) are graphs and charts that supposedly explain the plight of the "small market" ball clubs in Minnesota and Oakland, Kansas City and Pittsburgh . . . and let's not forget Milwaukee. One of the commissioner's arguments, based on the report, is that those small-market teams cannot fairly compete and expect to be successful without radical revenue sharing. Actually, there is a fair amount of support from many corners, including fans, for some "trickle-down" economics, so long as it's a thoughtful and moderate plan that takes the future into consideration. But the commissioner swings blindly at each fat pitch, bemoaning the prospect of baseball's bankruptcy. And still he continues to astound.

"It has become clear to us that moving a club during this offseason, given our current industry economic environment, would merely be substituting one problem for another problem," the commissioner says. "Again, although we are very proud that no club has moved for thirty years, we may well find that relocation can become one part of our overall solution in the very near future, but it is not the answer to the problems we are facing this year." Which is a little like someone who owes you a hundred bucks saying, ad infinitum, that paying you one dollar today would make nary a dent in the debt. Has the commissioner totally forgotten that the Pilots were not exactly on a tourist flight into Milwaukee?

"These people did not get the wealth they have being stupid," says Ventura, referring to baseball's owners, including their commissioner.

"I cannot understand how eliminating the Minnesota Twins or any team will help the Arizona Diamondbacks draw more fans or resist the temptation to pay their players more than they can afford."

In the volumes of the *Congressional Record* that consume much of this country's legislative archives, this is the first time in which a wrestler has ever gone head to head with the leader of a major American industry. When a wrestler gets the best of the commissioner of baseball God is *not* in his heaven and all is *not* right with the world.

"Over the past couple of years," continues Governor Ventura, "the government has spent hundreds of millions of taxpayer dollars to prosecute Microsoft for alleged violations of antitrust laws. Why? In light of what baseball is getting away with, it just doesn't seem fair.

"I am fifty years old. The Minnesota Twins have been around for forty of those years. Every person in Minnesota who is my age or younger has had a hometown team to root for pretty much their entire life. And that is just going to end because thirty major league baseball owners and one commissioner don't have to play by the same rules as everyone else?" (Ventura, of course, never mentions that his beloved Twins were once the Washington Senators, for which Commissioner Kuhn, a Washington boy himself, could not find a buyer who would agree to keep the ball club in the nation's capital.)

The commissioner returns to dollars and cents, prompted, in part, by the written testimony of Donald Fehr, which refutes most of the commissioner's assertions this morning, including competitive balance, revenue sharing, and the need to "contract."

"As did many others," Fehr has written, "I learned through press reports that Mr. Selig planned to use this hearing to open the books and (supposedly) end any dispute about the accuracy of the owners' claims to great financial losses. Indeed, the account I read went so far as to quote him as saying there would 'be no secrets.' Like many, I was encouraged by this announcement. On the basis of those assertions, I wrote to MLB's counsel, explaining that, given the intent to release all the economic data, I believed the MLBPA was accordingly released from any pledges of confidentiality with respect to the same underlying data. I had hoped with such a release that we would be able to assist the Committee and the public in its analysis of the owners' financial representations.

"Unfortunately, we have been informed that the owners contend that the confidentiality provisions remain in effect and the Players Association will be sued if any of its representatives releases or discusses any information that Major League Baseball believes is confidential. As a result, while the owners will use their data and their accounting methodology to explain the financial position of each of the thirty teams and the MLB to the Committee, the Players Association, for now at least, is hamstrung and will speak about this data only in generalities. As a result, we suspect that the Committee's ability to analyze whatever it receives from MLB will be severely hampered, as well."

D. Fehr is so brash! He loves throwing those roundhouse sucker punches in absentia. Actually, it's probably pretty easy sounding righteous when your adversary is the ownership of baseball's thirty teams.

"Our figures are audited three different ways," the commissioner states, committed, it seems, to obfuscation. "Players Association gets all the numbers, including all related-party transactions. The Blue Ribbon Panel . . . got the audited statements."

"Don't you know the union can't give these statements to anybody?" questions Conyers. "You just sent a letter, your lawyer, that you would sue Fehr."

The exchange that ensues pounds another nail in the commissioner's coffin.

Selig: Congressman Conyers, you have the audited financial statements for six years. The only reason you don't have them for the seventh year, it is not over yet. . . .

Conyers: What about the stuff I just asked for, sir? We don't have that.

Selig: All the audited—all the related party transactions have been audited by Coopers over and over again.

Conyers: We don't have any numbers. Staff keeps whispering in my ear we don't have the numbers . . .

Selig: I'd like to know, since they've been audited three different ways, what information are you looking for?

Chairman Sensenbrenner: The time of the gentleman has expired.

Conyers: Could I see you immediately after this hearing?

Selig: It would be my pleasure.

Some pleasure!

"A legal curiosity," is how former commissioner Bowie Kuhn describes baseball's antitrust exemption. Kuhn might well have called it baseball's final "peculiar institution," given the long-overdue end to baseball's segregation in 1947 under Commissioner Chandler and the eventual demise of the reserve clause, which bound players to the whims of owners. But for the time being, it is enough for the exemption to serve as the visible tip of an iceberg that Sensenbrenner, Conyers, and their colleagues have been floating before the folks who run the game in the hope that someone with some common sense might sit up and take notice that the commissioner of baseball no longer seems to be one of us, that he no longer serves the best interests of the game, and that he no longer acts as a conscience for what is best for the game today and in the future.

"There are sights you don't forget," Thomas Boswell will write in tomorrow's *Washington Post*. "Bud Selig sitting next to Gov. Jesse Ventura at a House Judiciary Committee hearing is one of them. Sometimes the punishment actually fits the crime."

Boswell, of course, is right. But I for one, fan that I am, wish he weren't.

2. The Best Interests of the Game

When I was a youngster, I had an ambition to become . . . the man who was responsible to nothing except his own conscience. > **Kenesaw Mountain Landis,** first commissioner of baseball

"The best interests have got to be *for* the fans," insists Bob Lurie, former owner of the San Francisco Giants, who has been out of the game for more than ten years now. Time enough to mellow. Life after baseball can be better than the game itself, for the right people. Lurie's one of them. He's still in San Francisco, only now his game is golf. But like any decent person who has spent much time around baseball, Lurie takes to heart all questions concerning the game's best interests.

"The best interests of the game make sure that the fans understand that they're treated right and that the teams are doing the job that they're supposed to. Everybody might like football a little bit better, but baseball still is the national pastime, and it's got to be kept at the highest possible level."

The best interests of the game are as fundamental to the office of commissioner of baseball as a fastball and a curve are to a major league pitcher. In the minds of most fans, and probably the vast majority of players, "best interests" have defined the mission of the commissioner since Kenesaw Mountain Landis conceived it on the fly in 1920. Whether the issue was gambling (the Black Sox scandal of 1919 and Pete Rose's betting habits seventy years later), civil rights (Jackie Robinson's breaking the color barrier in 1947), or club ownership (Landis and Happy Chandler prohibiting the sale of the Phillies and Browns, respectively, to Bill Veeck), Landis and the seven independent commissioners who followed him—Chandler, Ford Frick, William "Spike" Eckert, Bowie Kuhn,

Peter Ueberroth, Bart Giamatti, and Fay Vincent—took a mostly open-minded tack in their interpretation of what was best for the game. For nearly fifty years in particular, through the innocuous reign of Eckert, the "Unknown Soldier," the office seemed almost formfit to a common-law conscience, a long stint in loco parentis. Landis deconstructed Branch Rickey's St. Louis Cardinals' farm system monopoly "in the best interests of the game." Chandler suspended Danny Gardella for jumping his Brooklyn Dodgers contract and signing with Jorge Pascual's Mexican League "in the best interests of the game." Ford Frick deemed an expanded schedule reason enough to dismiss Roger Maris's record-setting sixty-one home runs "in the best interests of the game." If conscience wasn't always synonymous with common sense, so be it; the commissioner would have his way and always in the game's best interests. The very expression, "the best interests of the game," has served as a virtual preamble to an oath of office. Though the extent of the influence of a commissioner's conscience was curtailed when players unionized in the 1960s, every commissioner, including Bud Selig, has invoked "the best interests" credo. How deeply have commissioners taken to heart this oath? The most famous story goes back to 1942, when Landis had the chutzpah to write President Roosevelt and, all but equating the game's best interests with those of the nation, offered "to close down [baseball] for the duration" of World War II. Almost fifty years later, in the wake of the San Francisco Bay Area earthquake in 1989, Commissioner Vincent's decision to resume the Oakland–San Francisco World Series was, in part, a healing gesture to a community coping with devastation.

But where do those best interests stand today? Commissioner Selig's first ten years in office were as an (absentee) owner for whom his (former) chums voted to negate the commissioner's "best interests" authority, a move that the then-acting commissioner described as having "strengthened" the office. Though ownership restored the best interests authority—did this thereby weaken the office?—when Selig's status was changed from acting to actual, that influence today remains secondary to his responsibility to ownership. And though Commissioner Selig has invoked "best interest" powers often enough, he has been criticized for having abandoned much of the independence that characterized most decisions of his predecessors.

"I've gone back and really tried to understand," Bud Selig explains. It's a beautiful day in Milwaukee, and the view from the commissioner's office stretches forever beyond the harbor to the horizon where blue sky meets the lake.

"You could see the metamorphosis of the office. It started in the Landis years, actually, and certainly accelerated quite a bit in the Chandler years and in the Frick years. Bowie [Kuhn], who I'm particularly close to, as well as Peter Ueberroth, had to face the players association that nobody else had to face."

I've seen and listened to Commissioner Selig before, in public settings, congressional hearings, brief sound bites on ESPN, and I've never been sure of the impression he was making on me. But in person, one on one, and without television cameras running, he's direct and carefully sincere, it seems. He is decisive in his choice of words, stressing his points and saying my name often, in an emphatic and inclusive whisper. He holds my interest.

"Life was changing. And as life changed, so did the office. But the one thing that didn't change was the commissioner being there to protect the integrity of the game, in every way. Whether it's economic integrity, integrity when it comes to social issues—gambling, whatever else—but, yes, you do feel the *great* responsibility of protecting its integrity in every intrinsic way."

But it's Fay Vincent who truly defines *how* great was the responsibility. "The best interests of the game?" baseball's eighth commissioner throws the question back at me, in coastal northeastern Florida, two weeks into spring training. "It's like 'due process' or any other of the wonderful statements that govern our lives. I mean, what does due process mean? The fourteenth amendment really has a huge affect on our daily life. And the same thing is true with phrases like 'the best interests.' The wonderful thing about the 'best interests' is that it is not susceptible to easy definition, and it was written by Landis, to generate authority for his ability to make rulings that he thought were [just]. He created this incredible position of the commissionership for his own purposes; but like all offices it comes out of its history."

Fay Vincent is living proof of the vicissitudes of the "best interests of the game." It was at the end of his brief administration that the standard by which a commissioner ran the office underwent a seismic shift. Vincent had succeeded A. Bartlett "Bart" Giamatti, his friend and former boss, who died just five months after he took office. It was Vincent who stood shoulder to shoulder with the commissioner the day Giamatti banned Pete Rose from baseball. Years after Giamatti's last moment of public eloquence ("Let it . . . be clear that no individual is superior to the game. I will be told I am an idealist. I hope so. I will continue to locate ideals I hold for myself and for my country in the national game, as well as in all of our national institutions. The matter of Mr. Rose is now closed.") Vincent, even now in retirement, continues to field, flawlessly, all questions concerning the once ever-popular Rose, his betting on baseball games while managing the Cincinnati Reds, and his betrayal of the best interests of the game.

Such was Fay Vincent's lot, first as Giamatti's chief assistant, a position he loved and excelled in, then as the man many believe to have been the game's last true commissioner. Unlike Giamatti, Commissioner Vincent was never afforded the chance to affect the ideals he shared with the former president of Yale University. In a little more than three years, he saw the impartiality that defined the office and the conscience that oversaw the game's best interests wrested from him.

"Jerry Reinsdorf [owner of the Chicago White Sox and the Chicago Bulls of the National Basketball Association] was very clear," Vincent explains. "'I hate commissioners,' he said. 'They don't own anything, they have no money invested. Why should they be given control of my economic future?' He said it wasn't personal, though it got personal. 'I don't like [NBA commissioner] David Stern, I don't like you, I didn't like Bart. I don't like anybody who's making decisions based on some criteria that are not in my best interests.'"

Vincent pauses, reflecting on the transition years of the office, between Bowie Kuhn and Commissioner Selig.

"I think that after Ueberroth and Bart and me . . . the owners had all they could take of the three of us, for different reasons. So they went to an owner."

Today, the best interests of baseball, which Giamatti defined as "that resilient institution," are buried, as we might infer from Reinsdorf's alleged remarks, somewhere beneath the bottom line. They've come a long way, those best interests, though the change strikes many as antievolutionary. Between two extremes—the conscience that Landis brought to the office he created for himself and today's corporate doctrine that seems to wag the very dog—nearly ninety years of history and precedent continue to affect the game and the office that might yet "come out of" its own history, whole and once again effective.

In 1920, in an act of unprecedented (and never replicated) unity and common sense, the owners of major league baseball's sixteen teams chose Kenesaw Mountain Landis as baseball's first commissioner. The decision to appoint an independent overseer of, in the words of Landis, "the best interests of the game" was born of a complex crisis of conscience and economics stemming from charges that eight members of the Chicago White Sox—Joe Jackson, Ed Cicotte, Lefty Williams, Chick Gandil, Swede Risberg, Buck Weaver, Happy Felsch, and Fred McMullin—had conspired with gamblers to throw the 1919 World Series to the Cincinnati Reds. What motivated owners to choose an impartial "high commissioner" the next year was nothing less than good public relations spiked with a healthy dose of fear. If it's stretching the truth to say that White Sox owner Charles Comiskey, parsimonious to a tragic flaw (as were most big league owners of the time), was an active conspirator in the Black Sox scandal, it's fair to say that he had more than a few opportunities to force the players' hands and halt the scam, or else challenge them as mutual investors in a common cause known as success and pay them equitably for their efforts.

"The owners weren't willing to crack down on what had to be cracked down on," Bowie Kuhn, the game's fifth commissioner and the man with the greatest personal perspective on how the office has changed over the years, explains of baseball's dilemma back in 1919.

"Everybody knew there was gambling in the game. Would an owner-commissioner crack down on it? They thought Landis would crack down a little better. Well, he promptly proved he could do just that."

Prior to Landis's appointment as commissioner of baseball, organized baseball had been governed by a three-man National Commission made up of National League president John Heydler, American League president Ban Johnson, and a chairman, Cincinnati Reds' owner Garry Herrmann. If the authority of the commission and its chair was concerned with anything more than telling players which clubs owned their contracts, there is little or no evidence of it. Before the commission was decommissioned in 1919, it had run organized baseball since 1903—for the owners. Best interests? That would have been those of the owners. The hiring of Landis and the acceptance of his terms for an independent commissionership was a brilliantly conceived public admission of collective guilt, the seemingly inevitable solution for getting organized baseball on track and ridding the game of any traces of corruption. It would be another seventy years, until the appointment of Bud Selig as interim commissioner, before major league owners would be so united again.

Nineteen-nineteen, the end of World War I: major league baseball is enjoying a popularity it hasn't seen since before the war. Babe Ruth, in his last year with the Boston Red Sox, sets a major league home run record with twenty-nine, more than the total of ten of the sixteen big league teams combined. Attendance at major league games is up, and the game of baseball is on the verge of assuming its enduring designation of national pastime.

But don't look for daily "betting lines" in the local—let alone, national—paper. Public lotteries, of course, are a phenomenon of the distant future, and casinos, either on riverboats or reservations, belong in other countries. In a world where gambling, if not the scourge of the day, is mostly illegal, baseball's call to conscience becomes one of the more fortuitous moves in the history of business in this country, totally anti-Enron. The owners take drastic measures after having determined that the public's perception of their game cannot be taken lightly and needing to prove, they believe, that the product they're selling is beyond reproach—that the game played by the most talented (Caucasian) professional ballplayers is truly a sport, something greater than burlesque and more "honest" than business. Baseball's legitimacy, that the game is on the "up-and-up," is at issue, not to mention profits, less court fees.

In choosing Landis and in granting him absolute power, the owners most likely overreacted—not unusual, as history has shown—but they reaped immediate rewards despite themselves, as they have ever since. In the wake of the Black Sox scandal, and generations before anyone coined the expression, baseball's owners took a decidedly proactive stance. They went out and hired a federal judge, anointed him High Commissioner of Baseball with infinite powers, and met his asking price of $50,000 a year. His name was Kenesaw Mountain Landis. Judge Landis. "The Squire." And for the next two decades and into the 1940s he preached with evangelical fervor from a pulpit the owners had built to his exacting specifications. Meanwhile, down in the box seats, Comiskey and his gang of owners, cried, "Save us!" responsively and in unison, to the Judge's message that he would tolerate no evil, either among players or owners. "Save our game!" they cried out again, "and," sotto voce, "keep us out of court." (It was their opinion that court would prove unkind to their kind—as owners have long since discovered, if not learned.) More than a judge, the new commissioner was the Mountain, which the owners believed they had moved unto themselves. Under the Landis influence baseball prospered for more than two decades.

Landis's sense of conscience—his virtual commitment to it—was terribly underestimated by the men who hired him. In his very humanizing biography of baseball's first commissioner, *Judge and Jury*, David Pietrusza offers a key to what made Landis tick. "I do remember," Pietrusza quotes the Judge, "that when I was a youngster, I had an ambition to become the head of something. I mean the man who was responsible to nothing except his own conscience."

True enough. Nothing characterized Landis's public service better than his devotion to his conscience. The best interests of the game became his way of life. Of course, in 1920 baseball's owners lacked Pietrusza's insights. To them, way back when, Landis was the federal judge who had stonewalled an antitrust suit by the upstart Federal League against organized baseball, also known as the American and National leagues, in 1915. In time—on the Judge's clock—the plaintiff ran out of money and the parties settled out of court. But the $600,000 "buyout" was too little too late to salvage the Federal League in time for the 1916 season, a much more public, and profitable, demise than that experienced by the Negro leagues some forty years later.

But the owners had clearly misconstrued what Pietrusza calls the Judge's "strategic inaction" as tacit support for their institution, which they quite self-righteously referred to as organized baseball. As Pietrusza and others note, from a purely judicial perspective Landis had been inclined to rule in favor of the Federal League; on the other hand, he also believed that any decision against organized baseball would have damaged the game beyond repair.

Strategic inaction was a common course for many of Landis's judgments, both on the bench and later as commissioner, as Chicago's Buck Weaver would learn. But though some of his judicial rulings were appealed and overturned in higher courts (the most notable being the U.S. Supreme Court's reversal of his $29 million fine of Standard Oil for antitrust violations) his conscience never wavered. And in matters of baseball, his was the final word. The banning of the eight White Sox for life, for instance, effectively overruled a court's decision that the players were innocent (a far-fetched but legally binding notion despite the fact that four of them—Jackson, Cicotte, Williams, and Felsch—had confessed and implicated the other four prior to their trial). Once again, the owners believed, Landis would bail them out, though ultimately they expected him to succumb to their economic best interests and whims. It would not be the last time owners were wrong about what a commissioner they elected might do.

Prior to the Black Sox scandal, the appointment of Landis as the game's first commissioner would have been as inconceivable as today's twenty-nine owners giving the nod to Ralph Nader to serve as their leader. But just as there are no atheists in foxholes, crisis often brings out the best in folks, even for the wrong reasons. If Landis was the right man for the job at the right time, he was also the absolute worst in terms of the owners maintaining unconditional control of their own (Reinsdorfian) interests. For the twenty-four years he served in office, Landis did precisely what the owners had hired him to do: he held baseball accountable to its public and to a sense of justice that extended beyond profit and loss. It's not enough to say that Landis created the office for himself; he created it *of* himself. The conscience he brought to bear in serving a game he loved gave birth to the concept of the role of the commissioner as custodian of the best interests of the game. This assumption would serve as the standard by which all future independent commissioners would be measured.

It's pure coincidence that a man named Kenesaw Mountain had a face carved from granite. After all, it was the Civil War *battle* of Kennesaw Mountain (where his father, a Union doctor, was seriously wounded in one of the Union army's most costly battles) north of Atlanta, not the mountain itself, that he was named for. Born on November 20, 1866, in Millville, Ohio, Landis was raised in Indiana. He quit school at the age of fifteen, studied shorthand (neither of which accounts for the fact that his first name, unlike either the Mountain or the battle, is spelled with one *n* not two) and became a court reporter. He graduated from Union Law School in Chicago (now part of Northwestern University) in 1891, and at the age of twenty-six was selected personal secretary by the newly appointed secretary of state, Walter Gresham, in President Grover Cleveland's cabinet in 1892. (Gresham had served with Landis's father in the Civil War.) Later, in 1907 and in the aftermath of his ruling on Standard Oil, there was a groundswell of support for him as a presidential candidate. (Four years after he assumed the commissionership, there were similar grassroots stirrings for his nomination as President Coolidge's vice presidential candidate.)

At 5'6" and 130 pounds, Landis had a face that spoke good conscience. Stern and weather-beaten, it was so much more unforgiving than the man behind it ever was. At home, he seemed to have been something of a cross between Mark Twain and JFK. An article from the *Chicago Tribune* in 1916 quotes him about his family life: "Every member of this family does exactly as he or she wants to do. Each one is his or her supreme court. Anything for the common good of the family is decided according to the wishes of the whole family. Each one knows what is right and each one can do whatever he thinks is best. It is purely democratic. I have nothing to say and consequently I say nothing."

Yet that public image, tinged just enough by his Hoosier roots, served his authority well, and he seemed to have taken enormous delight in that fact, both as judge and as commissioner. When the Judge's face appeared in the pages of the *Sporting News* sixty-five and seventy-five years ago, the cut line always seemed to read: "The best interests of the game . . . "

The focus of the Landis office was inclusive; he went after owners and players equally. Long before agents and a union, players were frequently called to the office of the high commissioner. Following the 1921 World Series, Landis fined Babe Ruth and two of his Yankee teammates for disobeying his order prohibiting big leaguers from participating in postseason barnstorming tours. (Too "unorganized," one might surmise.) Noting with sharply focused enmity that Ruth regularly received special treatment by American League president Ban Johnson, the commissioner called Ruth "just another player in this office." In addition to the fines, and to drive home the seriousness of the offense, Landis then suspended all three for the first month and a half of the 1922 season.

Tris Speaker and Ty Cobb were called on the carpet over much more serious allegations: betting on baseball. Six years after he took office, Landis in effect acquitted the two future Hall of Famers of laying bets—in Cobb's case, attempting to—on a game late in the 1919 season. The case only surfaced in 1926, when the Tigers' Hubert "Dutch" Leonard, angered that his longtime friend Speaker (who was then managing the Indians) failed to claim the thirty-three-year-old pitcher following his release from Detroit (managed by Cobb) the previous year, turned over incriminating letters to American League president Johnson. Correspondence among three of the principals (Leonard and Cobb of Detroit and Cleveland's "Smoky" Joe Wood—Speaker was implicated only in testimony) indicated that bets were placed (though not on behalf of Cobb, whose money had come in too late). The bet went down on Detroit, which won the game 9-5, primarily because the Indians, which had already clinched second place in the American League and normally odds-on favorites, were facing Detroit's Bernie Boland, a diminutive right-hander with a losing record—but *not* against Cleveland, a club he "owned." Though betting on baseball games was neither uncommon nor illegal in 1919, Landis's precedent-setting decision seemed to apply equally well here as with the Chicago 8, particularly in light of accusations that the Cleveland club had thrown the game.

But ownership had a Bill Buckner of its own, Ban Johnson, to hold down first base in the late innings. For whatever reason, Leonard's self-righteous revenge drove him to Johnson, not Landis, as confessor. Johnson, in a failed attempt to out-Landis the commissioner—and win back ownership's favor from Landis—promptly barred Cobb and Speaker, two of the game's most popular players, from baseball, then challenged the commissioner to honor his

own precedent and uphold his ruling. Johnson, always the annoy-
ing mocking bird during the early years of the Landis administration, was taking on the airs of a virtual corporation.

In answering Johnson's challenge, Landis assumed his best judicial posture, heard Speaker's and Cobb's denials (a fact that Cobb
himself had documented in a letter to Leonard shortly after the
White Sox–Reds World Series) then declared each man innocent
of the charges and announced that he would do nothing to change
anyone's status in major league baseball. It was the old Federal
League no-decision in different clothing. The commissioner out-
smarted Johnson at his own game. Leonard and Wood were already out of baseball (no team picked up Leonard's contract, and
Wood was already coaching baseball at Yale). As for Cobb and
Speaker, Landis's only caveat was that their managerial careers be
consigned to the American League, which, as Pietrusza points out,
proved to be the commissioner's final dig at Johnson's reign as the
American League kingpin. By the time Babe Ruth blasted all Black
Sox backlash from the air in the upcoming season, hitting a major
league record sixty home runs in 1927, American League owners
had replaced Johnson with Detroit's Frank Navin. It was another
key victory for the best interests of the game and its conscience, as
embodied by the office of the commissioner.

Baseball historians typically credit the combination of Landis's
fierce conscience and Babe Ruth's equally fierce bat with "saving"
the professional game.

Myth goes a long way in determining how history interprets our
public figures for us. And though the myth of Landis was great, it
was never greater than the man or his decisions. (You could de-
scribe Ruth's impact in the same fashion: what he did on the field
and then the larger-than-life persona off the field.) Baseball was
more fortunate than it knows to have had that interesting combination around. Ruth set the standards playing the game; Landis
took care of the ethics, the best interests of the game, and with a
mostly impartial judicial mind.

"The game was not 'saved' when Landis banished obvious crooks like Gandil and Risberg and Cicotte," writes Pietrusza. "Nor did it become simon-pure because the dim-witted Joe Jackson was bounced for taking $10,000. Landis' most important action in the Black Sox case was his most controversial: banning [Buck] Weaver.

"Unlike Jackson, Weaver took no cash from gamblers. From all accounts it appears that he took no action to purposely throw the Series. Nor did he give his assent in any manner to the plot.

"Landis knew all that. When he wrote that 'no player that sits in a conference with a bunch of crooked players and gamblers where the ways and means of throwing games are planned and discussed and does not promptly tell his club about it, will ever play professional baseball' he was referring to the hapless Weaver. . . .

"What Landis did in banning Weaver was to *ex post facto* place guilty knowledge of crooked play on the same level as the deed itself. Landis ratcheted baseball's moral code up several notches, making it akin to West Point's Code of Honor."

Though hardly a pioneer of players' rights, Landis opened his civil court to players who believed they had been wronged by ownership. More often than not they benefited from his counsel. Cal McLish, who pitched in the majors for fifteen years, told me his own tale of Landis a few years ago. Still in high school, McLish and a ball-playing friend of his, Leroy Jarvis, were paid a visit by Washington Senators scout Joe Cambria in their hometown outside of Oklahoma City in 1943.

Cambria, McLish explained, "had us sign an agreement in Leroy Jarvis's mother's front room that we would go to Washington DC for two weeks and work out with the big club. Work out with the Washington Senators! And we agreed to go. All expenses paid to Washington DC and work out with the Washington Senators? Hell, it was a big deal! We couldn't wait. But it was just that, to work out.

"Well, what had happened, Joe Cambria . . . tried to make a contract out of it. The Cardinals had me come to St. Louis so I could meet Judge Landis and explain what happened. I told Judge Landis, 'Well, we signed on a napkin in Leroy's house.' And that's exactly what happened right there. But we're the cause, me and Leroy Jarvis, of that rule being written that you could not sign a high school kid 'til he or his class graduated."

Though his authority did not extend to the independent operation of minor league ball clubs, the relationship of a major league franchise and its minor league affiliates did fall under the commissioner's purview, particularly when the game's best interests were at stake. Landis often took it upon himself to delve into the inner workings of ball clubs and their movement of players through the minors, where the practice known as "gentlemen's agreements" allowed teams to hide players on various farm teams in order sign them later.

With only his own quirky, unconventional jurisprudence as precedent, baseball's first commissioner learned as he went and made his calls on the spot, often on the run in trains between his Chicago office and any one of a number of major league cities. He was a czar, but a czar with a conscience. And it was none other than Branch Rickey, who'd felt the wrath of the Judge as often as anyone, who once said of Landis: "At no point did he temper justice with mercy. And today who is there to say that he did not act wisely?"

The conscience that Landis invoked in office extended well beyond the fields and front offices of major league baseball. Albeit unofficially, baseball's first commissioner enjoyed wielding his scepter whenever invited to. His was the prototypical "people's court." In 1928, despite the fact that he had absolutely no jurisdiction over the issue, Landis ruled that a girl on an American Legion team in Indiana was eligible to compete with and against boys. And though there was nothing in the American Legion rule book that prohibited girls' participation, neither the folks back in the Judge's home state nor anyone anywhere in Legion ball felt godlike enough to pitch in his two cents over what was yet to be known as gender issues. Landis gave the girl his blessings—and an autographed ball.

But for all he accomplished and for the many changes he implemented, Landis was not a baseball visionary. Most of the issues that would dominate major league baseball for more than sixty years after his death went unacknowledged by him. He did nothing to encourage the integration of organized baseball. He failed to appreciate the structure of the minor leagues and, in turn, the major leagues' dependence on that system of player development. He had no use for night baseball and was convinced it would never catch on. And the reserve clause, which bound a player in perpetuity to the club that owned his yearly contract, was never threatened during the twenty-four years Landis ran baseball. In an office that he created from his federal courtroom, the man knew how to choose his battles, the World Series being one of them. With his office born of a World Series, Landis chose that annual rite to publicly, and in good conscience, represent the game's best interests.

Nowhere was the first commissioner more at home than in a front-row box seat of a World Series game. Probably the single most impressive image of the man in his time, the picture that is burned into the minds of all baseball fans, is of his craggy face propped upon his doubled-up fists along a box-seat railing, red-white-and-blue bunting billowing about him, as he sits in judgment of sport's finest hour. *He* was in control, a permanent fixture at twenty-four consecutive World Series.

To avert a riot in Detroit in the 1934 Series between the Tigers and the Cardinals, Landis ordered Ducky Medwick removed from the game after Medwick and the Tigers Marv Owen exchanged punches during a Medwick at bat. (When the Cardinals took the field in the bottom half of the inning, the locals bombarded Medwick with everything that wasn't nailed down.) Following the 1938 Series, in which an umpire suffered a broken nose, Landis decided that beginning the next year six umps would work the postseason. Landis also ruled that umpires must consult the commissioner prior to throwing a player out of a World Series game, his logic basic: fans had paid their money to see the best and should not be denied what they paid for.

One of his most legendary moments came just prior to the 1934

World Series. Landis had recently sold the sponsorship of the Series' radio broadcast rights to Henry Ford. (It was the first such sponsorship of World Series broadcasts; Ford paid $400,000 a year over the life of the four-year contract for the distinction of being the first sponsor of a Series broadcast—Landis had a bit of Commissioner Ueberroth in him.) In that context, Landis addressed the announcing team of Red Barber, Bob Elson, and Quin Ryan. Barber, in his book *Rhubarb in the Catbird Seat*, quotes from the commissioner's performance: "Gentlemen, I congratulate you," Landis preached. "You are the best in your business, or you wouldn't be here in this room at this time."

"But, gentlemen, this afternoon on the playing field there will be two ballclubs that for this year are the best in their business. They know how to play baseball and they know it very well. They have demonstrated their abilities over the full season. . . .

"Gentlemen, I wouldn't presume to tell you how to conduct your business. But I will tell you to let the ballplayers play—they don't need your help. Let the managers manage. And above everything else, you let the umpires umpire.

"When you arrive in your radio boxes today, I want you to know that the full power of the Commissioner's Office will see to it . . . that you will not be disturbed in your prerogatives. I promise you that not a single ballplayer will interfere with you at your microphone. . . .

"Gentlemen, you report. Report everything you can see. . . . Suppose a ballplayer goes to the dugout and fills his mouth with water. Suppose he also has a chew of tobacco in his mouth. And he walks over to where I'm sitting in a rail box, he leans in to me, and he spits right in my face.

"Report each step the player makes. Report how much spit hits me in the face. If you can see it, report how much tobacco gets on my face. Report my reaction, if any. Report what happens thereafter. Report but don't feel disturbed about the Commissioner. That will be my affair after I have been spit upon. Your job is simply to report the event."

Though great theater, Landis's soliloquy drove home his point: the best interests of the game must be served by all involved; and for a broadcaster, as responsible for those interests as any umpire on the field, objectivity would be the standard.

A hundred years ago a ballplayer's "rights" essentially consisted of his signature on the back of his paycheck. That changed somewhat because of Landis, but it was under his immediate successor that the changes in the game were most profound. The best interests of the game under the Landis trust encompassed many aspects of baseball and its growth; civil rights was not one of them. Born a year after the end of the Civil War, Landis had no interest in bringing black ballplayers into the majors. Though he ostensibly kept organized baseball free of gamblers, he also did his part to keep it free of African Americans. Baseball would wait until the judge had died in office before a former U.S. senator from the parimutuel state of Kentucky—below the Mason-Dixon Line, as well—would support Branch Rickey's signing Jackie Robinson to the Dodgers organization in 1945.

Four years before Rickey signed Robinson to a Montreal Royals contract, Landis did open the door to integration just a crack. "Negroes are not barred from organized baseball by the commissioner and never have been in the twenty-one years I have served," Landis reminded anyone who might not want to believe that racism was already so ingrained into American life that a formal rule prohibiting black ballplayers from competing in organized baseball would have been redundant. In stating this truth, the commissioner was responding to a remark by Brooklyn Dodgers manager Leo Durocher, who took Landis and organized baseball to task over that unwritten law.

"If Durocher, or any other manager, or all of them, want to sign one, or twenty-five, Negro players, it is all right with me," said Landis in summation of his position to the press. "That is the business of the managers and the club owners. The business of the commissioner is to interpret the rules of baseball and enforce them."

And it was that last brief sentence that summed up the Landis position on race and the game. Although Chandler did not independently seize the moment, he did act on his conscience and in the game's best interests in upholding what Landis had so accurately stated. Baseball's second commissioner shared a number of qualities with his predecessor. He loved and understood the game (he was in his backyard playing "pepper" with his sons when he learned of the bombing of Pearl Harbor on December 7, 1941). He was schooled as a lawyer (initially at Harvard, though he received his degree from the University of Kentucky, in 1924). And, having served both as Kentucky's governor and as one of its U.S. senators, his influence extended well beyond the fields of play and the box office.

Chandler made no bones about his love for his home state and would bellow out "My Old Kentucky Home" at the drop of a hat, or less. (The complete text to the Stephen Foster song serves as an overly long epigraph to his autobiography *Heroes, Plain Folks, and Skunks.*) Apart from their nicknames—"Happy" versus "The Squire"—Chandler differed from Landis most considerably in his sense of politics and appreciation of compromise. When it came to gambling, for instance, Chandler was understandably sensitive to the livelihood of the folks who once had been his constituents, and he walked so fine a line when it came to such a pastime that Landis would have considered it clearly against the best interests of the game. Like the Judge, however, the ex-senator's conscience could flip-flop on a number of issues. On the one hand, Chandler banished Leo Durocher from baseball for a year for consorting with gamblers; on the other, he approved Del Webb's ownership of the Yankees, knowing full well that Webb, through his construction company, was affiliated with Las Vegas casinos. Had Landis lived, Chandler's approval of Webb surely would have killed him.

Anyone who answers to the name "Happy" is a sitting duck to detractors, and Chandler's impromptu musical interludes, those unabashedly sentimental tributes to his home state, only encouraged those owners who felt he was doing a disservice to his new constituency. Where Landis had been unassailable, Chandler was most vulnerable, and his "inappropriate" homespun persona—he publicly referred to his wife as "mama"—was as good an excuse as any to find fault with the man. Of course, the owners found more than song to be amiss when they ended his seven-year term of appointment six months ahead of schedule. They had been schooled on Landis, and despite the independent authority that remained part and parcel of the office, neither Chandler nor any commissioner who served after him would ever be granted the powers that Landis exercised.

Among Landis's successors, however, Chandler continues to command respect. Peter Ueberroth, who succeeded Bowie Kuhn as commissioner in 1984, told me that of all the commissioners who preceded him he felt the "most kinship with" Chandler.

"I got a chance to know him," Ueberroth explained. "I basically decided that for . . . any World Series or All-Star Game, he would be invited to . . . be in the commissioner's box, as would Bowie, as an ex-commissioner. He [Chandler] took me up on every single opportunity, and he liked the fact that he was returning a little bit to the public life."

Though baseball's owners outwardly mourned the passing of Landis, lauding the accomplishments and progress the game enjoyed under him, the grudges they felt entitled to harbor against Chandler seemed to fester for years after Happy got the ax. It took thirty-one years for the man who outspokenly encouraged the integration of baseball to be inducted into the Baseball Hall of Fame. Even Frick, his successor, was enshrined in Cooperstown before Chandler, a fact that did not sit well with the game's second commissioner, who acknowledged in his autobiography that he "felt like the forgotten man in baseball."

It is easy to argue that whomever succeeded Landis inevitably would have faced undue retribution from an ownership that wanted its autonomy back. But the owners were cruelly unfair to Chandler, who actually helped modernize the game. The decision to oust the second commissioner was perhaps the first of ownership's pathetically shortsighted decisions with regard to the office of the commissioner and the game's best interests.

"He made a lot of tough decisions that he's not necessarily credited with, and it gets blurred," said Ueberroth. "I respected him . . . And he also did other things with his life. So I had a kinship in that sense, too."

What Ueberroth admired most about Chandler was the latter's "unbridled enthusiasm when he felt something was right. . . . [H]e wasn't afraid to make difficult decisions. . . . I wouldn't always agree with him, but I could get a 'yes-no' [answer] from him. . . . [On] 'what do you think about . . . ' things which baseball considers very important, one of the issues that I call more 'surface issues' that were not life-and-death in the game. . . . Things like the designated hitter. Things like bringing Mantle and Mays back into the game. I got close to him as soon as I became commissioner."

If Chandler felt snubbed by baseball following his retirement, he should not have been surprised. His introduction to the office was fraught with a foreshadowing of the clamps that owners were beginning to place on the conscience of the office.

"The owners were screwing around to diminish the new commissioner's authority. I didn't know that," Chandler wrote of the owners' desire to shift the commissioner's focus away from the best interests of the game. "Their idea was that the commissioner would merely be the administrative executive; they would do the legislating, make the rules. A lot of them were plain greedy. Looking out only for . . . their own bank accounts. . . .

"On July 12, 1945, the owners gathered at the Mayflower Hotel in Washington—while I was, of course, still in the Senate—to informally talk things over with me. That session began to take the scales off my eyes. And give me at least a glimpse of storm clouds on the horizon . . . .

"We all cheat, if we have to," Cleveland Indians owner Alva Bradley confided in Chandler, whose reply was as direct as Landis's might have been. "'Well, Mr. Bradley, I wish I'd known that before I signed on for this voyage because I didn't agree to leave the United States Senate to preside over a bunch of thieves. . . . If I catch you, be prepared to belly up. I won't be easy.'

"The Cleveland owner didn't seem to be listening very well. He went right on, 'You've got to learn to wink at rule breakers.'

"I gave him a sharp look; probably something like Judge Landis might have done. 'There are sixteen teams in this game,' I said evenly. 'If I wink at one, I'll have to wink at fifteen others. That's not a wink, that's a twitch. . . . When you get caught, don't crybaby. Just come on up and take your medicine."

If that sounds too (out)Landish to believe, imagine how ownership responded. For nearly a quarter of a century they'd been preached to from the same parable. Just come on up and take your medicine? Not during the commissioner's Happy life. Still, Chandler's unique status in his office depended directly on the spirit of the law that Landis had established. Schooled in politics, baseball's second commissioner was the last direct recipient of "the word," which he defined as the man who coined it intended: the best interests of the game. The conscience of the office was on the verge of fifty years of dramatic and radical changes. But not before a fourteen-year interregnum known as the Ford Frick years.

Though Happy Chandler assumed the authority of office with the gusto and sense of conscience with which Landis also served the game's best interests, he should have been wary. In his book *Games, Asterisks, and People*, Ford Frick, who succeeded Chandler, notes that both the first and second commissioners ran their office mindful of "the same precepts. Both men insisted that baseball officials, individually and as a group, operate in compliance with the rules that they themselves had laid down." The difference, of course, is that Chandler was not Landis; the owners took pains to stress that fact in writing. The judge's body was still warm in the ground when owners added a new twist to the major league agreement: "No Major League rule, or other joint action of the two Major Leagues, and no act or procedure taken in compliance with such Major League rule or joint action of the two Major Leagues shall be considered or constructed to be detrimental to baseball."

"In other words," Frick wrote in his memoir, "the authority granted to the commissioner under the detrimental-to-baseball clause was restricted, as Landis surmised, to acts that affect the honesty, integrity, and moral standards of the game. Joint rules and actions are exempt.

"At the same time, there was stricken from the agreement a final paragraph that provided that all signers of the agreement waived their right to file court action against any ruling the commissioner might make. This paragraph was dropped at the suggestion of lawyers who pointed out that the paragraph was without meaning, because no court would uphold such an agreement. Maybe they were right, but the paragraph, legal or not, did carry a moral obligation that strengthened the commissioner's hand."

Whether the new wording escaped Chandler's scrutiny or he simply ignored the change is not the issue. What *is* important is that Frick did *not* miss the point. In his fourteen years in office Frick never gave ownership cause to challenge his rulings, particularly with respect to his interpretation of the "detrimental-to-baseball clause," which Landis had taken to extremes. So confident were the owners of their control over *their* commissioner that less than a year before baseball's third commissioner retired from office the owners actually restored the spirit of that paragraph, thereby clipping their own wings once again.

Despite his affection for the judge (and Chandler as well), Frick saw Landis as being "intolerant of opposition, suspicious of reform and reformers, and skeptical of compromise. He ruled the game as if baseball were a courtroom and the players and officials were culprits awaiting sentencing for their misdoings." To Landis and Chandler, what was detrimental to the game was, ipso facto, not in its best interests.

Landis had applied this very liberal interpretation of baseball's constitution with impunity. But Frick, who had observed baseball up close throughout his adult life, first as a sportswriter and baseball announcer then as president of the National League, saw

Chandler's relatively quick ouster as a clear indication of the direction owners wanted the office to take. No amount of inference could change the fact that with gambling no longer the great threat to the game's integrity, the owners were taking back at least some of the powers they had once willingly relinquished to the office and its conscience.

Frick unquestionably appreciated and honored the distinction between what was *detrimental* to the game and what was in its *best interests*. Likewise he knew that only a strict interpretation of baseball's constitution would earn him a second term. But there lies an interesting twist.

In his memoir, Frick relates a particularly revealing Landis story. Frick, as the newly appointed president of the National League, "was sitting in the judge's private office when the phone rang," Frick wrote. "The judge answered, and after an exchange of amenities, sat for a time listening to the voice at the other end of the wire. Then he interrupted.

"'Listen,' he exploded. 'I'm the commissioner—not a personal nursemaid. You got yourself into the jam. Now get yourself out. There's no baseball rule involved. It's just a case of someone lying—you or him. If you want to file formal charges, put them in writing. Meantime, why don't you call [American League president Will] Harridge. He's the president of your league. Goodbye.'

"As he hung up, the judge turned to me. 'Let that be lesson number one on your new job,' he said. 'Never go looking for trouble. Let 'em come to you. And don't start bothering me with your own.'"

It was a lesson well learned. As much as Happy Chandler was known to sing "My Old Kentucky Home" in public, commissioner Frick's mantra was monotone and much more direct: "It's a league matter," he said repeatedly regarding one impending ruling or another because, as he reiterated in his memoir, "It *was* a league matter" (Frick's italics). Frick quickly turned out to be a laissez-faire commissioner or, as Jerome Holtzman says in his book *The Commissioners*, "more a chairman of the board than a commissioner, which was, of course, preferable to the owners."

Though Frick learned as much from ownership's mistakes as from the owners themselves, baseball's third commissioner had a grasp of the game's history that neither Landis nor Chandler possessed. As a sportswriter, he'd covered both Ban Johnson's relinquishing of powers within the National Commission as well as Commissioner Landis's coronation and many of his ensuing pronouncements. Put another way: Frick's forebears were too busy making history to be slave to it. Still, while serving as National League president under both Landis and Chandler, Frick had proved himself capable of making some history of his own. It was Frick's idea to open a baseball hall of fame in Cooperstown, New York; and in 1947, during the Chandler administration, when members of the St. Louis Cardinals threatened to boycott rather than play on the same field as a black man, Frick's intervention threatened the future in baseball of any Cardinal who refused to play against Jackie Robinson.

As commissioner, Frick's measured responses to the nuances that distinguished *detrimental* from *best interests*, those slight interpretations of wording that sent Chandler spinning into baseball oblivion, effectively shifted the balance of baseball power back to team owners. Under Frick, the geographical alignment of the game, as well as its population, changed drastically. The Braves moved from Boston to Milwaukee; the Browns flew the coop in St. Louis and settled in Baltimore as the Orioles; the Athletics took up a new home southwest of Philadelphia, in Kansas City; the Brooklyn Dodgers and New York Giants expanded the western reaches of the game by three time zones, relocating to Los Angeles and San Francisco, respectively; and the Senators moved to Minnesota disguised as the Twins. Even more radical was the addition of four teams, two in each league, including a new Senators franchise in Washington to replace the departed one. Clearly, expansion benefited owners and was in their best financial interests, and despite the loss of three sites steeped in baseball history such growth was in the best interests of the game. Older players saw their careers extended by catching on with new clubs; new teams meant more jobs for players; and geographic expansion created new fans. Whether any of this was of concern to Frick remains unknown, but his rubber-stamp seal of approval assured baseball and its fans that relocation and expansion were at least not detrimental to the game. Undoubtedly Frick's most memorable nondecision was permitting the sale of the Philadelphia A's to one Arnold Johnson. A business associate of Yankees' co-owner Dan Topping, Johnson promptly bought the Kansas City stadium from the Yankees—the ballpark had just recently been overhauled and upgraded by the construction company owned by Del Webb, the other Yankees co-owner—and moved the ball club to Missouri, with Commissioner Frick filing nary a protest. And he would keep his mouth shut throughout the 1950s, as the Kansas City franchise served the Yankees American League monopoly by buying, selling, or trading the contracts of more than forty players.

When Frick died, in 1979, the great baseball writer Red Smith penned an obituary: "He was a good man but will be remembered chiefly as a reluctant leader. He didn't think baseball needed a house dick and didn't consider himself one. He regarded his employers as honest men capable of making their own decisions and felt he was there only to administer the rules."

Smith is 90 percent accurate. There remains one memorable instance when Ford Frick did indeed shift strategies and go above and beyond administering the rules. For all that Landis and Chandler did in the best interests of the game, nothing came close to Frick's pronouncement concerning Babe Ruth's seemingly invincible record of sixty home runs in a single season.

Among his other tasks as a writer, Frick ghostwrote an autobiography of Ruth, whom he had been close to during Ruth's first ten years with the Yankees. Midway through the 1961 season, with Yankees teammates Mickey Mantle and Roger Maris each on a torrid home run pace that threatened Ruth's record, Frick announced that for a record-breaking performance to count, a player would be obligated to set the record in 154 games, rather than the 162 games that expansion had necessitated that year.

Maris, of course, broke the record, but not until the final game of the season. For more than four decades, Maris's record bore a footnote that qualified his accomplishment. Frick's ruling—the first in the history of the office that dealt solely with accomplishments on the field of play—was a blatant abrogation of the extent of his own (self-acknowledged) limited powers. In 1992, seven years after Maris's death, Commissioner Vincent removed from the record books all evidence of Frick's single expression of the conscience of office, when he struck the mythical asterisk and turned the record over to Maris, fully, which he rightfully deserved though never enjoyed.

It's fitting that the most memorable and controversial action during Frick's administration involved not the behavior, either socially or financially, of a player or owner but an interpretation of the record book. Whatever his true reason for the Maris decision, it was a judgment pronounced, at least in Frick's mind, in the best interests of the game. Weak? Perhaps. But it kept the conscience alive. For the remainder of the twentieth century and six years into the next, the conscience of the office of the commissioner and each man's interpretation of the best interests of the game, while severely restricted by ownership's financial interests, bore with them an allegiance to conscience in matters concerning the best interests of the *game*, no matter what Jerry Reinsdorf says.

If Frick was laissez faire, he was an egomaniacal revolutionary dictator compared to his successor, Gen. William Eckert. The general had a nickname, Spike, that suited a catcher, say a Clint Courtney or a Thurman Munson. But that is about the only thing he had in common with the game he was chosen to govern.

"Some of the commissioners were misplaced; General Eckert was a mistake," Fay Vincent offered. "The owners went to get Zuckert and they hired Eckert. They couldn't even spell."

The story that Vincent alludes to, and one that continues to hold some credence, is that the owners actually *did* mistake Eckert for another Air Force general, former secretary of the air force Gen.

Eugene Zuckert, whose name was on the original short list of candidates. Whatever happened with Zuckert's selection, no one knows. As for Eckert, he hadn't a clue about baseball or its history and no sense of where it ought to be headed in the future. Baseball's introduction to its fourth commissioner, as much of an embarrassment to the men who chose him as it was to the unsuspecting commissioner himself, became the norm during his three-year administration.

"I was at the first press conference, where he pulls out his notes and he gives a speech and everybody wonders what it's all about," Cliff Kachline told me. "He had pulled out the notes for a speech that he was going to make to Air Force pilots. . . . He didn't know which group he was talking to."

Kachline, who covered baseball for the *Sporting News* for nearly twenty-five years before serving as historian of the National Baseball Hall of Fame and Museum in Cooperstown until his retirement, is as generous as anyone I've heard in describing the general: "He was a nice man. And that was about it, I guess. Essentially, he made no contribution to baseball."

For blunders similar to the above—the owners assigned longtime baseball insider Lee MacPhail as both company clerk and point man for the general, though often to no avail—Commissioner Eckert was treated as something of a clown prince of baseball, an Al Schacht in business formal.

"Despite his ramrod military posture, Eckert had the universal hunger for acceptance," writes Holtzman. "This final indignity [his early removal from office] ate like acid into his soul. More than any commissioner, before or since, he was completely without theatrics, a handicap greater than his lack of baseball lore. Dedicated to caution, to going by the book, he was unable to give the illusion of vigorous leadership, the quality the owners most wanted."

However, if, as Holtzman points out, Minnesota Twins owner Clark Griffith was telling the truth when he defended Eckert's appointment and claimed that the owners knew precisely who they'd voted for, then the lot of them are shamed on two fronts.

On a purely personal level, the owners never accorded the man the respect that was due the office. But even more telling than their unseemly character flaws is that knowingly choosing a man so ill suited for the job at a time when baseball was well on its way toward a 180-degree shift in economics and labor, and with precedents to challenge the reserve clause already in place or on the horizon (as in Marvin Miller and the players' union), reveals a motive light-years away from anyone's interpretation of the best interests of the game. What we know now, in retrospect, was best explained to me by Commissioner Selig: "The reserve clause should have been modified five or six decades ago. People had to know the reserve clause wasn't going to last. And *that*, I think, is the genesis of many of our labor problems."

Although the moniker Eckert carried from his first day in office, "The Unknown Soldier," defined his influence on the game, his legacy—tied as it is to ownership's blind pride—cannot entirely be dismissed. After nearly fifty years under the Landis model it was Commissioner Eckert's naive reign that served as the fulcrum for the office of the commissioner and instigated a battle of best interests that would challenge each of the next five commissioners.

"I remember saying to Bowie one day at lunch," Commissioner Selig told me. "It was about an issue in the seventies, and we were getting *pilloried* . . . I said, 'Bowie it's not fair, the other sports are doing these kind of things. . . .' And he said, 'You ought to feel complimented. They hold us to a higher standard.'"

But there are two sides to every standard. "In 1981, when we were in the midst of a long strike," the commissioner explained, "I remember Mr. [John] Fetzer [owner of the Detroit Tigers] and I walked into Bowie's office one morning. Red Smith . . . had written (this is the fortieth day of the fifty-day strike), 'If Kuhn were still alive this wouldn't be happening.' Now some will say that's pretty funny, but Bowie did not. Bowie didn't think it was the least bit funny. And he was pained by it."

Kuhn's commissionership was filled with pain, much of it self-inflicted, some would say. But when Bowie Kuhn came to the commissioner's office in 1969, he was following almost twenty years of neglect of the game's best interests by commissioners Frick and Eckert. In addition, the new commissioner confronted the most radical changes in baseball since Landis had all but warned ownership: "You'll be sorry!" Kuhn wanted to pick up where Landis had left off, which is all well and good, but not when your model has long since faded from the consciousness of your employer, the owners.

All his life, Kuhn has loved baseball. As a kid he held a summer job hanging numbers on the scoreboard of Washington's Griffith Stadium, home of the Washington Senators. Years later, as he assumed the office of the commissioner of baseball at age forty-two, he still held fast to a vital image from his childhood.

"Landis was, I think, a hero for kids," Kuhn told me, "as President Roosevelt was a hero for kids. We were in tough times. The Depression. The war was coming. The war came. To me, the two greatest figures in the country were the president and Landis. I'm not kidding. Of course, I was a big baseball fan so I knew who Landis was, even though I was just a kid. . . . Those great pictures where he posed—he knew where the camera was at all times—were effective. I felt I knew who Landis was, just the way I knew who Roosevelt was. I think that Landis was a model for reasonably well-informed people who knew what was going on in baseball, the dominant sport."

But that was Landis, with maybe a dash or two of Chandler. And that was 1920, when baseball *was* the dominant sport. By the time the game's fifth commissioner took office, his beloved Washington Senators had long since moved to Minnesota, and the city's expansion ball club was just three seasons away from packing its bags for Texas—an event that would pain the commissioner because of his failure, despite genuine efforts, to secure a local DC buyer for the club. With two diverse interpretations of the best interests of the game at loggerheads, Commissioner Kuhn learned that running the office he believed every American kid dreams of could be a nightmare.

Kuhn came of age as counsel for a private law firm that represented the National League. With his insider knowledge and legal background, which was fast becoming a prerequisite for anyone seriously worth considering for the office, Kuhn seemed to have been groomed for the job.

"I grew up in a family of lawyers and judges and politicians. I was going to be a lawyer. If you're going to be a lawyer, why not be commissioner? It was in my head.

"I was going to be president, too, incidentally," he added, perhaps only half in jest.

Kuhn entered office hellbent on upholding the game's best interests, and during his first year he seemed well on his way to achieving his goal. He met with Marvin Miller, the legal mind behind the players union, to settle players' pension funds issues and vesting disputes. He also arbitrated two significant trades that were complicated when at least one player in each instance opted for retirement rather than switch teams. Encouraged by the commissioner, and in celebration of professional baseball's one hundredth anniversary, President Richard Nixon opened up the White House to all of major league baseball prior to the All-Star Game at Washington's RFK Stadium. Unfortunately, 1969 was the exception, not the rule. The following year, Curt Flood took baseball to court, and the reserve clause was five years from being challenged in federal court. By that time, Kuhn was still facing nine more rocky years in office, tilting at windmills that sported neon signs reading: Best Interests of the Game.

Given his legal mind and his sense of the game and its history, Kuhn should have been Joe Page coming out of the Yankees bullpen to save the 1947 World Series against the Dodgers. Instead, he was Brooklyn's Hugh Casey, who despite two wins and a save in that same Series, is remembered for the pitch that got away from Mickey Owen, in the bottom of the ninth of Game 4 of the '41 Series against New York. Bowie Kuhn might have had his moments, but his failures are what became the indelible memories of his time in the limelight.

"Bowie certainly loved baseball and knew a lot about it, and he really cared," says Vincent. "I think he tried very hard. I think he loved the job more than anything else. It's hard to do that. If you're so caught up with how wonderful it is to be commissioner you can't take any position that rocks the boat.

"Bowie had a lot of trouble. He did some good things, but he made some of the pivotal mistakes that cost baseball to this day," Vincent says. "The decision in the [Andy] Messersmith arbitration not to settle? They begged him to settle but he was an arrogant lawyer, he said we'll win in court. . . . And of course what happened is that created free agency and blew baseball apart."

Whether Kuhn was arrogant in choosing to represent baseball in court is moot. Free agency was inevitable. Besides, Kuhn's hands were tied: he was indeed working for the owners. All free agency did was make that fact very public. As Jerome Holtzman explains, it was during Kuhn's first meeting in 1970 with Marvin Miller that the union redefined, in writing, the scope of the commissioner's best-interests authority.

"Miller insisted Kuhn and his predecessors were employees," writes Holtzman, "selected by the clubs, paid by the clubs, and responsible only to the clubs. In May 1970, while most of the owners slept, Miller won a crucial victory: Hereinafter, player grievances would be adjudicated by impartial arbitration, and the commissioner's 'best interests' powers would be limited to protecting the 'integrity of the game.' It was the cornerstone for a sequence of stunning Players Association victories climaxed by the Messersmith decision which forced modification of the reserve system," that is, that a player could play out the option the team had on his contract for one year, after which he would become a free agent bound to no team.

Kuhn, himself, admits to some regrets. "The commissioner has the power, under the collective bargaining agreement as it existed in 1975, to withdraw from arbitration any issue if he felt it affected the best interests of the game. The free agency question should never have been resolved by arbitration, was never intended to be resolved by arbitration. If you read the agreement, it was specific on that question. And yet the arbitrator brushed it aside and said there was an overriding consideration, and he decided. And once he decided, trying to reverse it on appeal was difficult. I seriously considered taking that grievance and deciding it myself. I would have decided it in favor of retaining the system as it existed, but I would then have had the leverage to insist on modifications to the system, which would have been fair to the players.

"I had already put my shoulder behind a very important change, salary arbitration, and the reason I did it was to make sure the system was fair to the players. And that was a great help to balancing the system. But it was inescapable by 1975, '76 that you had to have some element of free agency. And if you didn't do it one way you'll get it another way. In hindsight, I probably should have taken the grievance and resolved it in a more orderly way, which I think I could have done."

That Kuhn bore the brunt of the blame was inevitable, though circumstances were certainly mitigating. Hardly a fan of Kuhn, Vincent acknowledges that the office had changed radically by the time Kuhn was elected.

"Remember," Vincent told me, "the commissioner's best-interests power is limited by the law. The union is protected by federal statutes; the commissioner is perceived to be an employer, a part of the ownership; so the commissioner's ability to say it is in the best interests of the game that some of the economic realities be changed, that power doesn't exist. Compared to what Landis could do, a modern commissioner is very sharply restrained by the Taft-Hartley Act and by the legislation that protects the right of unions."

But shouldn't Kuhn, of all people, have recognized that? If he did, that knowledge did not influence his interpretation of the powers of the office.

"The commissionership was *founded* on something very akin to a conscience-of-baseball concept. . . . I think Landis had to wrestle with conscience questions," Kuhn explained. "He wasn't running down to Washington to lobby the Congress on issues [like] television and franchise locations."

"I haven't agreed with Marvin Miller on much of anything," Commissioner Selig admits. "But Marvin said years ago, when he was tussling with Bowie on a daily basis, 'I don't care what they say, I represent the players.' Well, that didn't happen in the Landis or Chandler or Frick or Eckert eras. So all of a sudden it began as a huge shift in the office and Bowie got unfairly blamed . . . [by] people who really, to this day, don't comprehend it. I think it's horribly wrong. A month before he passed away, Bart and I were having dinner in New York, as we often did, and he said to me, 'You know, Buddy, I only have suasion over one side here.'"

To this day, Kuhn prides himself on having held firm his position. "I was the commissioner. I thought I had responsibility for whatever went on in the game that might adversely affect public perception of it. But you're talking to an old-line commissioner, so of course I prefer the model that began in 1920."

Despite sixteen years in office, a tenure second only to that of Landis, Bowie Kuhn was a frequent scapegoat of fans, owners, and the press. "Landis never had anything approaching bad press, on any subject that I've ever heard of," he says.

"There wasn't much bad press on anybody in baseball, if truth be known. Ruth, by today's standards, could have come in for a lot of bad press. He didn't, and so could some other people. They didn't. The press . . . almost viewed baseball as beloved as The Judge did."

Today, Kuhn's legacy strikes me as solid, though noticeably tarnished. Tarnished by baseball's first general strike and spring training lockouts. Tarnished by his battle with Oakland A's owner Charles O. Finley, who sued baseball when the commissioner negated, "in the best interests of the game," his sale of three players, Joe Rudi and Rollie Fingers to the Red Sox and Vida Blue to the Yankees, for $3.5 million because it would have subverted the game's "competitive balance." (Yes, that same competitive balance that Commissioner Selig has persistently invoked.) Tarnished by his head-to-head battles both with the union and the owners.

Tarnished by the advent of salary arbitration. Tarnished by his defense, in court, of the reserve clause. And tarnished by his own legal background, which often seemed at odds with the game he loved. Perhaps the greatest indictment of Kuhn, however, can be found in a moment of ironic testimony by Walter O'Malley during the Finley versus Kuhn trial late in 1976. O'Malley, the game's most influential owner, testifying on behalf of the commissioner, whose critics called him a pawn of the Dodgers owner, defended Kuhn's ruling as the act of a strong commissioner.

"My opinion," O'Malley stated, "is that we need a strong commissioner and that we would not be a self-disciplined, self-governed sport if we did not have one."

But Kuhn continues to stand tall in his defense of the powers of the office. Nearing eighty years of age he is still fit and strong. As the elder statesman of the office, he questions the direction it has taken over time, particularly the Bud Selig template: "I think that, inevitably, the powers have become more distributed, in the game. . . . A lot of people would say that's good: we're not an imperial country; we don't believe in things imperial; there's more democracy, you might argue, more decision makers.

"But I think that is a bogus comparison. Certain organizations need, and would be most effectively led by having, a strong hand at the top. . . . I've always thought in sports having one strong hand was desirable. Keeping in mind that if he was ineffective—or you can say, today, she was (I used to promote the idea that Margaret Thatcher ought to change her citizenship and be the commissioner of baseball)—if the strong authority doesn't function well, you fire that person and put somebody else in there to do the job."

And for that alone I commend him. Kenesaw Mountain Landis testifying in court in defense of his actions is unimaginable, yet it was Kuhn's only recourse as commissioner. By doing so, Commissioner Kuhn was putting the office and the entire notion of the best interests of the game to their sternest test ever.

As Vincent reminds us, "The wonderful thing about [the term *best interests*] is that it is not susceptible to easy definition."

The court agreed. Judge Frank J. McGarr succinctly concluded *Finley v. Kuhn et al.* by noting that, "the questionable wisdom of this broad delegation of power is not before the court. What the parties intended is. And what the parties clearly intended was that the commissioner was to have jurisdiction to prevent any conduct *destructive of the confidence of the public in the integrity of baseball.* So broad and unfettered was his discretion intended to be that they provided no right of appeal, and even took the extreme step of foreclosing their own access to the courts" (italics added).

Was the court right in upholding the commissioner's authority to nix Charlie Finley's garage sale? Probably not. Forty years before, another Athletics owner, Connie Mack, sold off a number of his stars, including Lefty Grove and Mickey Cochrane. But Landis did not move a muscle to halt the breaking up of a contending team, which would fall from third place to fifth in 1934, and for the next ten seasons never finished above seventh place, six of the seven spent wallowing in the cellar. Mack's defense was basic.

"It costs money to win championships," Mack stated in his memoir, *My 66 Years in the Big Leagues.* "You have twenty-five men on your team who feel they should advance, and deserve to get raises in salaries. If you can afford to reward them, it is the best investment you can make. If you can't afford it, there is only one thing to do—sell these players to someone who has the money to pay them what they are worth."

If Mack's motivation seems too above board to be true, it is. Finley would have quoted his senior verbatim if he thought the court would have bought it. But he knew better. Besides, his argument carried precedent: selling players had always been an option of team owners; it should have been an open-and-shut case.

After managing to stay out of court for years, being *in* court had become baseball's newest ritual, as common as spring training. Bowie Kuhn's entire term as commissioner was challenged on every front imaginable. And the commissioner responded in equal passion for all, often sounding more like Landis than the judge himself. That may have been his downfall. Clearly, the only true issue of the time involved players' rights (via the union), including Curt Flood's challenge of baseball's reserve clause. Everything else should have been addressed by league presidents or subordinates within the commissioner's office. Yet Kuhn lit into Jim Bouton for his insider's tell-all *ten years* after the publication of Bouton's (then) controversial *Ball Four*. As for the suspension of Mickey Mantle and Willie Mays for signing contracts for promotional positions with casinos, Commissioner Kuhn was much too Landis-like for the times. It has been argued that Kuhn, with his legal background inside baseball, was an equal match for union leader Marvin Miller and might have effected significant changes had he not been so dogged in his allegiance to the Landis conscience of office. Still, if Bowie Kuhn was quixotic as commissioner, at least it was because he was blinded by his love for the game and what he genuinely believed to be its best interests. There was a lot working against him.

In December 1984, I had dinner on the infield (it might have been the outfield) of the Houston Astrodome along with hundreds of other guests at the banquet of baseball's annual winter meetings. Unaffiliated with any official baseball organization, I was seated through a space-available agreement with the "front office" of a California Angels rookie league affiliate, Medicine Hat, if I remember right: a general manager and his wife, the club's office manager and her husband, and three summer interns from the local community college. The highlight of the evening was the crowning of The King of Baseball 1985, Donald Davidson.

Davidson was a midget, the perfect size for a king, particularly the King of Baseball, it seems to me, but not in the Eddie Gaedel mode. Davidson, I realized, surely was a man larger than size alone, as his newly acquired pedigree required. You could say of him that he was a man unconstrained by his size. Isn't that what we want from a king? Would the crown even fit, otherwise?

Davidson had spent his entire life working in baseball, mostly for the Braves. As a kid he was batboy for the old Boston club. Then, by way of Milwaukee, he moved down to Atlanta working wherever he was needed, mostly in public relations. It was clear enough from Davidson's selection that the King of Baseball must unabashedly love the game, at all costs. The previous summer I watched in awe as the longitudinally challenged Davidson frightened a 6'2" three-hundred-pound electrician to tears in a press box after a ballgame. Something to do with the latter's knocking a cup of ballpark beer onto Davidson's color-coded-with-felt-tip-pens scorecard. The colors ran like something Biblical, the Red Sea after the Israelites had safely reached the other side. Davidson had that kind of passion.

The commissioner of baseball that year in Houston was Peter Ueberroth. Just six months earlier, he had marketed the Los Angeles Summer Olympics to international acclaim. He won awards. His picture was on the cover of every magazine in the country. There was talk of him running for president. Hell, these were Landis qualities! To major league baseball owners in search of a replacement for Bowie Kuhn, Ueberroth was the prototype celebrity of the changing economic times. He came across as a marketing genius with a Midas touch. He was a practical-minded yet imaginative man—also somewhat aloof (very un-Landislike), which the owners delighted in, aloofness being a quality they shared, to a man and in corporation. I have no recollection of Ueberroth's presence at Davidson's coronation, though given his public relations acumen I cannot imagine him *not* being there.

On the Friday night of those meetings I attended a party hosted by Jack Kent Cooke, late owner of the Washington Redskins, who was trying to lure a major league baseball team to DC. (Talk about tilting at windmills!) But most of the cocktail chatter that night involved Ueberroth, as in: Did you hear, the commissioner *is* supposed to show up? And so he did. And everyone called him Mr. Commissioner. Never had "mister" sounded so regal. Though not king, he was kingly indeed. He had an aura about him that seemed to emanate directly from his title, commissioner of baseball: conscience of the game, if not the spirit.

As far removed as Ueberroth was from Landis, the office (as we like to say when we speak of presidents and other distant elected officials who rise to some significant occasion) would be the measure of the man. Ueberroth, in his own unique and strong fashion, was stepping up to the challenge, just as the five previous commissioners had. As Bowie Kuhn acknowledged, over the years the commissioner's expression of good conscience has changed with the man and the times. For Peter Ueberroth, a good measure of that expression was the bottom line, which always seemed to be written in black. So despite his occasional public derision of them and their antics, the owners loudly applauded Commissioner Ueberroth's vision, and though they ought to have benefited from the man's common sense and foresight, they found his most appealing quality to be one he shared with Eckert: concerning baseball, both were deemed distant outsiders.

That ownership could so consistently misread and not profit from—yet again—the man it elected to office is utterly astounding. The knock against Commissioner Ueberroth has always been that he didn't love the game, and I think that's wrong. He hasn't loved the game his entire life, like Selig and Vincent and Kuhn, but as commissioner he loved the game as much as anyone (certainly as much as he loved the Olympics). Which is what he was paid to do.

It wasn't until Ueberroth left office, however, that the owners appreciated—after first overcoming their outrage concerning "collusion"—how much he had in common with Landis. "I made it clear that they were asking me to work on drugs, work on economics, and work on the popularity of the game," he told me. "And those were going to be the three [goals of] the one term."

If his goals sounded lofty, Ueberroth wasted no time in meeting the challenge. Taking office on October 1, 1984, the day after the regular season ended and the day before the National League Championship Series began, the new commissioner faced an umpires' strike that potentially threatened the World Series. After the Cubs beat the Padres 13–0 in a game called by umps from the collegiate ranks, Commissioner Ueberroth brought the real men in blue back to work. At the same time he also warned the Cubs that unless management installed lights in the perpetually "dark" Wrigley Field, all future Cubs' playoff games would be played in St. Louis. Less than a year after taking office, Ueberroth instituted mandatory drug testing for all minor leaguers; and in 1986, in the middle of spring training, he suspended seven major leaguers for drug use. (In point of fact, the seven—Keith Hernandez of the Mets, Dale Berra of the Yankees, Joaquin Andujar of the Athletics, Jeff Leonard of the Giants, Lonnie Smith of the Royals, Enos Cabell of the Dodgers, and the Reds' Dave Parker—opted for a 10 percent forfeiture of their annual salaries, one hundred hours of community service, and random testing.) Three years after Ueberroth took office, attendance at major league games reached an all-time high of 52,029,664 in 1987. Unfortunately, that was also the year that independent arbitrator Thomas T. Roberts ruled that major league owners had colluded in refusing to sign 1985 free agents. And there would be similar findings concerning the '86 free agents by another arbitrator the following year. Blindly, the owners had followed their commissioner's advice: to refuse to bid on the contracts of free agents. They would pay dearly: $280 million in fines to the Players Association.

Ueberroth was always an independent-minded commissioner. Though the owners hired him and paid him, they did not own him. Lyndon Johnson once said: "Bobby Kennedy couldn't pour shit out of a cowboy boot if the directions were written on the heel." Commissioner Ueberroth's variation, which he voiced during the collusion years, was much more accurate than LBJ's one-liner. "They aren't capable of colluding," Ueberroth said of the owners. "They couldn't agree on what to have for breakfast." Once again, the owners underestimated a commissioner's conscience and his belief in the game's best interests.

"When I took the position," Ueberroth told me, "I met with the owners. I told them that, basically, I was not going to come sit in their boxes and watch ballgames; I would not attend . . . bar mitzvahs or bat mitzvahs of their children or their birthday parties or be social with them in any way, shape or form. . . . I would not call them because there were too many of them and there was only one commissioner; they could call me and I would return their call instantly. I would also give them very, very clear yes-no answers; I'd always want their input but I . . . didn't have any sense of being popular. And I also would only take [the position] for one term, a five-year term . . . start to finish. It wasn't necessarily received well, but I basically told them that before they elected me so they had a chance not [to] elect.

"Authority is 20 percent given and 80 percent taken, and . . . any . . . leader in any walk of life has a responsibility to *take* the 80 percent. And I think that's available, as any of the commissioners of any of the sports have that ability. . . . I certainly decided that I had that authority, . . . the authority to make independent decisions."

Ueberroth's most memorable act as commissioner (certainly his most popular) was his reinstatement of Mickey Mantle and Willie Mays. Two of the greatest centerfielders of all time, Hall of Famers, and icons of baseball's golden age of the 1950s, Mays and Mantle had been barred from the game by Commissioner Kuhn for taking public relations positions with two Atlantic City casinos. Ueberroth saw the positions for what they were: grip-and-grin jobs, photo opportunities, and for the most part considered harmless by the baseball public.

Their reinstatement, Kuhn told me, was "from a public relations point of view a very good decision; a terrible decision from baseball's point of view. For him [Ueberroth] it was probably OK; bad for baseball. But Peter really saw things . . . [as] almost like a commercial decision: Baseball doesn't need the cloud hanging over Mays and Mantle; they're two of the great stars; let's get rid of that cloud. That was more [about] making baseball more commercially attractive."

Ueberroth stands by his decision, which, oddly enough, is in keeping with the spirit of his predecessor's verdict. "At the time I had . . . a summer home, in Laguna Beach, and I took the entire file and read all of the Mantle-Mays information," Ueberroth told me. "Sat on the beach, and it took me the better part of the day.

And I kept waiting to turn a page and find . . . something that was damning or something that was wholly illegal, and frankly finished the last page and they just did not exist. Did not exist.

"I agreed with Bowie that it was unseemly for these two individuals to work in casinos . . . or be used in advertising, [and] it allowed me to work with the casino and the gaming industry to remove them from any advertising and not have them work the casinos. They would basically go on golf junkets and golf tours. . . . [N]either one had any meaningful amount of income or money saved, and yet they were two of the most revered individuals in baseball and did not deserve to be removed from the game. So I wasn't close on that one. And I respect Bowie's opinion."

Ueberroth is not without some second thoughts concerning his term in office. Reflecting on the changing office of the commissioner, he feels he "didn't fight hard enough with the Players Association regarding [the drug problems of] Darryl Strawberry and Dwight Gooden.

"Both of those guys," he told me, "needed constant monitoring and restriction on a year-round basis to enable them to stay in the game. Any drug expert knew that, and I gave up fighting to have them tested twice a week for the rest of their careers. And that would have kept them out of harm's way and they, in my view, both would have been Hall-of-Famers. More importantly than Hall-of-Famers, they would have had better lives, and their families would have had better lives. . . . [But] being in New York and listening to the media and listening to all the pressure every day, I gave up that fight too early. I may have lost it in the end, but I still gave it up too early. I think they would probably, in an honest interview . . . both confirm that. These guys were both intelligent; they both had God-given skills, and we just missed. . . . Baseball, the institution of baseball, missed for both of them."

Publicly, Ueberroth, like every commissioner before him, believed his role was to improve the game for all concerned: "Most important, for the fans," he pronounced upon taking office. But when asked for his personal assessment of his tenure the night he announced his resignation, a year and a half before his contract expired, he said, "When I took over, baseball wasn't healthy financially. Now it is." With the bottom line in the black, again, and his conscience clear, Ueberroth rode off into his personal California sunset (not unlike Eckert, though the general's exit was marred by his equally unmemorable entrance). Not surprisingly, Ueberroth is the only commissioner to leave office on his own terms.

Peter Ueberroth entered the office as "up-front" as any commissioner before or after. What he didn't tell his bosses is that he "would work hard on a successor—because I wasn't thinking about that at the time.

"But we did try and find a terrific person, more talented, . . . to take on the commissioner's role. Because it had been very sloppy with Bowie. They let him go then they brought him back then they had him on temporary . . . and all the rest. They basically, in my view, kicked him around, and he didn't deserve that; he devoted a great deal of his life to the game and he deserved . . . better reaction [from] the owners."

A. Bartlett Giamatti was that "terrific person."

A passionate fan of the game and a scholar, Giamatti had served as president of the National League during Ueberroth's commissionership. In fact, if he had not been mired in a most unbecoming strike by employees of Yale University, where he was president, Giamatti, not Ueberroth, might have succeeded Kuhn. Instead, shortly after the strike at Yale was settled, Giamatti was named president of the National League. In baseball parlance, it was Bud Selig who "scouted" and "signed" Giamatti.

In accepting the National League presidency, Giamatti romantically announced: "I am almost 50 years old, and I have fallen in love. I'm running away with a beautiful redhead with flashing eyes whose name is baseball." Being named commissioner must have been like waking on his honeymoon to the redhead *and* her twin sister. Conscience and the game's best interests, it seemed, had drawn new life.

Despite Ueberroth's presence (including his effectiveness as commissioner), Giamatti, according to many, was all but groomed for the job of commissioner of baseball. Others will say that his resolution of the strike at Yale established Giamatti as a union buster and merely placed him at the front of the line of candidates when Ueberroth stepped down. Both are exaggerations.

"When Bart took the job [of president of the National League] I asked him if it was a real job," Vincent told me. "He said, 'No, there's nothing to do there. All you do is supervise the umpires.' . . . Bart wanted to be commissioner and . . . eventually the owners got fed up with Ueberroth, the way they always do with everyone, so he was encouraged to move on."

Notwithstanding Jerry Reinsdorf's full disclosure and the obvious exception of Pete Rose, everyone loved Bart Giamatti. When he died of a heart attack five months after he took office, the loss, coupled with the banishment of Rose just days before, was monumental.

"That was a great loss to the game," Lurie told me. "He was a gentle guy. He could be very firm, but he was a fan at heart. That was the main thing. But he could also be very tough, in a very nice way. His whole demeanor, his whole attitude of how much he loved the game and what he did and how hard he worked at it. I think he accomplished some things, and he could have accomplished a lot more."

Gentle is not the word that comes to mind when we think of Landis, or Commissioner Selig for that matter. Yet gentle is how others have described Giamatti. Bowie Kuhn, for instance: "I don't think we ever found out what he could have been. I think he would have been a very, very good commissioner, with a traditional view of the office. Probably somewhat more gentle than my view. . . . Bart had lovely soft edges. He was a lovely man. I don't know anybody who ever knew him that didn't like him."

"Bart might have been my best friend in the world . . . ," Commissioner Selig told me, sounding wistful. The commissioner gazed across the room to a bookshelf and nodded at an eight-by-ten frame within which the two commissioners are, indeed, friends, glancing back at us, their eyes sparkling with a love of baseball that's palpable.

"He was a very good friend of Bart's," Vincent says of Selig. "He loved Bart. They were very close." As was Vincent, whose loss is inexpressible.

One of Giamatti's first acts as commissioner was to name Francis T. "Fay" Vincent Jr. deputy commissioner. The men had been friends for some time, and they appeared to genuinely balance each other out. In his memoir, *The Last Commissioner*, Vincent recalls the press conference following Giamatti's announcement that "the banishment for life of Pete Rose from baseball is the sad end in a sorry episode."

"Many questions were posed, from all directions, and Bart, naturally loved it," Vincent writes. "'Please, please, one at a time, ladies and gentlemen,' he said. 'All your questions will be answered. We'll stay here all day and into the night, if need be. Please, there are many of you, and only one of me. I'm just a baseball commissioner, wandering, as the poet said, *lonely as a cloud*.'

"Of all our moments together, this was my favorite. It was a little wink from Bart to me, a line from the Wordsworth poem, 'Daffodils,' which we both enjoyed: 'I wandered lonely as a cloud / That floats on high o'er vales and hills, . . .'

"We had long had a private game in which the opening line of that poem was a signal between us, a way to acknowledge our love for Wordsworth, a private acknowledgement of each other in the most public of settings. To me, it was Bart saying, 'Good to be with you, old pal.'"

One obvious measure of the friendship the two men shared is the level of responsibility that Giamatti had transferred to his deputy. Previous commissioners had also appointed deputies—Landis, for instance, had Leslie O'Connor—but none commanded Vincent's authority.

"Bart's idea," Vincent explained to me, "was that he wanted to be much more the public figure, he wanted to be involved in the external world—that was his great strength—and I had run big businesses. So, he said, 'You run the business and I'll do a lot of the public relations; the public work.' For the two of us, that was perfect.

"It was a good model. It worked for us. . . . I was a lawyer . . . and a lot of baseball, unfortunately, involves legal stuff. He didn't want to be bothered with any of that, [and] I could deal with it. When we got to Rose, I could both negotiate the problem with Rose's lawyer and write the contract, which I did. . . . [T]he organization has to suit the people, and in this case the organization suited Bart and me.

"I really was in on everything that Bart did, and I think any good deputy will be. . . . It's just that Bart's strengths were not worrying about the details of licensing or worrying about running the office or worrying about 401(k) plans for employees or . . . legal ramifications. He was much more interested in the policy, the major initiatives that he . . . wanted to focus on and lecture about."

It was spring training, and major league baseball was just beginning its exhibition season when Vincent hired a friend, John Dowd, to investigate allegations passed on to the new administration by outgoing Commissioner Ueberroth, that Pete Rose had bet on baseball games, including those involving the team he managed, the Cincinnati Reds. "Peter handled these early discussions with admirable patience," Vincent wrote in his 'Baseball Valentine.' "Ueberroth felt it would be best if he could deal with the Rose matter before he left office, which was decent of him, but unrealistic.

"Bart admired Rose. Early in his career, Rose was a second baseman, and Bart always liked second basemen, who are often less physically gifted than their teammates, but overachievers in every other way. Bobby Doerr was Bart's childhood hero. Bart admired the way Rose accepted the thirty-day suspension Bart handed him for bumping Dave Pallone, the umpire. Rose was enough of a baseball man to understand Bart's message in handing down such a severe punishment: *Nobody touches my umpires*" (Vincent's italics).

Dowd pursued the allegations against Rose with a diligence that Rose himself possessed and was loved for. Dowd, Vincent writes, "had experience as a head of a Justice Department strike force conducting Mafia investigations. [He] advised us that the baseball investigation would be difficult because, in a private proceeding, baseball does not have the power to subpoena. Still, Dowd said there are always ways to get information. Dowd was a pro; a former Marine with a towering physical presence, he had the charm of the Irish and the hard-edged tenacity of a big-time prosecutor. He knew what he was doing and therefore had a calming effect on Bart, on all of us."

The betting life of Pete Rose consumed Giamatti's entirely too fleeting commissionership. The stress the commissioner felt over the potential implications of the Rose investigation was apparent and, as Vincent acknowledges, it tested their friendship.

In response to Rose's suit against the commissioner, a Cincinnati judge issued a restraining order against baseball while he considered the merits of the case.

Commissioner Giamatti began to worry enough for all of baseball.

Vincent attempted to assure his friend that eventually they would have their injunction to move the case to federal court and a neutral field. Which, of course, is what happened. But not before the press and the public built up their own case of outrage over the commissioner's audacity: Pete Rose had 4,256 base hits in his major league career, more than anyone who ever played in the majors, more than that other equally lovable legend, Ty Cobb. A. Bartlett Giamatti may have had more degrees than a thermometer and a dozen initials after his name but nary a cup of coffee in big league—any league!—baseball. Or, as writers used to say about the longtime backup catcher Moe Berg, who served as a spy during World War II: he spoke seven languages and couldn't hit in any. To those inside the game, Pete Rose was Mr. Baseball; Bart Giamatti may have been the commissioner of baseball, but he was *only* the commissioner.

The Rose investigation tested Bart Giamatti's patience as never before; not even the strike he faced as president of Yale compared to this. Neither he nor the little patience he brought with him to the office were faring very well. This was baseball, and at issue were the best interests of the game that Landis himself invoked when he banned another of the game's great hitters, Joe Jackson.

"I kept saying to Bart: 'The system works. You have to have faith in the system. We will prevail,'" Vincent writes. "I had been saying that to him for so long it ultimately became a standing joke between us. Bart would say to Dowd or to anyone who happened to be in the room, 'Here is a man who believes in the system, who believes the system will prevail!' Typically, he would say this with mirth. 'Can you believe this, a man of Mr. Vincent's abilities who believes in the system!' It was funny. But soon the mirth disappeared and his mood darkened."

Fay Vincent was schooled on patience, in part, from his training in the law, but more importantly as the result of a forty-foot fall from the roof of his dormitory at Williams College in 1956. Vincent, a standout tackle on the Williams's freshman football team, suffered spinal cord damage and substantial paralysis. His athletic career was over; he was fortunate to be alive. Hospitalized and suspended in a contraption that kept him virtually motionless, Vincent became depressed, a condition his mother helped resolve by playing Gershwin's "Rhapsody in Blue" "loudly and saying above it, 'Isn't that lovely? Isn't that beautiful?'" he writes.

"I have never since enjoyed a piece of music as I did that afternoon in my hospital room. She had made her point. On that day I abandoned my life as an athlete, forced though the departure was, and embraced the life of the mind."

But Vincent's dear friend Bart Giamatti was putting a strain on his deputy's hard-won endurance. Vincent considered quitting: "to save the friendship," he writes. Eventually, Vincent's belief in the system prevailed, and the friendship, if anything, strengthened. In time, Rose was banished and Giamatti, perhaps, achieved a small measure of the patience his friend seemed to command. Did the

Rose investigation and everything that surrounded it kill Bart Giamatti? Not entirely. Officially, the cause of death was a massive heart attack, not an obsession with something as fuzzy as "the best interests of the game" or the conscience of office. The gentleness that so many saw in Giamatti was a complex quality, but it did not conflict with his resolve in upholding those interests.

"I think Bart would have left baseball in a year," Vincent told me. "I think baseball would have driven him crazy. And the union labor problems. . . . He had problems with the union at Yale and that's what drove him away from Yale. I think after 1990 he would have left baseball immediately. . . . I think he was ready to move on. I think he would have run for office. He was looking for a bigger stage."

The emptiness that baseball felt following Giamatti's death was as heartfelt as the void the game experienced following Landis's death, twenty-four years after he was sworn in. Though Vincent was the logical choice to succeed his friend, he was practically doomed from the start. By the time Vincent took office, the owners had learned to see through their commissioner, finally. This one was the lowest of the lot: he was nothing more than a fan.

"The problem is that every commissioner, the minute he gets there, someone tries to get rid of him," Vincent explained. "And you have two choices: you can either do the job, in which case you get in trouble. Or you can . . . do anything they want, to hold onto the job, and that makes you a eunuch and a joke. And eventually they throw you out anyway."

"Fay was different than Bart in style," Bowie Kuhn told me, "and very different from Peter. I think Fay was more of a throwback to the Landis approach or the Kuhn approach. Yet . . . Fay lacked the political touch to pull it off. I may not have been the world's best politician but I wasn't a bad one. I did a lot of things that the clubs didn't like, but when push came to shove they were standing behind me. And not with knives in their hands, at least not yet. Fay didn't have the benefit of a group of owners that, by and large, supported him, and when he behaved in imperial fashion, as I feel a commissioner has to do from time to time, he got in trouble."

Commissioner Vincent never really had a chance. Less than a month after taking office in 1989, he faced an immediate Armageddon in the form of the San Francisco earthquake, which resulted in a ten-day postponement of the World Series. It might have been his finest hour.

Like all earthquakes, the one that hit San Francisco in 1989 came fiercely and violently from deep down under. For Fay Vincent, the new commissioner, managing to actually complete the World Series amid the tragedy and chaos was his single public triumph in office. Though he rose eloquently and righteously from those ashes, things just got worse in a hurry. It must have been quite clear to Vincent that the source that was rocking the commissionership was as unforgiving and long brewing as that of any earthquake. Every which way Commissioner Vincent turned he seemed to anger the owners. Three years after he took office, he was out. Even Spike Eckert served longer than Fay Vincent.

For better or worse, when Fay Vincent's name is mentioned in the context of the office of the commissioner of baseball, many other faces also come to mind. As in: Bart Giamatti, whom he succeeded but whose stature he would never attain. As in: George Steinbrenner, the Yankees' owner, whom Vincent suspended for more than two years for hiring Howard Spira, a small-time mobster, to spy on Yankees outfielder Dave Winfield. As in: Donald Fehr, with whom Vincent tried to improve owners-players relations. As in: twenty-three of twenty-six owners who wanted the commissioner totally removed from labor negotiations. But those memories strike me as mostly superficial when compared to what Vincent himself told me he remains proudest of.

"I did two things no other commissioner ever did," he explained. "I apologized to the black community for the exclusion of blacks from baseball. No commissioner had ever apologized—I couldn't believe it, it was a front page story in the *Times*!—and, secondly, I got them in the health plan. . . . I also brought Len Coleman to baseball [as National League president], who was a distinguished black executive. . . . As I was leaving, he, with some help from me, got them a pension, the Negro Leaguers, so they get $10,000 a year pension and they're covered by the health plan. And that's significant."

Vincent's great regret was his inability "to persuade the owners that what they were about to do—both to get rid of me and have a war with the union—was going to produce just what it produced. We're ten years later and they've not made a single inch of progress."

Ironically, under different circumstances, Vincent's qualifications as a businessman who had worked in the upper corporate echelon of Columbia Pictures and Coca-Cola, should have made him perfect for the job. But Vincent held fast to his sense of the commissioner's responsibilities for the game's best interests. To diminish the powers of the commissioner in office is not an option the owners have, Vincent repeatedly told his employers. This was not what the owners wanted to hear.

"Any time you mix morality into an economic issue you make it very hard to resolve," Vincent writes. "If you are bad and I am good, it's difficult for us to come together to do something that's advantageous for both of us."

Like Martin Luther, Vincent refused to recant. At least at first. "I have always believed that the proper role of the commissioner is to look out for the interests of" the owners, players, and fans, he wrote. It's no surprise, then, that his coup de grâce was something he pulled straight from baseball's Major League Agreement, which the owners have tried their best to ignore ever since the death of Landis.

"The campaign against me culminated in a vote in September 1992," Vincent writes, "in which a majority of the owners expressed their lack of confidence in me and called upon me to resign. The implied threat was that if I didn't resign, they would force me out of office. And here I found myself the unhappy participant in a battle of principle. . . .

"I firmly believed that under the Major-League Agreement, the owners do not have the power to fire a commissioner. (As far as I know, they still don't.) This part of the charter was written by Judge Kenesaw Mountain Landis when he first took the job; he knew his decisions might cause him trouble with the owners, and he put in provisions that would prevent a disgruntled group from forcing him out. He had been a federal judge, and he certainly wasn't going to give up a lifetime appointment for a job from which the people whose conduct he was judging could fire him whenever they wanted.

"The owners like to say that baseball is a business where the commissioner is the chief executive, and you can always fire the chief executive, but that analogy doesn't hold, because in business a chief executive is not expected to make rulings on the actions of his board of directors; a commissioner is in charge of keeping the owners in line with the game's rules and regulations."

Despite his inclination "to stand up for this principle and to fight the owners' actions in court," Vincent chose not to pursue a legal battle. Sounding very much like his friend and predecessor, Vincent announced his retirement: "I strongly believe a baseball commissioner should serve a full term as contemplated by the Major League Baseball Agreement. Only then can difficult decisions be made impartially and without fear of political repercussions. Unfortunately, some want the commissioner to put aside the responsibility to act in the 'best interests of baseball'; some want the commissioner to represent only owners, and to do their bidding in all matters. I haven't done that, and I could not do so, because I accepted the position believing the commissioner has a higher duty and that sometimes decisions have to be made that are not in the interest of some owners.

"Unique power was granted to the Commissioner of Baseball for sound reasons—to maintain the integrity of the game and temper owner decisions predicated solely on self-interest. My views on this have not changed. What has changed, however, is my opinion that it would be an even greater disservice to baseball if I were to precipitate a protracted fight over the office of the commissioner. . . . Simply put, I've concluded that resignation—not litigation—should be my final act as commissioner 'in the best interests' of baseball."

"It's an impossible job," Vincent told me. "St. Francis of Assisi couldn't solve the problems. If you try to do the job you're going to irritate a third of the owners. A third of the owners are negative about you to start with, a third are undecided, and a third of them are for you. And that undecided group moves back and forth. You can be sure a third of the owners today would vote to throw Selig out. And he knows that. He used to say that to me: 'A third of them are against any commissioner the day he takes the office.'"

That was knowledge that Vincent gained the hard way. Although his appointment to the office of commissioner should have offered baseball a seamless transition from the brief Giamatti regime, the game's owners, particularly Milwaukee's own Bud Selig, were doing much behind the scenes.

"We had a decent relationship," Vincent says of how he got along with Selig. "But I missed one fact. One of the lawyers in baseball, a guy named Chuck O'Connor, early on said to me, 'Fay, Bud wants to be commissioner, and he said he's going to get rid of you and you don't even see it coming.'

"And I said, 'I can't believe that, he's too smart, he doesn't want to be commissioner. Why would he want to do that?' O'Connor was right. I missed that completely."

When he titled his book on the 1919 Black Sox Scandal *Eight Men Out*, Eliot Asinof wasn't thinking of commissioners Landis through Vincent. But by the time baseball's ninth commissioner took office, at first on an interim basis, "eight men out" served as a fair description of the vacancy that Bud Selig assumed in 1992.

Bud Selig's skill is sales. His gift is his passion. If the face of Landis belongs on Mt. Rushmore, Selig's probably belongs on a car commercial. But that's all right, a fact of life that should flatter all car salesmen everywhere. True, after graduating from the University of Wisconsin he went to work in his father's car dealership, but that wasn't his calling. As much as Landis was called by his conscience, Selig was called to baseball. Landis was a czar, Selig an Everyman. But an Everyman who sold Milwaukee to baseball's owners—a sales pitch that took four years to close—when he rescued the year-old Seattle Pilots franchise and brought the ball club to Milwaukee's County Stadium as the Brewers on April Fool's Day 1970. Selig will remain forever a hero in Milwaukee for the devotion he applied to the task at hand, that of finding a ball club to replace the Braves. In Holtzman's words, "Selig dedicated himself—no, more than that, he dedicated his life—to the quest of obtaining a replacement franchise for Milwaukee."

Selig's appointment as interim commissioner seemed to make as much sense as that of Vincent following Giamatti's death. As Holtzman points out, Selig is "the quintessential insider. Nobody had matched his devotion, serving on all of the owners' committees, big and small, some of them for two and three terms."

"I'll tell you why I finally did it," Selig explained to me. It's an old story, but it bears repeating. "I really debated. And I never thought I was going to take it.

"Two to four months, I'll be out," Selig told his wife. "And I meant it. Never would have changed."

"But, Larry," the commissioner offered, "the owners felt there were some commissioners who came in who did not understand the game, either its business or its history, and they really kept after me. 'Bud, you *can't* bring a newcomer in right now. Because no matter how smart the newcomer is there's going to be a two- to three-year learning curve, and we don't have two to three years.' And you know, at first I rejected it and then I began to think about it. . . . I had to say to myself that as much as I thought we had one or two other very good candidates . . . they had never been in baseball.

"You wouldn't make me the chairman of General Electric coming from the outside with no experience, would you? So people say, 'Well, an owner shouldn't be a commissioner.' And I agonized over that; I understand it's the genesis of a lot of comment today. But I know where most of that comes from, so frankly that's people who have a different agenda. I say the opposite. I say if Mr. Fetzer were here today, Mr. Fetzer would say, 'Why not. You've been trained. There isn't a problem in the game that you don't know about. You have lived it yourself.'"

Bud Selig is a self-professed historian who will celebrate the lore and heroics of the game in a heartbeat. But he'll also defend the course his commissionership has taken. And on one level his position is defensible. "The other great unwritten power of the commissioner is persuasion," Ford Frick wrote in his memoir of his years in office. "Any commissioner assumes added stature the minute he dons the official robes of office. People in baseball, and the general public, may question his judgment or disagree violently with this or that decision, but they do respect the office. That's where persuasion comes in. A telephone call or a man-to-man conversation frequently will head off a sticky situation before it develops into a reality. Nor is that merely a personal philosophy."

As the consummate hunter for a consensus—almost any consensus—Selig projected that power of persuasion better than any of the previous eight commissioners. He rode that capacity into office, and it is what keeps him in office today. But the robe of office that Selig wears so comfortably, the very one that Landis tailored for himself, is worn and threadbare in spots, altered and realtered to suit the conscience of the eight others before him. Selig, who professes that he doesn't have to try to make it fit, has probably entertained the notion that maybe the best thing to do would be to retire the robe. (Surely the owners—many, if not all—have wished often enough that Landis had been buried in it, an appropriate shroud.) When Landis created the office he knew two things: his public and his word as law. It was his office, and it was his conscience. In effect, baseball from 1920 until his death in 1944 was his game. Bud Selig, for many reasons, can only dream of such luxuries.

"There's a lot more litigation today," Commissioner Selig rightly acknowledges. "The agendas are far different today. They're far more intensely disparate. So that makes the commissioner's job, sitting in the midst of all that, *very* painful."

True, though the scope of the first commissioner's powers included all facets of the game on and off the field, many of the legal restraints that Selig sees as defining his powers were nonexistent when Landis took over. But that position is shortsighted. Commissioner Selig knows more about baseball than any other owner—and for a while it looked like he would resume an active owner's role when he left office. In the simplest of words, he should know better. Certainly he knows that the conscience that Landis brought to the office extended well beyond the fields of major league play. Surely the commissioner knows that Landis's successors in office, though never commanding the powers the judge assumed, were well aware of the ambassadorship—the responsibilities of conscience to the best interests of the game—that the office still carries with it.

Today's commissioner, like Bowie Kuhn right through to Fay Vincent, suffers from the age we live in, the instant messaging of who's to blame and why. Knowing the game as he does, Commissioner Selig surely appreciates how well the Landis image would serve his office and the game he too loves. Eighty-six years ago, the decision to create an office of commissioner of baseball that was subject to Landis's absolute power was the only viable solution to getting organized baseball on track. Today, under Commissioner Selig, that "option" seems like fantasy. When Landis died in office on November 25, 1944, five days after his seventy-eighth birthday, a week after owners had renewed his contract through 1953, baseball was on the verge of entering a golden age for which Landis was, in large part, responsible. He left behind a method and an ethos that would serve as the basic template for the game's eight subsequent commissioners for going on one hundred years. To honor Landis and his best-interests legacy (the rich estate from which they prospered) baseball's sixteen humble and appreciative owners promptly began slashing away at the authority of their commissioner, slowly at first, but consistently. Thus, despite—often because of—his accomplishments and the independent-minded precedents of his administration, Landis made the job increasingly difficult for the men who held the office after him. The owners took care of that—see Reinsdorf and *hate* above. And though the combination of changing times, both socially and economically, further restricted the conscience of the office and the unwavering allegiance that Landis commanded from day one, his successors—with the probable exception of the anomaly known as Eckert—were always aware of the ambassadorial and attendant best-interests responsibilities that came with the office.

Lately, when fans bemoan the absence of a true commissioner, they are, in effect, speaking of the commissioner's having severed diplomatic relations with the game's best interests. The greatest criticism anyone might fix on Landis is that he made it impossible for any of his successors to ever match him. But he set a standard, one that has remained in place even to this day of players' and owners' "disparate interests." The greatest criticism anyone might throw at Commissioner Selig is that he claims he had no choice in accepting the impossible task as his predecessors had.

Ironically, in the minds of owners the strength of the office comes from the owners' complete disregard for the notion of the best interests of the *game* and the logical support of that concept by the commissioner they elect. They go out, identify the man they want and need most—and they've been successful six of eight times, excluding commissioner Selig—then impose their arrogant and self- serving attitude on him and think he won't respond. Six out of eight times! This is baseball: the owners are hitting .750!

For more than eighty years the owners of major league baseball teams claim they have opted for the principle of "the best interests of the game" when naming a commissioner, even Eckert. Why they abandoned that notion in appointing Selig as their commissioner is attributable to more than the their desire to have *their* commissioner represent only *their* interests. In refusing to understand or appreciate the history of the office and its relationship (including its benefits) to themselves and to players, ownership has exhibited a bullish collective stubbornness that defies the best interests of the game, including their own.

"I warned the owners that they had no cards, that going to war with the union was stupid," says Vincent, "that the only way to do it, to make progress, was incrementally. I said, 'You're apt to be satisfied with a thirty-year program of five percent improvement. It will take forever, but that's all that's available. . . .

"That was my biggest failure: I couldn't get them to understand that a war was going to result in tragedy for them. And it has."

Despite the shift from Landis's autonomy, despite even the most glaring failure of the current administration—the 1994 strike and cancellation of the playoffs and World Series—most fans, to paraphrase Lurie, actually believe they hold a stake in the affairs of the state of baseball, both sides of which are obligated, to some extent, to their common audience. If Lurie's perception that the best interests have to be "for the fans" sounds like the wishful thinking of a sentimental duffer, that alone does not make him wrong.

3. Baseball's Peculiar Institution, part 2

FEBRUARY 13, 2002

Senate Hearing 107-427, re "The Application of Federal Antitrust Laws to Major League Baseball"

Spring training begins tomorrow. Not a day too soon considering what the off-season has been doing to the office of the commissioner of baseball. A month ago, barely a week into the new year, Michigan representative John Conyers put his money where his sarcasm lives and publicly called for Commissioner Selig's resignation—"in the best interest of baseball" being Conyers's coup de grâce. Conyers's attack was fueled by the commissioner's disclosure that in 1995, as the owner of the Milwaukee Brewers ball club (and then-acting commissioner), Selig borrowed $3 million on behalf of the Brewers from a bank in which Carl Pohlad, Minnesota Twins owner, had significant interest. Given all that any reasonable upper-Midwesterner might infer from so much smoke and fire along the horizon of a thousand lakes (could contraction of the Twins mean a handsome buyout for Selig creditor Pohlad?) perhaps Conyers's behest deserves consideration. More than a conflict of interests, the loan itself, secured as it was without the knowledge and approval of the other owners, has the commissioner breaking one of the rules he was hired to enforce. But there's more, or less, to wit: Commissioner Selig's "apparent unwillingness," according to Conyers, "to reveal other financial information that you [the commissioner] assert supports your decision to eliminate two baseball teams."

Normally, the histrionics and threats of congressmen over baseball amount to little more than Lou Pinella going jaw to pate with any of a number of long-suffering American League umpires. But in any direction you look from Capitol Hill, Conyers's statement back on January 8 resonates with intimations of something historic, a fair warning shot across baseball's bow: Fix it and make it work. Congress is running out of patience, and baseball's excuses are growing thinner by the minute. As Sen. Paul Wellstone, Conyers's Senate ally on behalf of the antitrust bill under consideration, would soon testify: in light of "our country's . . . urgent priorities [less than six months after 9/11] . . . we should not have to be concerned about protecting our fans and communities from unilateral, self-serving decisions by major league baseball owners."

One of those owners, of course, happens to be the commissioner of baseball.

In case you haven't been keeping score during baseball's winter of discontent, the commissioner's defense of his and Major League Baseball's actions since the Diamondbacks knocked off the Yankees in seven games has been loud and singular: the antitrust exemption. To which Florida attorney general Robert Butterworth responds in opening testimony this morning: "It is nothing less than a betrayal of the public trust to now conspire behind closed doors about the future of baseball in those communities that welcomed the major leagues."

Butterworth assumes, with some cause, that Major League Baseball, Inc. had the scope of its contraction hopes focused on the Sunshine State, whose courts have held major league baseball's antitrust exemption inapplicable to issues of franchise movement. (Never mind that for eons baseball has been pumping big bucks into the Florida economy via spring training and developmental minor league ball clubs and ballparks and would likely continue to do so without the state's perennially embarrassing Tampa Bay franchise and it's bipolar National League cousin in Miami. An infusion that would not be the case, say, in either Montreal or Minnesota.) The tack of senators this morning is necessarily extreme and surprisingly on the mark. Not surprising, but most vehement, is MLB's defense that the sport's special place in American culture—and, by extension, the business of the sport—depends in large part on the game's antitrust exemption. But such strategy only calls attention to the fact that their's is a privilege enjoyed by no other professional sport, and that the infamous exemption is but a Metrodome shadow of its former self, applicable only to the big leagues' working relationship with the minors and providing no authority whatsoever to unilaterally eliminate or move a franchise.

And *still* Congress wants baseball to win. Ultimately, Congress is rooting for baseball to see the light, to come to its senses, and, in accepting with deference the courtesy its business has been granted, quit whining and begin to act honorably. At least as honorably as the man who created the office and the owners who allowed him to do so (notwithstanding their temporary loss of sanity), intended, eighty-three years ago.

When last we gathered on Capitol Hill, in December 2001, Steven Fehr, outside counsel for the Major League Baseball Players Association, announced that his brother Donald M., executive director and general counsel for the MLBPA, "would be eager to testify in the future if you so wish." And low and behold he is here, and most eager. (That's the first thing you want in a union man, enthusiasm.) But forget a seventh-game matchup of Spahn versus Ford or Martinez and Clemens: there is no Bud in Mudville today.

It has become a longstanding tradition for the commissioner to represent baseball before Congress, particularly with respect to the game's antitrust exemption. Which brings us back to the very birth of the office of the commissioner of baseball—from the womb of the antitrust exemption. In federal court five years before he assumed office in 1920, Judge Landis, by choosing not to rule against organized baseball (the American and National leagues) in an antitrust suit filed by the Federal League, gave major league baseball the corporate muscle it needed, if not the papers it is now written on. It also put into ownership's collectively porous mind the idea that this judge was on *their* side, even as Landis was inclined to rule *for* the Federal League and that by stalling his decision he was acting in what he felt to be the best interests of the future of the game of baseball, which were not exclusively those of ownership. Two years after Landis became commissioner, of course, Justice Oliver Wendell Holmes, speaking for the Supreme Court, made the exemption official. These facts go unmentioned this morning, though they're surely worth considering in light of the ensuing repartee between management and labor, in light of the absence of a true voice speaking on behalf of the game's best interests.

Perhaps the commissioner is learning to pick his battles, albeit slowly (he still must host what will prove to be one of the most memorable All-Star Games ever, and there will be a major settlement with the Players Association to celebrate). More than likely the commissioner's December performance humiliated baseball's fragile corporate psyche to the point that someone big and at the front of the line decided: Let's turn it over to legal. I'd like to think that MLB, Inc., is just a designated hitter today, though I get that acid-reflux feeling that it's the corporation calling the shots. Doesn't the corporation, like the union of players, deserve its moment of testimony? Perhaps. But where's the commissioner? Who rewrote *his* job description?

"Many critics of Selig's tenure retain a romantic vision of the Commissioner as some sort of philosopher-king looking out for The Best Interests of Baseball even when those interests conflict with those of the owners who hire him. The experience of Happy Chandler, Bowie Kuhn and Fay Vincent shows the limits of this view," writes Doug Pappas in his "Business of Baseball" column on baseballprospectus.com. "But the commissioner is uniquely positioned to act in the collective interest of MLB as a whole, whatever that effect may be on individual teams—and Selig has abdicated this responsibility."

True or not, the very perception of acquiescence diminishes the stature of the office and its conscience. And that's what hurts. Because the morning will be full of innuendo and accusation, with the office of the commissioner—not the players, not the corporation—taking all the hits.

Today's main event pits Donald Fehr against Robert DuPuy, baseball's executive vice president and chief legal officer, in a judicial sparring match that is filled with pointed barbs and parries, contradictions and counterclaims, and even a comical gaffe or two, as when committee chair Patrick Leahy of Vermont introduces DuPuy as the "Executive Vice President and Chief Legal Officer of the Major League Baseball Players Association." For the most part, though, there's a lot of reading between the lines in search of moments of concision and lucidity and the occasional accidental stab at logic. There will be no chivalric jousting between committee members and witnesses today, no wildly clashing personalities, no Jesse Ventura, no John Conyers; if the commissioner isn't in the house, the targets are illusory. Donald Fehr? Robert Dupuy? Please! What do *they* have to lose?

In his opening remarks, Leahy notes that "in 1998, Congress culminated decades of hearings on labor strife and other problems in major league baseball when we enacted the Curt Flood Act. . . . It was a bipartisan effort to clarify the law. The principal purpose of the law was to make sure that federal antitrust laws apply to the relationships between major league baseball owners, teams, and players."

Though there is but one professional baseball team in Leahy's home state, the Vermont Expos, a short-season single-A team that plays its home games in Burlington ("Their mascot is Champ," my brother, who lives up there, tells me, "the Lake Champlain Monster . . . like the Loch Ness Monster only without a good agent."), Leahy's position is not provincial.

"When the Committee was engaged in hearings in 1995 that led to passage of the Curt Flood Act, after the work stoppage in 1994 and the lamentable and historic cancellation of the World Series," Leahy continues, "David Cone, an outstanding major league pitcher, testified and asked this question: 'If baseball were coming to Congress today to ask us to provide a statutory antitrust exemption, would we [get it]?

'Of course not.'"

The Curt Flood Act, which reasonably defines the limits of the antitrust exemption, summarizes itself as follows: "that major league baseball players are covered under the antitrust laws (i.e., that major league baseball players will have the same rights under the antitrust laws as do other professional athletes, e.g., football and basketball players), along with a provision that makes it clear that the passage of this Act does not change the application of the antitrust laws in any other context or with respect to any other person or entity." Specifically, the act's protection applies to minor league teams and ballplayers.

"We have seen owners approve a merry-go-round of ownership swaps," says Leahy, "with the owner of the Montreal Expos being approved to buy the Florida Marlins, while the owner of the Marlins and a former owner of the Padres were approved to buy the Boston Red Sox, and the other owners joining together to buy and operate the Expos and prepared to pay the owner of the Minnesota Twins a hefty fee to kill that team's existence. To an outsider, it seems that the major league baseball team owners take care of each other pretty well."

Clearly, the picture Leahy paints has a very corporate profile, and there is no escaping the fact that MLB believes itself to the distant manor born, well beyond the law. During frequent recesses one can overhear Rich Levin, MLB's senior vice president for public relations, working his cell phone and reassuring someone—the commissioner back in Milwaukee?—that the hearing is going according to game plan. Frankly, it's disconcerting to know that baseball is putting such a positive spin on the proceedings. Equally troublesome is the inference that whatever Commissioner Selig brings to the boardroom of owners does not translate well when he appears in public. Which raises the question: if the commissioner truly is the "consensus builder" among owners, what is it he's building consensus on? That the commissioner is not in the house this morning reinforces the growing impression that the office is a paper tiger and lends some authority to Rep. Conyers's call for the commissioner's resignation.

Following Butterworth's testimony, Lori Swanson, deputy attorney general of Minnesota, demonstrates her knowledge of baseball's rule book. In questioning the commissioner's loan from Pohlad, she will cite Major League Rule 20 (c), which prohibits loans made directly or indirectly between owners without the approval of their colleagues.

"In the past, Commissioner Selig . . . has made certain representations to Congress about what major league baseball would do if the so-called exemption were allowed to remain in place," Swanson begins. Referring to then-acting commissioner Selig's 1993 congressional testimony, Swanson quotes her absent adversary: "Baseball has continued to uphold its unique covenant with its fans and it deserves to retain its current status under the antitrust laws." However, as Swanson notes, "Mr. Selig's reported response to a question as to why the possible violation of league rules [prohibiting the loan] was not discussed at a recent owners' meeting: 'We decided it was an antiquated rule.'

"Well, the baseball antitrust exemption is also an 'antiquated rule' from a time when major league baseball was more a pastime, not just a business. If the owners are willing to ignore their own internal governance structure when an 'antiquated' rule gets in the way of doing business, that certainly calls into question whether Major League Baseball can be trusted to conduct itself in a responsible manner with an antiquated antitrust exemption (if such an exemption exists)."

Wellstone adds fuel to the fire: "The application of the antitrust laws does not prevent a league from working to keep a team in a city," he says. "But insulating that league from the antitrust laws absolutely prevents cities, fans, and other interested parties from challenging a league decision to move a team. . . .

"I want to emphasize . . . that I think relying on the 'good will' of major league baseball to protect Minnesota's interests with respect to relocation would be foolhardy. I think that our state, our communities, fans across the country need to have the right to challenge these decisions. They ought to be able to challenge anticompetitive practices when it looks like it is just a cartel that has gotten together."

Cities, fans . . . our state, our communities . . . Wellstone's appeal clearly concerns the best interests of the game, which according to baseball's own constitution falls within the purview of the commissioner. Who is not here.

Although Commissioner Selig's absence can be interpreted as a betrayal of the office he represents, DuPuy's presence as the embodiment of corporate baseball does nothing but disservice to the office of the commissioner. After all, this is not Leslie O'Connor representing the conscience of the office under Landis, nor Fay Vincent standing in for same on behalf of Bart Giamatti. With Dupuy solely representing ownership's interests, the collective lot of owners has seemingly removed the commissioner from the equation.

So Donald Fehr will make his stand alone. He will shoot from the hip, and he will remain standing. And Robert DuPuy will hold his own; *not* being the commissioner makes him somehow invulnerable and therefore much more spirited than one would have imagined. Likely DuPuy knows something no one else does: that in a matter of weeks he will become president and chief operating officer of Major League Baseball, Inc., while Paul Beeston, president and CEO of the entity since 1997, disappears across the border, back home into Canada.

With Commissioner Selig's absence deferring issues of conscience to a later hearing, Sen. Orrin Hatch tacks in a new direction. "I am not opposed to redefining or even repealing baseball's exemption if the arguments and evidence presented indicate the need for such action," he says. "At this time, however, I personally am not convinced that the limited antitrust exemption is, as some claim, the root cause of the problems identified by opponents of the exemption." Three cheers for the man from Utah!

Hatch then suggests "that two basic questions need to be addressed at this hearing. . . . First, in what specific ways do the antitrust laws and baseball's limited exemption from these laws actually affect or contribute to the problems that have been repeatedly identified by industry participants and commentators? Second, how would legislative action modifying or clarifying baseball's exemption ameliorate or even eliminate some of these problems?"

The questions make far too much sense—and will never be answered. So much for the challenge from Utah. With the corporation of major league baseball owners legally protected and the union of players always within its rights, the senator seems to be setting the stage lights for nothing more than some entertaining shuck-and-jive from Messrs. Fehr and Dupuy. But not before the most provocative testimony of the day, from the little-known vice president of minor league baseball, Stanley M. Brand.

Brand is an expert on, and a vigilant advocate for, baseball's antitrust exemption as it affects the sixteen minor leagues (180 minor league teams, *professional* ball clubs) that comprise the association in this country and Canada.

"I can tell you this," Brand testifies, "on April 10, 1994, Mr. Fehr was quoted in the *Los Angeles Times* as stating [and sounding an awful lot like Commissioner Landis, of all people]: 'Too much money is being wasted in the minor leagues.' Since that time, the Players Association has been the principal proponent of total and outright repeal of the antitrust exemption. During consideration of the Curt Flood Act, the players' representatives resisted adding language to this legislation, making clear . . . the protection to the minor leagues. I can only conclude that the Players Association seeks repeal in order to diminish minor league baseball so that they can lay claim to the money they say is wasted on the minors and divert it to major league players."

According to his boss, CEO and president of the National Association of Professional Baseball Leagues Mike Moore, Brand is "not really a lobbyist . . . [But] if I have something of concern in Washington, Stan's the point guy to take care of it for us, because he knows the people there. He knows how things work. He knows where to go, who to talk to." (As does Major League Baseball. As Doug Pappas points out, "Major League Baseball is the only one of the four major team sports with its own PAC." Founded in 2001, it is officially titled Office of the Commissioner of Major League Baseball Political Action Committee. Last year alone, according to Pappas, "MLB spent $278,000 . . . on campaign contributions and soft-money donations to the political parties.")

Brand, former counsel to the House of Representatives, lost in the running for president of the minors, but he can carry the moment here where his legal background informs his eloquence. It's something Commissioner Selig could never have pulled off. The minors' "man in Washington" has now ignited Fehr, whose remarks concerning Fehr's testimony today and the actions of the corporation of major league baseball owners in recent months provoke DuPuy, who in turn throws his own transmission into overdrive. Back and forth they go, the player's union boss and the man we're to infer represents baseball's highest office, if not its conscience. Sometimes they respond to one another, sometimes to a question or comment from the committee. But always their remarks are pointed and strike at the heart.

As in DuPuy's statement that "contraction is an attempt to face up to the economic realities of the industry so as to deliver a competitively balanced product at the highest level to as many fans as possible." (The man *dreams* of red herrings.)

Or Fehr's: "Mr. DuPuy makes a compelling case—although without examination of it—that baseball needs to do what it is doing. With all due respect, that is exactly what everyone about whose conduct questions are raised under the antitrust laws does. It says, 'My conduct is reasonable. It is not unreasonably anticompetitive.' That is not a reason not to have the antitrust laws. That is a defense."

If it's difficult to tell who's winning, at least the target is unmistakable: their adversary's negligence of public trust.

In his written statement, Fehr states: "In a very real sense, the entire debate about the number and location of franchises simply comes down to . . . [s]hould the public policy of the United States be that the owners have unlimited discretion—regardless of the action taken or the motive behind it—or should such decisions be made against the backdrop of the antitrust laws, with the courts able to ascertain the facts and determine whether the conduct passes muster?"

In virtually the same flourish, however, Fehr divorces his union from anything close to the best interests of the game, particularly with regard to its fans and the communities that identify with their respective teams.

"We do not . . . represent the broader community interest," he wrote. "The Players Association of course represents and is authorized to represent only its own membership."

It only *sounds* like Fehr is going after MLB, Inc. Does Major League Baseball need any greater clue that the answer to Fehr's position that the union does "not represent the broader community interest" is the commissioner of baseball, who is still "uniquely positioned to act in the collective interest [and conscience] of [major league baseball] as a whole"?

Sen. Mike DeWine of Ohio, stating his belief "that baseball will never be truly healthy, will never be truly competitive, will never truly be the sport that we all love so much and that we know it can be again, unless we solve this competitive problem," then closes the hearing.

"So, Mr. DuPuy and Mr. Fehr," Dewine concludes, "I think you have a big responsibility, and it is a responsibility, quite candidly, that goes beyond your responsibility to your respective parties, beyond your responsibility to the owners, beyond your responsibility to the players. I think that is the great tradition of baseball and the history of baseball, and I believe some obligation—a compelling obligation—to the fans."

Ah, the fans. By virtue of numbers, the House has traditionally been the people's court, the Senate's contribution to democracy reeking of a supposed decorum. Perhaps that's why there is no ragged line of fans this morning snaking endlessly down the corridor outside the hearing room; and the history buffs and that most common of migratory birds, the curious tourist, have taken refuge from the cold in the Smithsonian Castle or the National Gallery. During the House hearing in December the Bring-Back-the-Washington-Senators contingent seemed to be well represented on both sides of the gavel. But not here in the Dirksen Building. With their faded ball caps, red letter *W* in script, they are as out of place this morning as ball gloves left on the field of the Skydome between innings. These are the guys who for years have tried to do for Washington what Bud Selig did once for Milwaukee, give a team their home.

It's hard not to love these Joe-Hardys-at-heart who remember the old Olympic Sporting Goods store, over on 7th Street between F and G and Wagman's deli and grocery, where legend has it that whenever concessionaires across the street at Griffith Stadium ran out of franks they'd dispatch a messenger to Wagman's to buy out the store. There's no question this group of grass-roots defenders of Washington's right to a ball club deserves some mention in Cooperstown, at least as much as Marvin Miller. In my heart of hearts I want to believe that the commissioner commiserates with their struggle. I want to believe that he remembers the caveat offered by the Wisconsin Supreme Court when it ruled in favor of the of the National League and the Braves' right to move to Atlanta: "There ought, we think, to be included in any law which Congress may pass upon this subject some provision which would protect communities, either those who have or hope to have home teams, from arbitrary and unfair dealing."

But the commissioner and his conscience ain't in.

As conspicuous as Commissioner Selig is by his absence, there is another hole equally troubling: where are the players this morning? It's like one of those errors of omission that pops up every so often in a baseball game, when a player forgets to tag up at third on a long fly or when an outfielder misses the cutoff man: a failure to do what should have been done. In the good old hearings of days gone by we had ballplayers present. In 1958, less than a year after he retired from baseball, Jackie Robinson testified before a Senate committee that ballplayers ought to have a say in selecting the commissioner of baseball. (Imagine so outrageous a thought! And from Jackie Robinson, of all people!)

I know, I know . . . there's a reason the players pay Donald Fehr more money than can fill Miller Park. But I also know there's a *reason* they call it "The Curt Flood Act." Just as there's a reason the commissioner has traditionally been the steward for the best interests and the conscience of the game.

Not for three weeks, when Robert DuPuy is named president and chief operating officer of Major League Baseball, is the state of the conscience of office apparent. DuPuy will be "responsible for all phases of baseball's central offices, including licensing, sponsorship, international, broadcasting, publishing, marketing, public relations, government relations, baseball operations, legal affairs, finance, baseball's Internet operations and the labor-relations committee." Which leads one to ask: Just what *is* it the commissioner does out there in Milwaukee, since what's "in the best interests of the game" itself seems so irrelevant to the corporate attitude and influence behind the office.

Based on everything we've seen today, if you are not a lawyer, no matter how much baseball you know (and Bud Selig *knows* his baseball), you don't really stand much of a chance in a congressional public forum. At least that's what MLB, Inc.'s defense seems to be.

But how refreshing it would have been to have had a baseball voice, embodied by the commissioner of baseball himself, speaking, not in legalese, but in baseball terms and on behalf of the game and its fans. Major League Baseball, Inc., does not need the commissioner of baseball—even if he were blessed with the mind and know-how of, say, Donald Fehr—to provide a legal brief.

There is nothing revolutionary in what I'm saying. Baseball is a game of rules, unwritten as well as written: a foul-ball bunt attempt by a batter with two strikes is ruled a strikeout; in the clubhouse before a game, everyone avoids today's starting pitcher. The first and most important unwritten rule for holding the office of commissioner of baseball is that the occupant be—and remain—a fan. I am rooting for the commissioner to come to his senses and, like Warren Beatty's Bullworth in the movie by that name, stand up and sing the game's praises. For he knows better than anyone that his own dear friend Bart is also cheering him on, from down the right-field line, to say it right and talk about the game. Eloquence be damned. Speak in Stengelese if you must. Make it easy on yourself: become a fan again.

4. Separation of Church and State?

"The baseball people, the game itself, is magic," Fay Vincent told me. "The business of it is terrible. It's like two worlds. When the game is on, you love the game. When it's not—off-season—it can be ugly. And the politics in baseball, the people you're required to spend a lot of time with, people like Reinsdorf and Steinbrenner. . . . It's not exactly the front row of St. John's Cathedral. It's a group of people that takes some getting used to."

Absent Steinbrenner and Reinsdorf, it's not all that different for fans.

No matter which side of the field you're shouting from, the business of baseball stinks. It's as true today as ever. Kenesaw Mountain Landis didn't know *bupkus* from Reinsdorf and Steinbrenner, but by the time he took office he knew oh so much more than he wanted to know about Charles Comiskey and company. Happy Chandler spent the better part of his last year in office lobbying the game's businessmen for a vote of confidence. And to listen to owners today, Peter Ueberroth's only legacy was a $280 million ownership payout to cover the sin of collusion.

Arguing the business of baseball is never any fun. Although both the game and its business are about numbers, those on the ledger side of the sport rarely add up, and when they do they boggle the mind. Once, numbers had substance—batting averages, winning percentages, ERAS. Numbers were everything. Today—and putting aside whatever steroid use has done to the legitimacy of baseball's true numbers—when a player gets traded or signs as a free agent you need H&R Block to navigate the news stories' dollar signs of deferred payments, signing bonuses, incentive clauses, and guaranteed charitable write-offs. But try and find last year's batting average in that same story. Good luck.

The business of baseball is *not* baseball, just the clamorous evidence of the dull and divisive part of the game we have learned to live with. Unfortunately, it's the business side of the game that has begun to alienate its core fans, even those who appreciate that business has so much to do with making the game we love possible. Who's to blame? Owners, players, agents (whose names never come up at hearings), the press, even some fans, share and share alike. This may come as a surprise to some, but baseball players weren't always millionaires. Fifty-five and sixty years ago, when Leo Durocher was selling Chesterfield cigarettes on the back page of the *Sporting News*, the only time dollar signs ran inside the paper was during the late fall and winter, when those were the only numbers available. Some guys were making almost $100,000 a year!

Major league baseball has always been big business, no matter how many exemptions Congress and the Supreme Court grant and deliver. In sociological terms, players today are the nouveau riche, the owners, "old money." True, the best players in every generation were well rewarded. Speaking for others back before free agency, Milt Bolling, the longtime scout and former shortstop for the Red Sox in the 1950s, explained: "When I signed, I never even thought about making the big leagues. I just thought that playing professional baseball was a job, and if you didn't have a job, and you weren't educated, you went home and worked in a factory and carried a lunch pail, as they said. . . .

"That's why you had a lot of baseball teams: a lot of guys kept playing baseball in the minor leagues 'til an older age because there was more money and it was an easier lifestyle than working in a factory. . . . We all knew that when we finished we had to go to work. And guys were glad to see baseball start again because . . . it was easier than carrying the lunch pail."

Though baseball may have been a job, it wasn't work. Better than that, it was *baseball* and as Bolling says . . . Imagine!

In contrast to the ever-growing economic distrust that separates owners and players today, forty and more years ago, when the disparity between their incomes was most noticeably disproportionate, the two groups shared a more or less mutual respect based precisely on their differences: the guys on the field were playing *major league baseball*! And earning a living, too; those upstairs were making serious money (most of them, anyway) and had been for some time. Remarkably democratic! So, that's how it works: "separation of church and state."

Of course, the reverse of the formula—"in dreams begin responsibility"—applies as well: the more that players' earnings began to approach those of individual owners, the less respect and appreciation either side seemed to accord the other. In 2006, one is still buying the other's product and complaining that the cost is too high, though cost alone has not hurt sales.

We follow baseball now in a time when the respective influences of both players and owners are virtually equal. The lines between the business of the game and its best interests frequently blur. Conscience and economics tend to ride the same breath when folks talk baseball these days, with emphasis too often on the latter, though that's hardly a new phenomenon. Two of baseball's most significant business decisions also happened to be in the best interests of the game: Jackie Robinson signing with Branch Rickey and the Dodgers organization, in December 1945; and the creation of the office of commissioner a quarter century before. When Landis took over baseball—and that's essentially what he did—the game on the field was mostly identical to what we're used to seeing today. So it's more than the game we're talking about when we praise Robinson's presence and influence—he was an immediate drawing card wherever he played, money in the bank, among other, more important things. And Landis's peculiar demand for carte blanche (he would have made a hell of an agent) over matters both on and off the field was driven as much by his appreciation of how poorly the game and its owners would fare in the court system he knew so well as by his appreciation of the virtues—the necessity—of impartiality.

It's no coincidence that when the American Football League and the American Basketball League merged with the NFL and NBA, respectively, the model for their commissionerships was the one that Landis put in place, not the three-man committee that was dissolved in his favor. It was a model that worked.

"When I was commish," says Bowie Kuhn, who takes justifiable pride in using the contraction, "I used to do a lot of lobbying. . . . I represented the other sports in certain issues, and they were perfectly happy to have [me] do it. But the only sport that ever sent anybody was basketball. 'I've got this young lawyer who might be a help to you,' [then-NBA commissioner] Larry O'Brien told me. It was David Stern."

"He has done a great job," Kuhn says of the current NBA commissioner. "I think that, by dint of his own personality and brain power, he still holds, legally [and] effectively, a lot of power.

"But, can you ever fully restore that [Landis] model in any sport? I don't think so. . . . In the past, if the commissioner made some decision and it had an adverse financial effect on a club, well, so be it, you could live with it. But today when the commissioner makes a decision it may have millions of dollars' worth of impact on one club."

For the first time in memory, fans, players, and management can all agree with Bowie Kuhn.

The office of the commissioner of baseball has always been a job. The purpose of the job has always been to oversee a business. But an unusual business. Confined mostly to the eastern half of the United States through the mid-1950s, major league baseball has since grown international. As in conglomerate. And, in hearing after hearing, at press conference ad infinitum, everyone—from the commissioner and the owners, to agents, union leaders, players, and members of Congress—refers to the game as an industry. And surely it is. Today, approximately 350 people work in the main

New York office of Major League Baseball, Inc., on Park Avenue. Another 60 work in its Chelsea office, known as Major League Baseball Productions. Additionally, 200 people are employed at MLB Advanced Media, which oversees the corporate web site as well as the sites of all thirty teams. What do they all do, those more than 600 people (I've heard the number might actually be closer to 800)? The majority, I'm told, are involved in marketing, licensing, and all of the other awful legal aspects of the game. Is that possible? Bowie Kuhn recalls there being about 60 people working in the office during his years. Throw in an additional 25 or 30 folks from the two league offices and you're still talking small business. Though longtime fans have traditionally viewed the commissioner's office as a safety net for both the clubs and the players, many now wonder if today it's not the teams themselves that have been left holding the net and keeping the corporation, not the game, afloat. And to what ends?

The corporation of Major League Baseball is structured as a "limited partnership" owned by all major league teams and with a five-owner board of directors and two "independent members," Robert DuPuy and John McHale. (I'm not exactly sure of the corporate definition of *independent*. Dupuy, of course, was Bud Selig's lawyer for more than a decade before moving over to MLB, Inc. McHale, the former Montreal Expos owner, served as Commissioner Eckert's deputy—talk about combat pay!—and, according to Holtzman, withdrew his name, on the advice of National League counsel Bowie Kuhn, from consideration to succeed Ford Frick because his position with Montreal represented a *conflict of interest*.)

Until Commissioner Selig sold his beloved Brewers in 2004, the business model for today's commissionership was frighteningly similar to the three-headed monster that Landis slew. That the commissioner is no longer an owner is not enough, in and of itself, to revive what the office was as recently as Fay Vincent's tenure. Remind me again: why was it that professional basketball and football adopted the "independent" model?

Traditionally, the business of the commissioner has been to interpret and enforce the rules of baseball, yet the common thinking now is that the commissioner serves the owners and the owners alone. And for good enough reason. As stated in Article II, sections 1 and 2(a), of the Major League constitution: "The Office of the Commissioner of Baseball is an unincorporated association also doing business as Major League Baseball and has as its members the Major League Baseball Clubs.

"The functions of the Commissioner shall include: (a) To serve as Chief Executive Officer of Major League Baseball. The Commissioner shall also have executive responsibility for labor relations and shall serve as Chairman, or shall designate a Chairman, of such committees as the Commissioner shall name or the Major League Clubs shall from time to time determine by resolution." You don't have to be a lawyer or Judge Landis to see that the commissioner, as defined in a constitution that remains in effect until December 31, 2006, is no greater than the sum of ownership's will.

For accepting such concessions, Commissioner Selig's annual salary is in the neighborhood of $3 million, give or take, compared to the $650,000 that both Vincent and Bart Giamatti made. However, as the constitution is "originally adopted as the Major League Agreement on January 12, 1921," there continues to remain a germ of that eighty-five-year-old agreement in which a significant function of the job is *still* to investigate "either upon complaint or upon the Commissioner's own initiative, any act, transaction or practice charged, alleged or suspected to be not in the best interests of the national game of Baseball."

Today's commissioner of baseball conducts his end of baseball's business affairs in his hometown of Milwaukee. In the reception area of his office, the signature woven into the fabric of the rug on the floor reads Alan H. Selig, just like on an official major league baseball, which the rug, probably fifteen feet in diameter, is cut to resemble, even down to the red herringbone stitching and the ubiquitous MLB logo. The space is stately and only somewhat imposing, with the commissioner's selected memorabilia—autographed balls, two straight-backed wooden benches crafted from Louisville Sluggers, signed photos of many of the greats of the game—adding to the showplace. In his office, the commissioner can swivel 180 degrees and take in the Lake Michigan harbor and coastline, the gentrified Midwestern sprawl, and the Milwaukee Art Museum with its stunning Santiago Calatrava–designed addition.

Bud Selig is not the first commissioner to situate his office outside of New York City, only the first since Chandler, who ran the show out of a three-room suite on the twenty-sixth floor of the Carew Tower office building in Cincinnati. On a clear day he could see clear across the Ohio River into "the promised land" of Kentucky and his home in Versailles, ninety miles south. Landis, of course, held court—both on and off the bench—in Chicago.

Among other things, Fay Vincent is critical of today's arrangement: "Bud didn't want to come to New York. He wouldn't leave Milwaukee. [But] he has to have a major presence in New York, because that's where everything gets done, and that's where the staff is. So here you have a commissioner who won't come and really run the office of the commissioner. He didn't move it to Milwaukee . . . because he would have lost a lot of people, and that would have been very disrupting. So you have this sort of crazy organization, where he sits in Milwaukee and no matter how he tries he can't be involved in the *running* of the operation."

Commissioner Selig, naturally, disagrees. "I travel a lot. I'm wherever I have to be. . . . I go to New York when I have to. . . . One of the things I felt is: I'd rather stay here because there are a lot of days, like today, I can get work done here.

"And my being here or New York is nothing. I spend most of my day on the telephone. I've talked to everybody in the [New York] office already, at least two or three times. The owners did that as an accommodation to me. But I would *not* have done it if I thought it compromised anything at all. Because it hasn't."

Regrettably (for all concerned) the perception among fans is that the distance *has* compromised the office as conscience of the game. When Judge Landis was initially approached by baseball's owners they wanted him to believe he could serve as commissioner without leaving the federal bench. Not a problem, his suitors told him, the commissionership won't be a terribly busy job. Wrong again. (In fact, Landis did remain on the bench for more than a year without pay after he became commissioner.)

Commissioner Selig's thirteen years in office (six in an interim capacity) have been a peculiar hybrid of Landis, the seven men who succeeded him, and the American League's first president, Ban Johnson, who was the true power behind the National Commission, which governed major league baseball from 1903 until 1920. If the office of the commissioner of baseball seems to have come full circle, it may well have, since the question on the minds of most fans today is not all that different than the one owners were asking themselves more than four score years ago: Is this any way to run a business?

Complicating that question is that even until this day—despite Commissioner Selig's and union boss Donald Fehr's repeated public use of the term *industry*, despite all evidence to the contrary—baseball remains a sport (or at least more sport than business) according to Congress (whose collective patience is running on empty) and to the imprimatur of the Supreme Court. That's a fine high wire to walk. Even if Commissioner Selig does "feel the *great* responsibility of protecting the game's integrity," as he says, there is too much evidence to suggest that given his salary, given the powers of the Players Association, and given the corporate power and reach of that New York entity, MLB, Inc., integrity in terms of the game itself, should no longer be a concern of the commissioner.

Commissioner Selig's appreciation for the history of major league baseball is both his strong suit among owners and his Achilles heel from out here in the cheap seats, among fans, where his love of the game was born. Unfortunately, because the commissioner may be the last person to realize it, he is the office's first real victim of that very history. Not the casualty of the truism that those who haven't learned their history are condemned to repeat it, but the prey of, and sucker for, a history that reveals an ever more tenuous grip, from administration to administration, on the influence of the conscience of the game. Still, five of the seven commissioners since Landis, from Happy Chandler to Fay Vincent, have recognized that though the differences between the business behind the game and the game's best interests have always been profound, that distinction does not make them mutually exclusive.

"Did we expand too fast?" the commissioner asks, rhetorically. "We did. Yes. No question. And that's why, when Jerry McMorris, [owner] of the Rockies, who was the first guy to call me about contraction—I'll never forget, I was sitting right here—said, 'Commissioner, I've got a great idea for you!' I said to him, 'You must be nuts. That's the *dumbest* thing I've ever heard?' But in the next year it gained; man, it gained. And people said, 'Look, the second expansion is wrong. We just expanded too much.' And I think we did.

"But, as I say, contraction [was] one of many responses to solve this problem, Larry. But it *wouldn't* have been needed if we had solved it earlier. It's like everything else in life: the longer you let problems go the tougher they are to solve. And I think some of my predecessors understand that. Don't they? Don't you think so? I know two of them do. Clearly."

I would like to believe the commissioner on this one, yet his very own Blue Ribbon Panel on Baseball Economics of July 2000 stated that "if the recommendations outlined in this report are implemented, there should be no immediate need for contraction." MLB chose to ignore its own sage and sanctioned advice, implemented none of the panel's recommendations, and then proceeded to call for the elimination of two teams.

"I don't have the option of Scarlet O'Hara anymore," the commissioner argues. "Today, the economic issues are stunningly different because you have no reserve clause. You have free agency [and] a whole series of things that you didn't have then. So I would say to you that, 'Yes, I think the commissioner's job has become more complex with each decade.' And sometimes people really didn't understand that. And the one thing that we *haven't* done as well as we should is to solve our problems.

"When I look back on things—even though I've been part of this now for [thirty-five] years, a long time—you wonder why things weren't done. Address what you can see coming! Quite frankly . . . we *didn't* do a good job of adjusting to some of our problems. Some of it was due to arrogance, some of it was due to maybe not comprehending that life was changing around us."

The commissioner's remark brings to mind something Ford Frick wrote in his memoir back in 1973 concerning the same issue, that "In these wild days of inflation, any workman—common laborer or baseball personality—is entitled to all he can get." I love the notion of sticking the "baseball personality" in the same soup line as the "common laborer." Frick was ahead of his times—after the fact. Back in the 1950s, ballplayers who played under Commissioner Frick were, to a man, like Milt Bolling: they held down jobs in the off-season. But I seriously doubt that Commissioner Selig would agree with Frick's equation. He loves the game too much, and his passion for it is tangible as we speak, one on one, just the two of us, high above the lake.

"There's a story that I've told that others have written about that I'll tell you quickly," the commissioner says. The tale is almost mythical by now and concerns his introduction to life behind the scenes of major league baseball's ownership. "My first meeting, 1970, and I was thirty-five years old, a kid from Milwaukee and this is big stuff, going to a major league meeting." And here the commissioner pauses, as though recalling that moment, more than thirty years ago, continues to take his breath away. As if he still can't quite believe that what he's about to tell me actually took place. This is the side of the commissioner that most fans have also heard about but have never seen or shared, a side that every living former commissioner—everyone inside of baseball for that matter—recognizes as genuine.

"Bowie called me and said, 'We have a meeting.' We had just

gotten a team [the Brewers, nee the Pilots from Seattle], so this is all happening, I think, in the second week [of the season]. I went to New York, not knowing what the meeting was—didn't care—just glad to be going to a meeting, a *major league* meeting.

"Bowie sat me between Phil Wrigley [of the Cubs] and [Cardinals owner] Gussie Busch . . . and they couldn't have been nicer. There was always very great support for Milwaukee from both of them; Mr. Wrigley had a home here in Lake Geneva, so he was very happy. It was a joint meeting [of both American and National leagues] so people sat interspersed."

The commissioner leans closer and in a virtual whisper of shared confidence lets me know that "It was all about *labor*, the beginning of the pension squabble and it was the ugliest, *nastiest* meeting. I left there stunned. And I remember saying to Mr. [John] Fetzer [Detroit Tigers' owner] on the way home, 'Wow!' And he gave me all the history, and also was very prophetic in much of what he told me about what was going to happen. . . . It was *bitter*, I mean really nasty. The owners obviously were not adjusting well to Marvin Miller and the players' association.

"Now, you can go back in history and look at that meeting. And the line I use about it is that it never got any better. It went from bad to worse. Every meeting, every commissioner, every labor negotiation. . . . It was sad, sad to watch, to see the anger and the hatred.

"The question that people ought to ask is, 'What's been going on for the past thirty-something years?' And that's a fair question. I'm not critical of anybody, because I know what Bowie went through . . . in a period of, really, a lot of upheaval. And Peter [Ueberroth] tried . . . and I know Fay has a lot of thoughts on the subject . . . but the fact of the matter is if we had confronted all these problems, they wouldn't be what they are today.

"There's no question that the thing that you always feel the strongest about is the game itself, whether they are economic issues, social issues, integrity issues, whatever. You worry about what is its impact on the game. It's something I talk to the owners about all the time. I was raised in the business. I watched people like John Galbreath, who owned the Pirates and who was the same kind of very classy man, who never let their own myopic interests get in the way of what they thought was in the best interests of the game."

Commissioner Selig relishes his longevity in the game. "I'm sort of what it used to be," he says. "When I first walked into a meeting, there was Calvin Griffith, Walter O'Malley, Horace Stoneham. That was their business; they *had* no other business. Tom Yawkey, that was his business. There was a lot of that around."

No more. The clubbiness of those times has vanished—in much the same way that it has vanished among ballplayers—along with the very individuality of ball clubs that often seemed to reflect the unique personalities of their respective owners, as the commissioner is well aware. Instead of ownership being something of a sport itself—a rich man's sport, yes, but a sport—the teams themselves have turned into mini-versions of Big Brother, that is, MLB, Inc. When Bill Veeck ran the Browns he lived in a small apartment in the ballpark and where he liked to throw parties. When the Red Sox were on the road, Tom Yawkey would gather local kids from the Fens to pitch batting practice to him in Fenway Park. Sometimes I actually find myself wishing for the return of old Charlie Finley with his mule and his mechanical rabbits and his penchant for exotic nicknames. Even Peter O'Malley has left the game. It's not terribly hard to imagine what the commissioner does, indeed, miss. Unfortunately for baseball, he's one of the few in the game's upper echelons who do. Bud Selig has witnessed it all, and other than a handful of old-school front-office folks, he stands alone in terms of experience and history. But by serving for so long as an owner and as commissioner he seems to have compromised both his understanding of the game and its history as well as the conscience that necessarily governs the office of commissioner.

"The owners have been wonderful with me, as you well know," the commissioner says, with a sigh of appreciation. And why shouldn't they be? Until very recently, he was one of them, but one of the few who have any sense of baseball, its business or its history. Which is something I'm not convinced the commissioner appreciates. Bud Selig is known as a "consensus builder" among owners, having done what no other commissioner could accomplish. Today, for the first time in memory, the owners are united. But for what purpose?

"I grew up with a lot of these people," the commissioner says, "so I know them well. The other thing—and I have to go back to Mr. Fetzer again, and a lot of people—I *watched*. There's a skillful way to do things. Just because you're the commissioner, you're not omnipotent. The fact is that if you want to get things done, you need a consensus. One of the problems in the past is they didn't have a consensus, so *nothing* got done. . . .

"I knew the system would have to be changed. So I set out to make sure that *everybody* knew what the problems were. I'll spend a lot of time with clubs; they'll agree, they'll disagree, but nobody can say that they're not heard. So I've been lucky. I've been luckier than any other commissioner because my eight predecessors had a pretty rocky road, as you well know. I found, years ago, there was always a rather significant group who felt out of the loop. Not me. I was close to Bowie, and I was chairman of the search committee that picked Peter Ueberroth. And Bart and I were . . . Bart might have been my best friend in the world. . . . But there was always a significant group that thought they were detached, and I made up my mind that I would try to not have that happen if possible. And, I might say, knock on wood, it has worked out great."

Great from the owners' standpoint, no doubt, but what about the fans and the game itself? Doesn't the commissioner remember when he was one of us? Doesn't he recognize that he came to ownership, and in turn the commissionership, by first being like you and me? Doesn't he recall that, long before Milwaukee had a team, it was the game itself he loved? And doesn't he remember back in 1966, when the Wisconsin Supreme Court overturned a lower court's injunction to keep the Braves in Milwaukee that it recommended that in the future communities be protected "from arbitrary and unfair dealing"?

Surely the hearts of Wisconsin's supreme jurists had Bud Selig, and millions of other passionate fans, in mind.

"One thing I've said over the last ten years is that I have no doubt that historians will say [this has been] the most active decade in baseball history," he says, referring to interleague play, the three-division pennant races, the wild-card entry in the playoffs. Those new wrinkles, along with doing away with the American and National league presidents and the league offices and the permanent retirement of Jackie Robinson's number forty-two, are Commissioner Selig's most noteworthy accomplishments. And three years ago, in an attempt to restore a greater sense of competition to the All-Star Game (as well as to exonerate himself somewhat from the mess that came of his "calling" the 2002 game after eleven innings), the commissioner announced that the winning league would gain home-field advantage in the World Series. Under any other commissioner these changes would be significant. Instead, they seem mostly cosmetic. Perhaps the commissioner feels he needs to compensate for being the first owner in history to serve as commissioner, and for retaining the position despite his claims that it was never something he wanted in the first place.

"If this were fifty years ago, the idea of a strong, independent commissioner . . . Independent of whom?" the commissioner asks rhetorically. "Many a night I'll sit here and daze and I'll think, 'What would Mr. Fetzer have done?' Or John Galbreath? And what they all would tell me . . . when they were teaching me the business was, 'Just do what's in the best interests of the game.' You've got to determine that. Is it *best*, for instance, to have a[n unlevel] economic playing field?"

With due respect for the commissioner's affection for old-time owners, I would bet dollars to donuts that the majority of today's owners haven't a clue who John Fetzer was.

"But the solutions may be *incredibly* painful. And you know that the commissioner is going to take a beating. I don't like it, I don't like the office taking a beating. I worry about that more than myself, because I regard myself as a custodian for this generation.

There'll be somebody next, and I only want to do things to make his or her life easier."

Of the three living former commissioners of baseball, Bowie Kuhn is Bud Selig's biggest supporter, though he is clearly wary of the precedent that the Selig administration may have already established. Kuhn was openly critical of the choice of an owner to replace Fay Vincent as commissioner.

"Not because I was against Buddy as commissioner," Kuhn explained to me. "I thought Buddy had some real potential as commissioner, still does. I criticized it because I felt it would make it harder to be commissioner because people would question your decision. The Minnesota [contraction] thing is a perfect example.

"I don't think there's anything amiss in terms of contraction in Minnesota, really, but the way people saw it. . . . He creates an impression that the commissioner is maneuvering things for his own financial benefit. So I don't think it's ideal. I think Buddy would agree with that. But at the time they gave Buddy the job, both as temporary commissioner and functioning as chairman and then as full-fledged commissioner, there was nobody else who could get the votes. I mean, they looked around. . . . Buddy could get the votes."

Of course, even baseball's owners were aware of potential conflict-of-interest claims against the office. But the office itself—despite seventy years of conscientious effort and real sweat equity by six or seven (depending on which side of the fence we stick Ford Frick) dedicated servants of the game—was of no concern to them, and still isn't, by all accounts. Granted, the Landis model that Kuhn and Ueberroth and Vincent recognized and leaned in favor of whenever possible had been pared down to the core, but at least the seeds were intact. And as Arthur Miller wrote of Willie Loman, they "deserve attention." But Miller was writing from a very different generation, wasn't he?

Kuhn continues: "'Well,' they said, 'at least it will be open; nobody can claim there's any subterfuge here. Everybody knows Buddy owns the club, and we all agree that that's all right and we're going to hire him anyway.'

"So, there was no hidden conflict of interest, but the suspicion remains, and it also makes it harder for Buddy to generate national support because I think it . . . undermines the office of the commissionership, in appearances if not otherwise. I don't think it's ideal."

Despite his skepticism, Kuhn understands the motive.

"The owners had gone restive with the powers of the commissioner. Buddy was an owner. . . . I think they had a greater sense of comfort. Buddy was, in a sense, the chairman of the board. Great communicator. I mean, some owners in my times [said], 'We don't hear enough from the commissioner! He doesn't call us up!' Nobody ever said that about Buddy. Buddy calls you up. And the owners had an immediate sense of comfort with Buddy. Still do. In the strike [and the subsequent cancellation of the league championship series in 1994], they held together. Remarkably. Nobody had held together like that before in the ownership. Buddy as the chairman of the board has had considerable effectiveness. I don't think he's given enough credit for it. But it's a different kind of commissionership. It's one where: 'I'm the chairman, but the board has the power.' Before, there was a board but the chairman had the power—over everything."

Ohio Republican senator Mike DeWine grew up a Cincinnati Reds fan. He's still a Reds fan, but he's also a baseball fan with a sense of the game's history, both on the field and as it is—and has been—governed through the office of the commissioner of baseball. He sounds deeply troubled by the way the business end of the game has been conducted.

During the Senate hearings in 2000, DeWine pointedly asked of commissioner Selig: "How will the Commissioner of Baseball convince the owners and the players, especially the owners of larger market teams, that the future of the game is tied to the health and survival of the sport?" He's still waiting for an answer, though his perspective is more acute today and more valuable.

"I think it goes back to basics," DeWine told me, "and the basics are that competition is what people want to see. The great thing about baseball is that traditionally [when] a team wins the pennant they only win six out of ten games. Traditionally, at least . . . the pattern that has emerged is so obvious: only the teams that make the money or the teams that have the big revenue streams [and] big salaries have a chance to get into the playoffs and then into the World Series. In the long run it's not good for baseball.

"So what you have to get people to think about is their long-term interests. What are their long-term interests, as opposed to their short-term interests? And that's not necessarily an easy sell. But . . . as far as the owners, you have to convince them of the obvious, that, yeah, everyone wants to see the Yankees, but they have to *play* somebody. And it's a lot more fun if they're playing someone who is competitive and who can beat them two out of every five games, maybe, or maybe a little more. That's a tough sell.

"The Yankees are probably a bad example," the senator admits. "We go through stretches in history when the Yankees reel it off. When I was growing up, in the 1950s and '60s, it was a Yankee-dominated period. You can go back to Babe Ruth and Lou Gehrig, and there's another Yankee-dominated period. There are several, and the sport survived just fine. What we're now seeing, though, what with thirty teams, is there are . . . a handful of teams that are going to win every single year. They may switch around a little bit but they will win year after year after year. . . . It is simply not going to be healthy.

"I think it is [a matter of] convincing people of that fact. Maybe it's a tough sell, but the more teams that you want to go see. . . . I will see seven or eight Reds games every year, no matter where they are [in the standings]. But that's not the way for most people."

And has Commissioner Selig been forthcoming concerning his understanding of these problems?

"From everything he indicates to me," DeWine says of the commissioner, he has been. "But what he says to me privately isn't significantly different than what he says publicly: 'We're working on it, and you have to allow me to work. Don't [let] Congress mess anything up. You have to allow me to work internally with the owners and keep them all on board so then I can go out and work with the players.'

"A couple of things have happened," DeWine continues. "One is with . . . expansion . . . you now have baseball in communities where the roots are not as deep. I think baseball will always exist in Cincinnati. I think baseball will always exist in Chicago, in St. Louis. These are great baseball towns. These are *baseball* towns.

"When I was growing up they'd always pitch the tickets: See Stan Musial and the St. Louis Cardinals. It was always, 'Stan Musial's coming in.' Now, it's saturated over the air. The other thing with the expansion . . . there are some cities that if they weren't winning or if they didn't have a shot at it I don't think they could sustain a team. [And] the disparity now is so great, in revenue and in salaries, much more than it has ever been before. . . . Even to *field* a team today takes, what, $40 million probably? Well, that means you've got to *make* $40 million. And if you're in a small market and if you're not winning and if you don't win year after year . . . I don't know how you do that. And I think what you're going to see . . . is that type team in the future never being able to win, not having the long baseball tradition. Our society doesn't just look to baseball as a sport. [It] now has all kinds of diversions, a million ways to spend their money, and they can see the best baseball in the world for nothing, on TV. That team won't survive.

"We're up to thirty [teams] now. . . . [H]aving the Yankees dominate in the 1920s or the 1950s was okay; whereas today having five teams or six teams that totally dominate and twenty-four that *don't* isn't okay."

Three years later, however, in an article ("not subject to the approval of Major League Baseball or its clubs") on MLB.com, Jason Beck reported that Commissioner Selig, speaking before a gathering of the Detroit Economic Club, referred to the Tigers as a "'dramatic manifestation' of the competitive balance allowed under the sport's current system of revenue sharing." Two years after small-market Detroit's 119-loss season, the commissioner declared the

Tigers and nineteen other (unnamed) teams divisional contenders. "You couldn't have dreamed this scenario in Detroit under the system we had ten years ago," Beck quoted the commissioner as saying. Headlined "Selig Says System Is Working," the story ironically calls to mind Fay Vincent's comment about Commissioner Giamatti's playful refrain—"Here is a man who believes in the system, who believes the system will prevail!"—during the investigation of Pete Rose's betting on baseball. But there was nothing either playful or ironic in what Commissioner Selig had to say concerning Major League Baseball's vision.

I asked Senator DeWine for his take on the recent iteration of the office of the commissioner of baseball: having an owner running things. Referring to Landis, and the mythical proportions of his commissionership, DeWine said, "We all think the commissioner is supposed to be impartial and sort of up on a mountaintop and removed and making decisions, arbitrary or capricious or whatever they were, but he made them, in the best interests of baseball. As you know, there are some people who argue that really, throughout history, that has not been true. So I'm not sure that Selig is so far out of line. They've just now taken it to the extreme."

Extreme as in the interim commissioner's dismissal of MLB's "antiquated" rule requiring full disclosure regarding loans. Apparently twenty-eight owners were left out of the loop when the Brewers owner borrowed money from a bank run by Minnesota Twins owner Carl Pohlad. *Extreme* as in treating as equally antiquated the notion of accepting the highest bid for the Red Sox. *Extreme* as in how a member of the commissioner's heralded "Blue Ribbon Commission on Baseball Economics," George Mitchell, was also a member of those "low-balling" winners up in Beantown. How does someone on such a highly touted panel do a complete 180-degree turn and invest in an industry he had concluded was in serious financial trouble? All of a sudden, making more money is an antiquated business plan? And how in good conscience could the commissioner condone the ownership swap that took place in that smarmy Montreal, Boston, and Florida ménage à trois? How can a chairman of the board, as the commissioner is so commonly known as today, justify in good conscience rewarding a man who could not make a go of it in Montreal by handing him a team that's been run into the Florida swamp, then assign the Marlins owner to Boston where he could partake of the fruits of one of the game's premium franchises?

The answer? "Loria is a member of our club!" offers baseball historian Cliff Kachline, sarcastically. "And we take care of people in our club! Maybe we'd prefer—and I'm speaking from Selig's standpoint—maybe we'd prefer to have him [Loria]. He was not a bad member of the club even though he wasn't financially successful."

How is Congress supposed to treat an industry that, while claiming to be losing money, provides a congressional committee with financial data that differ from the figures that same industry provided its union and then places a million-dollar gag order on anyone in the union who releases those numbers? The last thing Congress wants to do is regulate baseball! But as far-fetched as that idea may seem, there is a case to be made.

"You're going to see Congress remain interested," says DeWine, "and pushing and prodding. How far Congress will go remains to be seen. There is certainly a reluctance to get very far involved in it, and I think it's a healthy reluctance. On the other hand, besides the fact that there are an awful lot of baseball fans in Congress, I think a much higher proportion than the general population (which is an interesting thing. It's amazing. I don't know why that is, but it is), the reality is that, unlike fifty years ago, today virtually all the new ballparks are built with tax dollars. They're local tax dollars, but the federal government's got a subsidy in there because we still allow the total write-off of boxes. . . . We still allow the total write-off of tickets. So, there's some indirect subsidy through the tax law of a lot of things that go on . . . [and] there's an interest, as taxpayers not just as fans. Taxpayers certainly have an interest in what's going on with the game."

What then should the role of the commissioner be? Is the commissioner's notion of the best interests of the game in sync with what the fans have in mind? "Well," DeWine says of the commissioner, "I don't know what he's thinking about. What I think the average fan is thinking about is someone who takes those words literally, the *best interests of the game*. And the best interests of the game means what's good for fans."

DeWine recalls the 1957 All-Star Game, when Cincinnati fans "stuffed" the ballot box and elected seven Reds to the National League starting lineup. Commissioner Frick stepped in and replaced outfielders Wally Post and Gus Bell with—of all people—Willie Mays and Henry Aaron in the starting lineup.

"Well, I didn't like the decision," the senator recalls. "I thought it was changing the rules after the fact. But it wouldn't have made any sense, in hindsight, to have that many [Reds] out there. So he changed the rules, basically. Voiding a trade, if there is something outrageous about the trade. That type of authority. That's what people think about, in the best interests of the game. I think most people focus on the game [but] if you ask me, it should also have to do with dealing with such things as revenue sharing. I happen to think that's in the best interests of the game, to deal with that, for its long-term future. It's essential. It's crucial."

I reminded DeWine that Fay Vincent said that baseball—and the office of the commissioner—is undergoing a major crisis.

"I think it *is* a crisis," DeWine agreed. "It's almost a hidden crisis though. I mean, everybody . . . *knows* about it, but it just sort of lurks, like this monster, behind the door."

In due time, a hefty dose of steroids will grow that monster through the doorjambs, uglier than anyone imagined.

"I don't think you have to have data, financial data, today to see where you are going to be in ten years. To me the only relevant figures are the payrolls. . . . [I]f you know *that* you know where the competitive problem is, and then you can start seeing with attendance and your local TV, cable, etc. If you put all of those together I don't think you have to know this team's making money, that team's losing money. I know I'm in the minority with that, but

... I think you've got enough of the pieces of the puzzle to see the picture, without this other thing [revenue sharing] that the union and the owners are fighting over, for their own reasons. That's not my problem. The rest of it's my problem, as a fan and as a senator. The rest of it: Where the sport is going to be in five or ten years when this team is sitting out here with no fan base and they're not winning because they stink and there's no real great attraction to bring [fans] to the ballpark, except the crazy chicken coming in. ... This is major league baseball. We do want some entertainment, but it's still major league baseball. And people are going to want to see major league [-caliber] baseball.

"I think you can see the crisis without seeing the bottom line. They all talk a good game. Fehr says, 'We understand, we're willing to make concessions on that revenue sharing.' Selig says, 'It's our top priority.' But whether they'll be able to put anything together? I'm not optimistic."

"I'm not a big believer in the commissionership," Stan Brand tells me. "He's like the original special counsel, the original Kenneth Starr."

As the vice president of the National Association of Professional Baseball Leagues—the minor leagues—Brand is, in effect, "small-business" baseball's lobbyist for the minor league game. Appointed to the position in 1992 by Mike Moore, the man he lost to when both ran for the presidency that year, Brand brings a keen knowledge of labor law to the table, while also being a very familiar face on Capitol Hill.

"[The owners] got in trouble in 1919 [and brought] in an outsider, created a Frankenstein," Brand says of the office of the commissioner. "They brought a guy in they couldn't control. He was an absolute terror on wheels, and as time went on they couldn't get rid of him. His czar-like powers actually got in the way, culminating, finally, in the owners taking back their own business."

But was it their *own* business? Landis *was* an outsider; he was also a judge who trained a piercing eye on the limits of fair business practices in his years on the federal bench. If there was little opposition to Landis's oversight of the business of the game, it was partially because the office of commissioner provided owners with some measure of protection—from themselves! (Too, the times were also far, far less litigious.) Were owners so much more ethical in their collective business practices than today's crew? Not likely. But they were smarter. Some people, inclined toward the romantic, will have you believe that the owners simply cowered before Landis. But much of that was charade; all in all, for the duration of Landis's administration, baseball's owners (and players) did all right by the commissioner.

As soon as he took the job—and having been hired during the game's greatest crisis—Landis was charting new waters. Every decision he made was, in effect, precedent setting. From the field to the box office to the bank and back, Landis established a conscience for the office and the game, setting a standard that baseball welcomed and needed. As Commissioner Selig and others believe is essential today, Landis was trying to level the playing field. Moreover, ownership was bound by contract to Landis.

"We, the undersigned," they promised, in 1920, "earnestly desirous of insuring to the public wholesome and high class baseball, and believing that we ourselves should set for the Players an example of sportsmanship which accepts the umpire's decision without complaint, hereby pledge ourselves loyally to support the Commissioner in his important and difficult task; and we assure him that each of us will acquiesce in his decisions even when we believe them mistaken and that we will not discredit the sport by public criticism of him and of one another."

That's a concession we'll never see again, and rightly so, particularly given the shared wealth that owners and players enjoy today. Landis's take on the limits of the game's best interests was unique, with business and ballplaying issues typically decided from the same perspective. For instance, in something of a foreshadowing of the 2002 All-Star Game, Landis bore the brunt of the blame for calling, on account of darkness, the second game of the 1922

World Series between the Giants and Yankees in the tenth inning. The problem? It was still light out. Convinced by umpire Bill Klem that a big top-half of the inning would make the home club's batting impossible, ump George Hildebrand briefly conferred with the commissioner, who agreed. Fans interpreted the commissioner's decision as a way for baseball to pocket some additional revenues, and he was roundly booed—many flipped him "the bird"—as he left the park. The next day, Landis turned over the entire gate, more than $100,000, to charity. He took the heat, while standing up for Hildebrand: it was the ump's call.

Fearing gamblers in attendance might sway players to give less than their best, Landis ordered American and National league presidents to forbid players from talking with fans prior to a ballgame. The fine for breaking the rule was $500. Landis also forbade managers from announcing starting pitchers prior to game time. Again, the commissioner saw this as a way to attack gamblers' influence. Fast forward to the twenty-first century and consider Fay Vincent's interesting twist to this argument in the matter of Pete Rose's betting on baseball.

"What's important is what's in baseball's interest," Vincent told me. "And what's in baseball's interest is for Rose to help coach people, teach them why it's a bad thing to bet on your own team when you're managing. And he could do that very easily, explain about why, some days, if [he] didn't bring in [his] number one relief pitcher because he wasn't betting that day and he'd hold the pitcher for the next day, when he knew he was gonna bet $2,000 and why he didn't bet on some starting pitchers, and why it's a corrupting thing for a manager to know that 'I have no money on today's game but tomorrow I'm gonna have two thousand, so today's game isn't as important and I'll manage that way.' The public doesn't understand it. Even some sophisticated fans think as long as you bet on your own team, what's wrong with it? Well, you don't bet every day, you can't bet every day at the levels he was betting, and when you don't bet every bookie that you talk to knows that Pete's laying off today. It's an entirely corrupting aspect."

Baseball's "last commissioner" has something uniquely in common with its first. As inconceivable as it is to you and me today that managers would *not* announce their starting pitchers prior to filling out lineup cards, so the context behind the Judge's decision, when gambling was the steroids of the time, becomes instantly accessible when scanned with Fay Vincent's contemporary logic. But don't be confused; Landis was not necessarily ahead of his times. In addition to his stonewalling integration and revision of the reserve clause, the first commissioner's take on a ballplayer "holding out" so as to force a trade is as distorted as any ruling that has come from the office in eighty-six years.

"The suggestion that by the hold-out process a situation may be created [that qualifies] a player from giving his best service to a public that for years has generously supported that player and his team, is an idea that will receive no hospitality here," Landis declared. "It is at war with the ABCs of sportsmanship and impugns the integrity of the game itself."

But the Judge's most infamous business decision involved a young Iowan named Bob Feller. In 1936, the Cleveland Indians signed the seventeen-year-old fireballing right-hander while he was still playing ball on the Iowa sandlots, then moved him straight to the big club, if you call Fargo-Moorehead to New Orleans to Cleveland *straight*. Anyone who tries to get you from Iowa to Cleveland by way of New Orleans either doesn't think much of you or has something to hide. And so it was that the Indians ticketed Feller, with nary a cup of coffee North or South, and his contract right into Cleveland where he signed with the Tribe then struck out eight Cardinals in an exhibition game. Cleveland's interstate exploits with Feller were hardly in violation of the Mann Act, but they were against baseball's rules. Until 1936, major league teams were prohibited from signing players directly from sandlot ball, a rule that teams routinely circumvented by "recommending" that a minor league club sign a ballplayer then sell his contract back to the major league club. After the season (Feller went 5–3 for Cleveland), when the Des Moines ball club blew the whistle on the whole sleight of hand, the commissioner faced a dilemma. If Cleveland had broken the rules, Feller would become a free agent, which was likely to lead to a bidding war, something the commissioner wanted to avoid. (Wouldn't today's owners praise such a high-minded motive? And so much the better if it serves the best interests of the game.) In stepped Bob Feller's father. His son's contract would *not* go to auction, not after his kid struck out an American League record sixteen St. Louis Browns in his first major league game. (He tied the then-major league record of seventeen his second time out.) The elder Feller threatened to sue baseball in civil court unless the commissioner validated the Cleveland-Feller contract. Landis knew he could not win in court. Then, of all things, the minor leagues' National Association voted that the rule prohibiting the "recommendation" practice was antiquated (heh heh! the office repeats itself, to paraphrase the prescient Commissioner Vincent) and that minor league teams would henceforth consider valid such contracts that previously had been "recommended." Landis conveniently honored the law.

The outcome of Feller's signing has much in common with the results of the Federal League's suit against organized baseball, which Landis had presided over before being named commissioner. In each instance, the matter ran its course, and both times good fortune intervened. In addition to not having a players' union to tolerate or a corporation of Major League Baseball to honor, Landis had his fair share of good luck working. That's baseball.

Lately, the disparaging of the Landis model for the commissionership, or one that even leans in that direction, has become the staunch legal defense of management. Of course, today's corporately endowed ownership lacks the insight of Vincent's belief that the office evolves out of its own history and simply fails to appreciate the potential of the office of the commissioner. Ownership prospered under Landis, and Major League Baseball's argument that the commissioner must represent only that elite mix of thirty corporations misses the point entirely, and probably hurts ownership more than helps it.

If history eludes today's corporate ownership, that was not the case among the sixteen owners who had to choose a new commissioner following Landis's death sixty years ago. If you think owners made life rough on Bowie Kuhn or Fay Vincent, if you think Bud Selig is being pilloried, you haven't heard of Happy Chandler. Initially, according to Shirley Povich, the late sports columnist with the *Washington Post*, ownership "was quite proud of being able to entice a man from the grand U.S. Senate into baseball as commissioner." But things changed almost before Chandler took office. As early as April 1945, someone leaked news that Chandler was all but appointed. Assuming the accustomed posture of a U.S. senator, Chandler told Mutual Broadcasting's Dave Driscoll: "I have not as yet relinquished my seat in the United States Senate. I am not responsible for the publicity that has been handed out by my prospective employers. I am still a member of the United States Senate. Don't forget that Judge Landis kept his job as a Federal Judge for fifteen months when he took over the position of baseball commissioner."

Big mistake. Better to let sleeping mountains lie. To some owners, there was a bit too much of Landis in the senator's tone; and for those who didn't catch it the first time around, the commissioner-in-waiting actually referred to Landis by name. It was as though ownership had just touched down from Rip Van Winkleville. It took them time to pick up where they left off, those sleepyheads, but they found their way. Thus, it comes as no surprise that when Chandler suggested, before he took office, that umpires should be paid additional money for working the World Series, ownership soured even more.

From the moment he began his new job Chandler seemed devoid of political consciousness. (Commissioner Selig might empathize.) Povich, in the same interview with Bill Marshall, author of *Baseball's Pivotal Era, 1945–1951*, said that he believed Chandler to have been "more of a baseball fan than a baseball man." Which was—and still is—a called third strike when ownership's behind the plate. (Fay Vincent might empathize.) Intent on reversing the course that Landis had charted, baseball's businessmen (now fully awake) were determined that their business would be none of the commissioner's. Realizing that any clear-cut pronouncement concerning the conscience of the commissioner's office would likely turn public opinion against them, the owners allowed Chandler to run a six-year sprint (aided in large part by a press that had turned on him) in which the foundation for today's social and economic structure was poured, at times unwittingly: the integration of organized baseball; the challenge to the reserve clause; the beginning of the players' pension plan; the players' attempt to unionize and a near strike in Pittsburgh; and the suspensions of Leo Durocher for moral turpitude and Danny Gardella for "jumping" the Giants to Mexico. And those are just the crumbs at the foot of the bed.

Beneath the covers, Browns owner Bill DeWitt had worked himself a sweet deal in which American League clubs were paying him one cent per home customer. How that arrangement was ever struck (and why DeWitt has never been acknowledged as a pioneer in revenue sharing) is a mystery, but Chandler ended the practice and ordered DeWitt to repay nearly a million dollars to the other seven league owners. (One owner' s vote lost.) Fred Saigh, who owned the other St. Louis ball club, was even more ingenious, simply choosing to refrain from paying all of his taxes. Chandler's discovery of some fraudulent Cardinals' accounting was the tip of that iceberg, which would eventually lead to Saigh's six-month imprisonment for income tax evasion. (Make it two votes lost.) The Chandler years were also packed with intrigue, in the vein of a Dana Andrews thriller. Chandler's assistant, baseball's secretary-treasurer Walter Mulbry, who was supposed to be serving the commissioner as Leslie O'Connor had served Landis, turned on his boss. Mulbry, as Marshall says in his account of the era, had been assigned by Chandler to investigate Yankees owner Del Webb "to learn more about alleged connections with Las Vegas gamblers and specifically about his role in the construction of the Flamingo Hotel. . . . Mulbry, Chandler's classmate at Transylvania University and his administrative assistant dating to his governorship, became friends with Webb and confided to him the details of the investigation." (Three votes shot.)

Shirley Povich offered Marshall a revealing insight into the second commissioner. As Povich told the story, when Chandler was asked by a reporter to hypothetically name his successor, he suggested Bill Veeck. "[H]e was selecting the most unlikely candidate for commissioner he could ever dig up, and the man who wouldn't get the first vote with the club owners. . . . He had no particular talent for judging public reaction and press reaction. . . . [H]e did not know how to handle the press except to profess his friendship for everybody."

Chandler's homespun mannerisms didn't endear him to the New York press, whom the commissioner managed to alienate even further by virtue of New York's distance from Cincinnati, where the commissioner maintained his office. More than anything else, however, as Marshall writes, "What really irked baseball writers was the commissioner's inability to handle criticism. Chandler was a man who demanded absolute loyalty—one was either for him or against him. Gray was a color he did not recognize. When a reporter penned a column he did not like, he often wrote him a pointed letter."

But what sealed Chandler's fate with the press was his refusal to approve Bill Corum, a popular New York writer, as a broadcaster for the 1947 World Series between the Dodgers and the Yankees because Corum had been critical of the commissioner's one-year suspension of Dodgers manager Durocher.

"If you want to be critical of me," Chandler told Corum, "you do it on your own time. This is my time. You're not gonna do it with my time."

"Happy had a tendency to over promise everybody everything," Povich told Marshall (something Commissioner Selig has also been accused of), adding that Chandler "naively put too much trust in people he thought were his friends," including Branch Rickey.

The story of Chandler and Durocher would make the greatest baseball movie of all time. (For the purpose of the subject at hand, what Chandler faced with Durocher was virtually the reverse of what happened when Landis took over but just as significant. Keep that in mind while we return to our movie.)

Truly, it's hard to say how it all started. Durocher's gambling exploits—more so those of Leo's friend, the actor George Raft—began under Landis and serve as this tragicomedy's back story, which includes a momentous shift in baseball ownership, in 1942, when Larry MacPhail left his Dodgers presidency for the Army Air Corps and Branch Rickey settled in behind him (opening the door to Mr. St. Louis himself, August A. Busch, and all but closing it on Mr. Browns, Bill Veeck). Following the war, Colonel MacPhail returned a hero and did what heroes long have done: he bought the Yankees.

The movie opens, in the 1946 postseason. The newspaper headlines tell us that MacPhail is wooing Leo to jump boroughs and join him for good times in the Bronx. Aaron Sorkin could not have penned a better opening line than what Durocher himself offered: "I hope to manage the Brooklyn Dodgers till the day I die." Hope died eternal that day.

By spring training of the following season, 1947, the commissioner, at the request of Rickey, had met with Durocher concerning Raft and others. The "commish" and "the Lip" had a remarkable meeting of the minds, with Chandler coming off as downright fatherly to the wayward Durocher. But when a pair of gamblers showed up in the box adjacent to MacPhail at a Yankees-Dodgers exhibition game in Havana and the commissioner took no action, Rickey cried, "Double standard!"

Enter Larraine Day. The Durocher-MacPhail war brewed in the New York papers, the slander aimed at Durocher being that he was at best a philanderer, at worst a bigamist. In truth, Durocher was twice divorced, strings no longer attached, and the actress was a Mormon, whom Jerome Holtzman calls "the diametric opposite of her new swain." Only recently divorced herself, Day's postnuptial bliss, that is, with Leo, was contingent upon a single ground rule: that for the next year she not live as a married person in California. How this equates to *Durocher* being the one who lives on the dark side only the ghost of Larry MacPhail knows. But the source of the story made no difference to the Brooklyn Catholic Youth Organization. When a local priest declared attendance at Dodgers games a venal sin, the dollar signs began to add up (or down) behind Branch Rickey's eyes. The commissioner had had enough; he suspended Durocher for a year for activities "detrimental to baseball." Thus it was, my children, that gentle Burt Shotten, in civvies, managed the great Jackie Robinson that first season—but that's fodder for the sequel. Durocher would get his revenge four years later through another moment of divine intervention, a miracle at the foot of Coogan's Bluff.

It's difficult to say who had the greater tenacity: Rickey for putting up with everything Durocher threw in his face that went against his principles or MacPhail, for reaching heights of skullduggery matched only by a few guys twenty-five years later in a building called Watergate. In either case, Chandler's decision to ban Durocher for one year was beyond extreme. At Yankee Stadium, on Babe Ruth Day, April 27, 1947, Chandler was actually booed. Once again, Happy had stirred the owners to thinking: Best interests? No, bottom line. Once again, big mistake.

Today, the name most of us identify with Chandler's is Jackie Robinson. In his autobiography, *Heroes, Plain Folks, and Skunks*, Chandler presents a rather high-toned defense of Branch Rickey's signing of organized baseball's first black ballplayer.

"As a member of the Senate Military Affairs Committee I got to know a lot about our casualties during the war," Chandler writes of his discussion of Robinson with Rickey. "Plenty of Negro boys were willing to go out and fight and die for this country. Is it right when they came back to tell them they can't play the national pastime? You know, Branch, I'm going to have to meet my Maker some day and if He asks me why I didn't let this boy play and I say it's because he's black that might not be a satisfactory answer. . . . It isn't my job to decide which colors can play big league baseball. It is my job to see that the game is fairly played and that everybody has an equal chance. I think if I do that, I can face my Maker with a clear conscience.

"So bring him in. Transfer Robinson [from the Dodgers' Montreal farm team]. And we'll make the fight. There's going to be trouble."

If the commissioner's account of his exchange with Rickey sounds over the top, the melodramatic was never out of Chandler's range. And he was still a politician. Coincidentally, Chandler's "consent" came just over a year after the death of Landis. What would the Judge have done? Would Rickey even have approached the commissioner if Landis had been in charge? And how fast would Landis have held to the transparent argument that integration of organized baseball would be the death knell for the Negro Leagues? In 1943, following Paul Robeson's address to team owners on integrating major league baseball, Landis all but renounced his own authority, telling the *Pittsburgh Courier* that signing black players was strictly the decision of individual clubs.

What Chandler did for Robinson and others was to break the "Negro question" down to its kernel: *to see that the game is fairly played and that everybody has an equal chance.* Forget about the meeting and The Maker, Chandler was doing his job, and in doing so heeded the distinction between lines of power. Chandler's position is crucial not because he permitted Rickey to sign Robinson, but because it acknowledged his *lack* of authority, an admission he loudly enforced. In this respect, Chandler's position is somewhat reminiscent of Landis's role in the Federal League trial, except that the Judge's passivity worked the limits of the law toward a conclusion he thought was necessary, though he knew it was wrong. For Chandler, it was just the opposite. He was anything but passive concerning his revered neutrality. And he remained a vocal proponent of the authority that was not his when Rickey landed Roy Campanella and Don Newcombe in the next breath.

Chandler's position affirmed the strength of the office and the role of its conscience both on the field and in matters of business. For the most part, Chandler was lauded for his support of Rickey.

And throughout his life, Jackie Robinson applauded the commissioner for his support. What owners quickly discovered was that African Americans and dark-skinned Spanish-speaking players, irrespective of the occasional outburst by some of their white counterparts, put money in their pockets. Regrettably, from ownership's standpoint, Chandler's sense of fairness to players ultimately was out of line.

"Yes, Jackie Robinson," they would concede. "But let's not forget Gardella and Murphy!"

Ah, Gardella and Murphy: the reserve clause, the antitrust exemption, and unions! Long before Curt Flood, there was Danny Gardella. Long before Marvin Miller, Robert Murphy had a cup of coffee in Pittsburgh.

Ask any owner or player today: Who was the most important player a commissioner ever banned from baseball? If they answer either Pete Rose or Joe Jackson they're wrong. It was Danny Gardella. At the tail end of the 1946 spring training exhibition season, less than four months after standing up for Robinson and Rickey, Chandler banned for five years eighteen major leaguers who had jumped their teams to play for considerably more money in Mexico. Gardella was among them.

Danny Gardella was a quixotic wartime outfielder who actually slew a windmill. As one of those uncanny people who seem to turn misfortune into opportunity, Gardella also turned the reserve clause—opposition to it—into a cause that would define baseball's labor relations for years to come. Ineligible for military service because of a hearing loss, it was his hitting (and his fielding) not his hearing that kept him out of the majors before World War II. But with the call to service of so many players, Gardella found a door open, and he entered. Going into spring training, Gardella could boast he was coming off a "career year" (.272, 18 home runs, 72 RBI in 1945, his second in the majors). Under most circumstances, the outfielder's request of $5,000 for the upcoming season was modest enough, but training camps throughout the majors were filled with baseball's returning servicemen. Gardella was expendable.

A native New Yorker, Gardella was something of a showman who enjoyed singing opera. "An impulsive character," according to Marshall, Gardella "entertained fans and players alike by eating dandelions in the outfield grass while walking on his hands or traversing the roofs of Pullman cars while pretending he was a tightrope walker." But when the Giants said no to his contractual demands, he did much more than entertain or pretend. He announced he was jumping leagues to Mexico.

The Mexican League was hardly a fly-by-night outfit. The league had operated since 1924 and featured high-caliber baseball that included such Negro Leagues' players as Ray Dandridge, Leon Day, Josh Gibson, and others who were spared the racism they experienced at home while earning more money than most major leaguers. Jorge Pasquel, the millionaire Mexican industrialist who had been blacklisted by the United States during World War II for providing refueling facilities to Nazi submarines, was the Mexican League's benevolent dictator. Pasquel enticed American players by footing the bill for comfortable living arrangements while offering (years ahead of his time) signing bonuses and incentive clauses. The league's surreal moments were frequent: Pasquel once overruled an umpire—from the stands; owner of both the Mexico City team and the one in Veracruz, Pasquel would frequently shift players from one team to another on a whim; guns were prevalent at games and loud. Still, the caliber of play was the equivalent of decent minor league ball north of the border. With the addition of eighteen Americans, Pasquel raised it a notch or two higher.

In his autobiography, Chandler vividly, and with a decided bias, describes how "the rich and colorful Jorge Pasquel saw the postwar upheaval when baseball veterans were coming back from the military as an opportunity to grab American players for his Mexican League. He was handsome, canny, articulate, and eccentric enough to sometimes go around wearing a silver encrusted gaucho gun belt with two gleaming pistols in the holsters.

"Bringing satchels of greenbacks and his four brothers, Pasquel swept north across the Rio Grande for his great *beisbol* raid."

Enter Gardella. According to Marshall, "a chance meeting between Gardella and . . . Pasquel at [Al] Roon's Gymnasium in New York set in motion one of the strangest chapters in baseball history. . . . Gardella was one of the National League's most productive home-run hitters in 1945. Nevertheless, he still needed to work at the gymnasium to make ends meet. When Pasquel . . . learned that Gardella had to work in the off-season, he was incredulous. 'That is when he [Pasquel] got the germ of an idea in his mind,' recalled Gardella. When baseball veterans returned from the war, Pasquel realized that a surplus pool of major-league talent might be available to play in Mexico at bargain prices. Gardella politely refused Pasquel's initial inquiry regarding his own employment, but they parted with the understanding that Gardella was welcome to a job in Mexico anytime he wanted."

So when the Giants said no to his request for a raise, Gardella called Mexico, collect. The next day, sounding more like Curt Flood than a two-sixty-something war-years' hitter, he told reporters, "You may say for me that I do not intend to let the Giants enrich themselves at my expense by sending me to a minor-league club. They have treated me shabbily, I have decided to take my gifted talents to Mexico."

Pasquel promised the moon and nearly made good on his word. A number of decent ballplayers were lured south for the money, including the Browns' Vern Stephens, pitchers Max Lanier of the Cardinals and Sal Maglie of the Giants, and Dodgers catcher Mickey Owen. (Not only was Owen the goat of the 1941 World Series, when he allowed Hugh Casey's third strike to Tommy Henrich to skip by him with two out and the Dodgers ahead in the ninth, he has the shameful distinction of being the only American Pasquel fired: Owen was player-manager of Pasquel's Veracruz club.) Others were tempted but declined. Ted Williams is said to have turned down a blank check and four strikes per at bat. Bob

Feller said no to $500,000. Despite the money, most Americans returned home to face their five-year suspensions almost as fast as they jumped in the first place. The Mexican League was a far cry from the majors.

Initially, as players returned, Chandler held firm, and the penalty, in light of the times, struck most people as reasonable. (Landis likely would have believed the punishment lenient, though the very election of Chandler—who as a Kentucky senator and governor supported horse racing—would have been unconscionable to the judge). Chandler reasoned that two years' suspension would not have been deterrent enough and that a lifetime expulsion would have been cruel and unusual punishment—to the players as well as team owners. In June 1949, however, he reinstated all suspended players. (Stephens's return to the Browns three days after arriving in Mexico preceded Chandler's initial decree.) But reducing the suspension should not be misconstrued as magnanimity. There had been a court case, with baseball as the defendant. The plaintiff was Danny Gardella.

Gardella, as it turned out, had never signed a contract with the Giants. (Landis might have drummed him out of the game on no greater charge than having been a holdout.) In essence, Gardella claimed that the reserve clause was unconstitutional since in his attempt to enforce it Chandler was denying Gardella the opportunity to make a living in his chosen profession. It really never gets more complicated than that. (From 1947 to 1949 the "outlaws," as the "jumpers" were called, barnstormed the country playing semipro teams. Late in 1948 the commissioner declared that anyone playing with or against the outlaws—including players in the Negro Leagues and the Cuban League—would also be banned from playing in organized baseball. The following season many of the outlaws signed with Drummondville, in Canada's Provincial League, over which the commissioner had no authority.)

"The Mexican League mess hung on for a few years," wrote Chandler. "Lawyers got into the thing. Danny Gardella went to court to challenge his banishment. . . . Danny, who had violated his reserve clause with the Giants, sued for $300,000. Finally a United States Court of Appeals turned down Gardella's request for automatic reinstatement, sending the case back for trial on its merits.

"I felt that vindicated the action I had taken," Chandler wrote in his memoir. "And now that the Pasquels had abandoned their foolish raiding, I could afford to be forgiving. The suspensions had been in effect three years. That was a stiff enough penalty. So on June 5, 1949, I let all the players come back."

More specifically, Chandler let those players return who no longer had suits against baseball. Max Lanier and Fred Martin, who were seeking damages totaling $2.5 million, agreed to drop their suits. Gardella did not.

Ultimately, Gardella wound up settling for $60,000, half of which he paid to his lawyer, Frederick Johnson. In the courtroom, Johnson was light on his feet and as sharp as Donald Fehr at his best. And, like Fehr, he threw everything about the business of the game right back into the face of baseball. But Johnson's plea was a matter of too much too soon. Still, if baseball wasn't quite ready for so drastic a change as doing away with the reserve clause, Gardella's victory posed serious questions about how the business of the game was conducted.

As Marshall recounts, in February 1949 the Second Circuit Appellate Federal Court for the Southern District of New York ruled on Gardella's appeal: "Three eminent jurists, Harry W. Chase, Jerome N. Frank, and Learned Hand" decided in favor of Gardella, 2–1, with Chase dissenting. "Organized baseball was shaken by the rationale employed by the majority. Both Hand and Frank maintained that baseball's connection with radio and television gave the game an interstate character that might bring it within the purview of the antitrust laws. Noting that the concept of interstate commerce had changed since the Holmes decision [of 1922], Hand also remarked that the Supreme Court had overruled many of the cases based on that decision during the previous twenty years.

"Even more devastating was Justice Frank's observation. Citing the thirteenth amendment, he described baseball and the use of the reserve clause as 'an enterprise holding men in peonage.'"

Quoted in the *New York Times* following the decision, Gardella said, "It's too bad if my case is hurting baseball because I've been hurt pretty badly myself. They say I'm undermining the structure of the baseball contract. . . . Let's say that I'm helping to end a baseball evil."

Branch Rickey believed that Gardella's entire case was a Communist plot. Four months later, when the U.S. Court of Appeals ruled that baseball was not obligated to take back Gardella, Lanier, and Martin, the court tempered its decision by advising that the antitrust suits be heard post haste.

Of all the people to try Chandler's wits, Danny Gardella seemed the most improbable. I have listened to Marshall's tape-recorded interview with Gardella, which was conducted in 1980. (He died on March 6, 2005, at the age of 85, and it's a safe bet that few if any member of the Major League Baseball Players Association offered a toast of their indebtedness.) In recounting for Marshall the events that led to his departure for Mexico and his suit against baseball, Gardella comes across as a man who recognized his place in history.

"All of these things," he says in a voice that sounds very much like Harvey Keitel (with a touch of George Burns thrown in), "tie in together to form a sort of strange magic carpet of destiny on which I rode into the arena of having to sue them.

"It was as though steps were leading up to it . . . sort of Alexandrian . . . I'm not trying to really say that I am a man of destiny, but it was very coincidental that certain things happened and [are] still happening. It's very strange, really. . . . Why should I have met the guy [Pasquel], in all of New York City, who was a Mexican magnate and who was that type of person . . . who had himself just escaped being killed in the Mexican revolution and had to run away and came back and was restored to his family? . . . And then . . . he tells me, like a father to a son, 'If you ever get in any trouble call me up and you can come down and play with us.'

"[Pasquel] was an opportunist, a man who was always looking for excitement, a man who had money, . . . a man who would have loved to take the very ego of the States, from a foreign viewpoint, and tease them a little bit. I guess he could sense the weakness of that whole thing. He was a big businessman. He was a revolutionist. He was a lot like Castro. I was the little guy who was in between Mexican baseball and the other thing. And undoubtedly this rich and powerful Mexican man had germinated the whole idea.

"It seemed like when I got on the Giants and I played those two years, it seemed those two war years were the things that I lived for, baseball, and that I felt [enough things] in my own life had occurred. I had the dream . . . for two partial seasons . . . the culmination of baseball fame that I had sought, had dreamed of as a child. So in a sense my dream had come true. I wasn't thinking of any long term remaining there. . . .

"It was fitting and proper that I should have been the wartime player, because that was the role apparently fate had fitted me for. . . . It was things like that that sort of announced each strange event that culminated in my being the guy to open the door for, or to give some degree of legal fresh air, liberty, to players in the game. It was a very strange thing. It was like the working of evolution."

Gardella's position on his court victory is very un-MLBPA-like. "I felt like a Judas in a way," he told Marshall. "I always thought it was quite wrong. . . . If you sue someone for something, why should money appease you? It's like a Judas taking money and saying, 'Well, I'm being bought off. So I'm bought off.' Apparently my lawyer thought it was all right. I agreed to give him half rather than have the court award him a certain amount of money, which is what he could have had, . . . a certain fee that was allowed to him. But I figured, I started with nothing—almost—and he was working rather hard at it, and since the legal aspect of it was so important I figured he was worth at least half."

As implausible as that oration would be today—Gardella actually received only $29,000 from the settlement, owing his lawyer an additional $1,000 in fees—and as insignificant as the settlement was, even then, Gardella had set wheels in motion.

Well before Lanier and Martin had dropped their multi-million-dollar suit, National League president Ford Frick and team owners put pressure on Chandler to reach an agreement with the outlaws, one that did not depend on money. Chandler, attempting to comply, sent Mickey Owen and two other jumpers to encourage Lanier, Martin, and Gardella to drop their suits. Owen went two for three, and ballplayers ever since have profited from that one miss.

Gardella entered the major leagues riding an asterisk (in 1941, he was among the nearly one hundred minor leaguers declared free agents by Landis) and left on a footnote. Actually, if you're keeping score, Gardella added another obscure distinction thirty years later, when jazz pianist and composer Dave Frishberg released his song "Van Lingle Mungo," the lyrics of which consist of nothing but the names of former major leaguers: Hal Trosky, Johnny Mize, Sigmund Jakucki, Barney McCosky, Mungo, and Gardella, among others. Ironically, the song found an audience on radio stations in 1981, when Gardella et al. were the only ballplayers' names one heard for two months as baseball endured its first in-season work stoppage.

If 1946 was an important year for baseball, Chandler, and the commissionership, the month of June was pivotal. In addition to the outlaws' return and Gardella's suit, on June 8 a union movement culminated in a near-strike of Pittsburgh Pirates players in a game against the Giants at Forbes Field in Pittsburgh. Behind the movement was a less-than-Marvin Millerish Bostonian named Robert Murphy. Harvard educated and with a background that included working for the National Labor Relations Board, Murphy saw the Pirates as rife with union potential and Pittsburgh, with its strong union presence, as the city that would be most sympathetic to players' demands. In addition, as Marshall notes, "With a team made up largely of journeymen ballplayers or veterans at the end of their careers, the Pirates were an easy mark.

"By May, they were in seventh place and obviously struggling.

Even the leadership of former Gas House Gang manager Frankie Frisch seemed uninspired. With such large rosters [to accommodate returning veterans, teams left spring training carrying thirty-five players] Frisch and other managers had a difficult time playing and keeping players happy. Moreover, players were increasingly uneasy, because the team had to pare the roster down to thirty in June."

Murphy almost pulled it off.

Murphy created something called the American Baseball Guild. "In a four-page press release," Marshall writes, "Murphy explained some of the Guild's goals, including (1) freedom of contract, (2) the right of a player to receive part of his purchase price if sold or traded, (3) the right of arbitration in salary disputes, and (4) the right to join a union. Observing that strikes would be rare because of his arbitration plan, Murphy asserted that players would not have jumped to the Mexican League if the Guild had been organized sooner."

With a strike imminent, the Pirates organized a team of "replacement" players (including Honus Wagner, by then in his seventies) to take the field if necessary. In support of the ball club's business, Chandler promised suspension to all players who walked off. On June 8, before the game, the union players gathered in the locker room and heard Murphy out—his advice: strike!—one final time. Then they called on the antiunion pitcher Rip Sewell, who'd been excluded from the meeting. Sewell had won twenty-one games back to back, in 1943 and '44, and he was in twenty-win form that night, giving an impassioned speech opposing a strike. Sewell won.

Concerning Murphy, Holtzman notes that "in retrospect, Murphy was a successful failure. . . . Before the 1947 season, the owners, now concerned with player unrest, approved many significant changes.

"A uniform player contract was adopted with a guaranteed $5,000 minimum salary, the first time a minimum was established (previously some players were paid as little as $2,500); moving expenses up to $500 if traded or sold during the season; no salary cuts from one season to another to exceed 25 percent; full payment for the season if injured and payment of all medical and hospital expenses incurred by disability directly resulting from injury; extension from ten to thirty days notice to a released player; a guaranteed total World Series player pool of at least $250,000; no doubleheaders the day after a night game; and a $25 weekly allowance advance to cover spring training expenses, which for many years thereafter was called 'Murphy Money.'"

All that from a guy who paid his own expenses. And with the support of the commissioner—and the *owners*! Murphy and Gardella, what a battery!

Chandler's final victory on behalf of players would be the pension fund. In a scenario that taxes the imagination today, Chandler, Larry MacPhail, and Marty Marion—a commissioner, a member of management, and a player—worked in common cause to bring about the plan, which tapped into World Series and All-Star Game television revenues for significant support. Though players were still not free of the reserve clause—at the time, most believed it to be an essential aspect of the structure of the business of the game—they had won, with relative ease, major concessions from the men who paid them, and with the commissioner's blessings. "For a brief period," Marshall notes, "the owners had an opportunity to assess the game and to develop a vision for the future."

Shortly after Chandler accepted the commissionership, Ed Danforth wrote a piece in the *Atlanta Journal* headlined "Careful, Senator! The Job May Be a Booby Trap."

"Wonder whether Senator 'Happy' Chandler has studied the new baseball charter," Danforth wrote, "which stripped the commissioner of the absolute powers held by the late Judge Kenesaw Mountain Landis?

"This department, long a friend of the amiable young Kentuckian with a country-boy smile and a genuine love for folks, prefers to believe that 'Happy' does not realize what he had undertaken. . . .

"There is just a chance that between campaigning back home

and touring the war fronts, Senator Chandler has not studied the new major-minor league agreement. He has taken a job that gives him absolute authority over players, but severely limits his authority over the club owners. He has taken over a game in which the cards are marked by 'the house.'

"The club owners have loaded the dice so they can commit burglary if they want to and, brother, they have been chafing for years under the cold blue eyes of Judge Landis, who held them transfixed with his glare.

"This department hates to see 'Happy' Chandler step into this booby trap, but wishes him luck, because he'll really need it steering baseball into the postwar era. Through the big money boom that is certain to follow, termination of hostilities would be a major undertaking, even if the commissioner held all the powers Landis did. Armed with only a cap pistol, 'Happy' will have to do a lot of bluffing to keep the club owners in line."

It never happened. Chandler was anything but a bluffer. William Marshall, who got to know Chandler fairly well through a series of interviews for his oral history project, told me that "Chandler devoted his moment to the person he was with. He made you feel important, as though you were the only person of consequence at the moment [a trait that Commissioner Selig commands equally well]. He remembered names, something he worked very hard to do, and he made the most of this." Ultimately, however, the commissioner's "most" would not be enough.

After more than a year of campaigning for an extension of his contract, Chandler found himself voted out of office by ownership during baseball's winter meetings in 1950. Vowing to serve out his term, Chandler addressed the owners the following day. Cardinals owner Fred Saigh told Marshall that the only owner to address the commissioner at the meeting was the Dodgers' Walter O'Malley, who said, "Mr. Commissioner—although I didn't vote against you, I think it is the prerogative of this group to have their own Commissioner."

Chandler continued to lobby, but when owners met again during spring training the following season, the vote went against him once again. Four months later, Chandler resigned.

"In all fairness," Red Barber told Marshall, "Chandler was almost a tragic case. He was the wrong person at the wrong time in the wrong job, and I don't know of anybody who is as stiff-necked as he is. He wouldn't give ground."

But Barber was wrong. Though Chandler's stubbornness, especially in business affairs, had much to do with his ouster, it also strengthened the conscience of the office, despite all odds. In August 1951, Cubs general manager Jim Gallagher wrote to the ex-commissioner: "I have only one thing to say as your term as Commissioner comes to an end. That is that you have done something that most people seven years ago, or even three years ago, would have thought impossible; no longer do the words 'Baseball Commissioner' bring to mind Judge Kenesaw Landis."

Exaggerated? Sure, but the sentiment was not exclusive. The day after Chandler's resignation took effect, July 16, 1951, Les Biederman of the *Pittsburgh Press* wrote to the ex-commissioner: "I'm sorry to see you leave baseball at the moment and I know baseball will lose by it. You've been a credit to the game and to the office of Commissioner. And I only hope your successor does half the job you did.

"The players are with you to a man and they all realize what a terrific job you did for them."

After Sewell "broke" the union in 1946, Chandler presented the pitcher with a wristwatch inscribed with a note of appreciation for his support during the threat of the strike. For his own efforts on behalf of the game, baseball's second commissioner received nothing but platitudes and a request from Congressman Emanuel Celler to appear before a congressional hearing on antitrust and the reserve clause. Both Chandler and his successor, National League president Ford Frick, testified that August. Also called to testify was Ty Cobb. When Chandler learned of Cobb's scheduled appearance he wrote the ex-Tiger offering advice. The letter concludes with a sad plea: "Mannie Celler, who is conducting this investigation, is my warm good friend. I know that you will be a good witness for baseball and

I hope you will tell them, if you feel disposed so to do, that you feel that they have made a mistake in their treatment of me. I am sure that Celler would like to have you say that if that is your belief."

It's easy to see Happy Chandler as a contradiction in terms: the Southerner supporting integration, the commissioner from the state where horse racing is king. With all the appeal of a great politician, local wherever he went, Chandler's charm was all too local where it mattered most, in baseball's cities and inside its business circles. For five years Commissioner Chandler refused to learn what owners trained to learn under Landis: how to take a punch. Without the broad and traditional party support that accompanies elected office (and forty-nine equal colleagues to share the pain), Happy Chandler's "failure" as emperor reflects ownership's failure to heed his senatorial wisdom. As Commissioner Selig said of owners circa the mid-twentieth century, Chandler "never let [his] own myopic interests get in the way of what [he] thought was in the best interests of the game."

They could not have been less alike, Landis and Chandler, nor could their respective times and the demands of those times. Baseball and its business in twenty-four years under Landis did not change half as much as they did during Chandler's five. And in terms of conscience, baseball's pivotal era—as Marshall accurately characterizes Chandler's abbreviated tour of duty—offered an alternative and productive model for success. Everyone—players, owners, fans—did better under Chandler than under Landis. And with integration, the game (and all of the aforementioned) prospered and supported the game as never before.

Why ownership did not sustain the business momentum gained under Happy Chandler remains less mystery than regret. A stubborn man nicknamed "Happy" can be a thorn in the side of even the most generous of us. Owners? Please! Concerning the game and its business, there has never been a greater consensus builder than Chandler, who managed to swing from players' to owners' camps as if he were back in the Senate. To those who label Chandler's vision small-minded: the beneficiaries of the consensus he forged were the fans. (Of course, it was consensus that did him in.) Granted, Chandler's inclusive approach was less unique to the man than to the times. Ownership's great failure during Chandler's administration was killing not just the messenger, but the very message itself. Whatever bolt of lightning struck in 1920 did not strike twice when it came to owners appreciating Chandler's accomplishments on their behalf. The greatest mistake ownership ever made was voting Happy Chandler out of office. But, in O'Malley's immortal words, it was "the prerogative of this group to have their own Commissioner."

"Their own" as in: Ford Frick.

It's difficult to tell whether ownership really knew who they were getting in Frick or if they just lucked out, but his appointment was the beginning of a seventeen-year hibernation of the conscience of office. An active and involved National League president, as commissioner of baseball Frick all but formally repealed Landis's methods and Chandler's standards. In one congressional testimony baseball's third commissioner threw up his hands and told committee members that "the men who own the ballclubs, the men who operate the leagues and the men who play the game must be inherently honest. If they are not, the commissioner, alone, regardless of his power would not be able to maintain the game's integrity." Then he went back to sleep, awakening just long enough, in 1961, to put Roger Maris in his place.

According to Holtzman, Frick's "most crucial service to ownership was in squelching the repeated attempts to remove baseball's immunity from the Sherman Antitrust Law; among other advantages, the exemption provided the umbrella that sheltered the controversial reserve system." Some service!

Though he testified "as a reluctant witness" before Congress seven times in his first year and a half in office, Frick did nothing to follow Chandler's lead in extending labor equity to players. Moreover, he did nothing to bridge the differences between ownership and the players' union, which was formed during his watch.

If baseball was without a conscience for the first time in thirty years, it was not without a leader. The Dodgers' Walter O'Malley was more than willing to assume the role of baseball's head mogul, grand poohbah, and senior minister of relocation. Frick kept in step as ownership called all of the business shots, most notably in the changes O'Malley and his tribe brought to the landscape of the major leagues.

In a period of twelve years, from 1953 to 1965, six teams relocated (the Braves to Milwaukee, the Browns to Baltimore, the Athletics to Kansas City, the Giants to San Francisco, the Dodgers to Los Angeles, and the Senators to Minnesota), and four new franchises were added in New York, Houston, Washington, and Los Angeles. None of which was the commissioner's doing. (How different things are today, as a *real* owners' commissioner is the point man in such business affairs as expansion, contraction, and relocation.) But in one of the game's great coincidences, owners, players, and fans all benefited as almost never before during the game's continental shifts. It's a given that the opening of the West Coast and Texas to major league baseball was the most significant—and beneficial—change in the game since Jackie Robinson broke the color barrier. But, as popular as relocation and expansion were everywhere west of Brooklyn, there were still those nagging congressional hearings, persistent reminders that labor issues—fair business practices when dealing with players—were being conveniently ignored, that something was amiss under the surface, that maybe ownership's faith in its ability to run the game was premature.

As William Mead points out in his book *The Explosive Sixties*, "to avoid competition, as well as to counter lawsuits and to soothe senators who were threatening baseball's antitrust exemption, jilted cities were given new teams. Far from planning its expansion, major league baseball was pushed, prodded and sued every step of the way."

By the end of the decade it had become apparent that Congress was not about to rule on the reserve clause. Celler's committee ultimately decided that "legislation is not necessary until the reasonableness of the reserve rules has been tested by the courts. If those rules are unreasonable in some respects, it would be inappropriate to adopt legislation before baseball has had an opportunity to make such modifications as may be necessary."

Ownership, in its infinite ignorance chose to interpret the ruling as a victory that the commissioner had crafted. Concerning the final clause, and particularly baseball having "an opportunity to make such modifications as may be necessary," owners saw themselves as synonymous with *baseball*, and they trusted their "own commissioner" to stonewall Congress in much the same way that Judge Landis had stonewalled the Federal League in its suit against organized baseball way back when. And not a one could foresee the coming of the Continental League.

Today, the Continental League is all but forgotten. And for good reason: it never was. Unlike the Federal League's legitimate challenge to baseball's antitrust exemption, the Continental League was nothing more than a threat concocted by Branch Rickey and William Shea, a lawyer appointed by New York City mayor Robert Wagner, to bring a new team to The Big Apple, in 1959. Rickey had been out of baseball for some time by then, but he was still a master of deception. Of two things he was sure: baseball's owners were still a self-serving lot; and baseball's commissioner was little more than a puppet. Rickey and Shea played the "antitrust card" at a time when ownership was most susceptible to such threats. In challenging the American and National leagues as baseball's third major league, the Continental League announced the awarding of eight new "major league" franchises: New York, Buffalo, Toronto, Atlanta, Dallas, Houston, Minneapolis-St. Paul, and Denver. In a brazen threat to the status quo, Shea announced, "There are enough good players around right now to staff a new league. You can't tell me that a nation of 160 million can't produce two-hundred more big league players."

No sooner did O'Malley and company agree to accept the new league's franchises in two installations of expansion (first to ten then to twelve teams) than Rickey and Shea closed up shop. Eight years later, Rickey was posthumously inducted into the Hall of Fame; Frick himself was inducted into the Hall in 1970, twelve years before his predecessor. (Hell, as president of the National League, Frick thought up the idea for the Hall—they had to let him in.) As for Shea, in 1964, the Mets named their ballpark for him.

If there is any doubt that ownership had completely missed the boat on Frick, we have only to look at his successor, Gen. William "Spike" Eckert. Within a year of his taking office in 1965, Marvin Miller was named head of the players' union, as the power structure of baseball's business began to noticeably shift in favor of the players. Eckert went from being the "unknown soldier" to the "forgotten commissioner," but his name does bear significance in terms of the office today. Eckert's appointment was the brainstorm of John Fetzer, the Detroit Tigers owner and Commissioner Selig's acknowledged mentor. And it was during Eckert's brief reign that Selig himself entered the world of major league baseball, first by opposing the Braves move to Atlanta then as the force behind bringing the Seattle Pilots to Milwaukee in 1970.

Major league baseball never recovered from the Frick-Eckert era, and during those seventeen years of malignant neglect neither did the office of the commissioner, despite the efforts of Kuhn, Ueberroth, Giamatti, and Vincent. For the next thirty-four years, the business of baseball would become a battle of wits in Congress and in courts of law over the game's antitrust exemption, the legitimacy of the reserve clause, the ever-increasing power of the players' union, and ownership's benighted attitude. From Curt Flood's challenge of the reserve clause in 1969 until Congress passed the Curt Flood Act almost thirty years later, ownership begrudged every concession that players earned in court.

"Nobody's saying that the players shouldn't make a good living," insists minor league baseball's Stan Brand, "but the Players Association ain't a union. I'm not denying their legitimacy, I'm not denying that they're the collective bargaining agent with players. . . . I'm just saying . . . every guy makes his own deal. No Teamsters that I know have agents."

Ah, the agents. Imagine how much less baseball's owners would have to shell out if today's professional ballplayers didn't have their agents to share with. Imagine how delighted Happy Chandler would have been if Gardella had had an agent to represent his best financial interests. Of course, if players had agents way back when, there probably would never have been a Black Sox Scandal and the need to hire an independent commissioner.

"I understand the modern reality of it," Brand assures me. "I'm not challenging it. I think it's fine to be organized, I believe in it. They just don't function like other unions that I'm dealing with."

It didn't have to be that way. A lawyer who loved baseball the way Bowie Kuhn did, someone whose own private law practice was regularly involved in National League business affairs; or a savvy businessman like Vincent, who also loved the game; or a Ueberroth, who probably didn't. . . . It's a fool's guess, at best, what others might have accomplished from 1951 to 1965. What's clear is that Chandler's common-sense attitude toward the changing labor-management profile was a solid model for continued progress for the right successor, which Frick was not, despite his history inside the game. The consequences of Frick's appointment, ownership's first and greatest miscalculation concerning the direction of major league baseball, are with us today, compounded by repeated attempts by ownership to block the course that players and the commissioner were gradually moving toward during that "pivotal era" from 1945 to 1951.

The solution today, as drastic as it sounds, is probably what owners and players would have arrived at years ago, if only ownership trusted in the conscience of the office.

"The players have to own a big piece of the game," Fay Vincent believes. "They have to own part of the team. For somebody to get that done, you have to persuade owners to give up a lot, and you have to persuade players to trust in the management and collaboration. So it's going to take some very strong leadership—it's probably well down the road, but until that happens baseball is going to have this continuing (and other sports are going to have it too) sort of nineteenth-century fight between capital and labor that most other businesses in this country long ago solved. And they solved it by making the workers partners.

"Eventually they have to come together. They'd have to form a big overall umbrella corporation, where the players own part of it and the teams own part. The players' future would be affected by the value of the franchises. If Maris and Mantle had a little piece of the Yankees in 1960, think of what [that] would be worth today. And it shouldn't be hard to work that out, mechanically; it's hard to work it out politically. But, players *should* own a piece of the future, because otherwise they don't care about it. All they say is, 'Pay me my $25 million a year. I want to get everything I can, and [when] I get out . . . then whatever happens, happens.' You know, après moi, le déluge. And that's unhealthy.

"Each commissioner creates his own model, just the way each executive creates his own organization. And you have to have an organization that suits the people.

"I've said many times, it's a unique American institution, the commissionership of baseball, because the owners tend to think of it as if they're the board of directors and the commissioner is the chairman. They like corporate imagery, but they don't know enough about it to think about it clearly. The commissioner is in charge of disciplining and controlling, if you will, the board. Well, there's no corporate precedent for that. No chairman has to worry about whether his directors are cheating each other or require discipline internally. It's a model that won't hold up. But a lot of the business-men that come to baseball say, 'Well, the commissioner should be the chairman of the board . . . we're like the board. We want a corporate model and [the commissioner] should be like the CEO."

Well, they surely have their corporate model today in MLB, Inc.

"But it's stupid," insists Vincent. "It's stupid because the commissioner has to tell George Steinbrenner that I'm going to throw you out of baseball for two years because you were cheating on baseball, . . . or you guys have been colluding, all of you, and I'm supposed to watch you and prevent you from doing something that's very harmful, not only to baseball, but to *yourselves!*

"I mean, collusion, in the recent experience of baseball, is the most significant fact and it's almost totally ignored. You never read about collusion. Nobody ever talks about it, but it dominates all of the modern history of baseball. Because without it there wouldn't have been expansion; without crazy expansion there wouldn't have been this stupid contraction.

"It was a $280 million mistake by the owners. Then to fund it, to pay off the money they owed to the union, they had to expand, sell franchises. Now they're saying: 'Well, we made a mistake!' Well, why did you make a mistake? You made a mistake because you've [been colluding] financially, then you had to cover that up financially by selling franchises. Now you have to contract because you've got too many franchises. . . .

"The real problem in baseball is the inability of the owners and the union to figure out any model for joint behavior. They're really following the old nineteenth-century labor-against-capitalist model. Now, Marvin Miller was an old labor union lawyer from the steel workers, and look what happened to the steel mills. They don't exist. The union attitude eventually kills some businesses. It killed the newspaper business in New York; it certainly killed the steel business, hasn't done much for the automobile business. But the most enlightened . . . is the partnership where the union and the management come together and say we've got to have some joint behavior, we have to work together, we have to protect our business; without the business there are no jobs.

"The genius, the great leadership, will be above the players' and the owners' sides to figure out how to construct a new model in a way that will give the players what they deserve and protect the business."

What the commissioner today is paid to do is really no different than what the game has asked of the first eight guys in the order—keep the inning alive. Otherwise, it's back to carrying the lunchpail. Or worse.

5. The Absence of Conscience

JUNE 18, 2002

Senate Subcommittee on Consumer Affairs, Foreign Commerce and Tourism, Hearing on steroid use in professional baseball and anti-doping issues in amateur sports

It's been less than a month since Ken Caminiti, the former Houston Astro and San Diego Padre told *Sports Illustrated* that he began using steroids in 1996, when he was named the National League Most Valuable Player. "It's no secret what's going on in baseball," Caminiti revealed in *SI*. "At least half the guys are using steroids."

Caminiti's confession has raised a fuss throughout baseball and the government. Some players have corroborated the *SI* piece, some have denounced Caminiti for lying and implicating the innocent, and still others have vilified the ex–big leaguer for airing their dirty laundry along with his own. More than one player went so far as to say that "management knew."

But within hours of the magazine hitting the streets, a disconsolate Caminiti decried *SI* for using him, saying that, in truth, he had no idea what percentage of major leaguers took performance-enhancing drugs. Essential to the story, however, and not retracted, was Caminiti's belief that steroids gave him an unfair competitive advantage.

Ken Rosenthal of the *Sporting News* responded by writing that "by ignoring steroid use, the owners and players have perpetuated [major league baseball's] biggest fraud since the 1919 Black Sox."

Rosenthal is absolutely right. Two years before the testimony of Barry Bonds, Jason Giambi, and Gary Sheffield in front of a grand jury investigating whether Balco, a nutritional supplements company, distributed performance-enhancing drugs to athletes,

I asked Commissioner Selig about this, if steroids might be the equivalent of gambling during Landis's day.

"Well, I don't think so," the commissioner offered, "because gambling is still there as an issue. Integrity is still there as an issue."

Perhaps the commissioner couldn't get Pete Rose off his mind, but the steroid problem in baseball, as we have since learned and as he surely surmised, is that the drugs in question can—some say already do—affect the outcome of games, not to mention some of baseball's most hallowed records and the integrity of the game itself. Indeed, throughout today's hearing we will hear senators repeatedly invoke the phrase *integrity of the game* in the context of performance-enhancing steroids.

I am reminded of what Bowie Kuhn said back in March, about Landis's "mission" regarding gambling, how "the owners weren't willing to crack down on what had to be cracked down on," how Landis was hired to crack down. Though Landis did not have a union and a corporation of owners to accommodate, the parallels are obvious; and the issues at stake once again include the game's credibility in terms of what fans *think* they're seeing on the field. Eighty-something years ago, the office of the commissioner of baseball was created out of that very concern.

My mind is jogged, too, to what Peter Ueberroth had conceded, that he "didn't fight hard enough with the Players Association regarding [the drug problems of] Darryl Strawberry and Dwight Gooden. . . . Baseball," Ueberroth said, "the institution of baseball, missed for both of them." The *institution of baseball*. At a hearing that is about so much more than a "lifestyle" or "recreational" drug, the late-twentieth-century answer to Babe Ruth's—and so many others'—drink of choice, who represents the institution of baseball today?

If it is true that performance-enhancing drugs did influence the home run output of McGwire and Bonds, in particular, then baseball, to echo Ueberroth's phrase, has missed for more than its players; it has missed for its fans. Which brings us back to Commissioner Landis and the origin of the office nearly a century ago, when management surrendered its conscience to the man they elected to govern such issues. Where is that conscience this morning?

Subcommittee chair Byron Dorgan of North Dakota opens the hearing with one of the more irritating observations of the day. Noting that "serious questions are being raised by baseball players themselves, both active and retired, about what some say is an epidemic about performance-enhancing drugs among many of baseball's most talented professionals," Dorgan adds a damning, if understated, indictment: "We invited a fair number of baseball players, especially retired players, to be with us this morning. None of them chose to want to be here."

Neither did the commissioner. And he kept his conscience with him. Given the commissioner's avowed commitment to the integrity of the game, his absence is troublesome at best. The past eight months, including two previous congressional hearings and breaking stories about Major League Baseball eliminating franchises and accusations of conflict of interest by the commissioner/owner, have been hell on the office of the commissioner. But this one's not about the business side of the game but the game itself, and it welcomes the commissioner like a batting-practice fastball that the commissioner should crush. Nothing in the previous two hearings has come, to paraphrase Vincent, "out of the history of the office" as much as the matter of steroid use by ballplayers. Nothing speaks to the commissioner's responsibility as directly as this morning's agenda. And nothing could boost the esteem of the office better than the commissioner defending the game's integrity. But it's not going to happen. Not today. Major League Baseball wants us to believe that it's capable of pinch-hitting for the commissioner, and nothing is further from the truth. Major League Baseball, much like the Players Association, is batting for itself. Conscience of the game be damned.

John McCain, who requested this get-together, offers up a straightforward appeal to morality. "Like it or not, professional athletes serve as role models," he says. "That's more important than whether a group of highly paid athletes are using anabolic steroids." It's a savvy political gesture on the part of McCain, but he's overlooking the matter of trust. Calling for a zero-tolerance policy, the Arizona senator reminds both management and labor that the subcommittee would "like to see . . . a fairly quick agreement of players and owners." Though there are no players in attendance, their leader is, and he has much to say.

"No one cares more about the game and the health of the game than the players themselves," asserts Major League Players Association executive director Donald Fehr. "In many respects, the players are the game."

He gets paid for this.

Purportedly speaking on behalf of the commissioner, yet with no sense of the conscience of the game *or* the institution of baseball, Major League Baseball executive vice president of labor and human resources Robert Manfred defends everything MLB, Inc., has done to combat the problem Caminiti unearthed.

"As I sit here today," says Manfred, "I cannot tell you whether all of the statements made by those former players are accurate. What I can tell you is that long before anyone was writing about steroids in the major leagues, our office, at the direction of Commissioner Selig, undertook a multifaceted initiative designed to deal with the related problems of steroids and nutritional supplements.

"The commissioner began this initiative approximately two years ago by convening a meeting of respected team doctors, as well as Major League Baseball's medical adviser, Dr. Robert Millman. This group of respected physicians came to the meeting burdened by two related concerns. First, they were concerned about what they perceived to be a growing trend of steroid use at the major league and minor league levels. The doctors also agreed that steroids were a threat to the health of our players and to the integrity of the game. Second, the team doctors were concerned that steroid use by major league players was sending a very dangerous message to young people who dream about becoming major league players. The doctors all agreed that steroid use by young people created health risks even greater than those faced by adults."

For the balance of the next two hours we will go back and forth—the "integrity of the game," the "credibility of the game"—in a friendly little ping-pong match in which everyone seems to be on the good side. Labor and management have never been in such accord. How can one *not* be in favor of maintaining baseball's integrity, its credibility, or efforts to "do the right thing" to assure its public of both? But there's an absence of genuine conscience in the voices of Fehr and Manfred, a conscience that speaks for the institution of baseball.

Today's hearing would have been a perfect forum for Commissioner Giamatti's eloquence or Commissioner Ueberroth's conviction. I can accept the fact that Commissioner Selig does not seem to possess either man's ease before a microphone. Besides, hearings have not been kind to him of late. But if MLB, Inc., yanked him too early, that's a shame because even Spike Eckert would have looked good on this one. After all, we're not talking about the Pirates' Dock Ellis pitching a freakish no-hitter while on LSD; we're not talking Babe Ruth hitting three home runs on a hangover. These are not the drugs of self-indulgence but of performance. It's a matter of cheating. And how can anyone support a cheater?

Of course, there is the not-so-small issue that Major League Baseball, in marketing its product, promotes the players and their historic feats so as to grow the game, we're told, to grow the industry—and to grow a few bank accounts along the way. If "management knew," as some players claim, is MLB lying to the public?

You won't find an answer by listening to Manfred. Instead, he cites statistics: the number of times players are placed on the disabled list during a season (up 16 percent since 1998, he says); the number of days players spend on the disabled list (more than 27,000 in 2001, he reports, up almost 20 percent since 1998); and the financial costs to teams (in 2001 alone, $317 million, he claims).

"While the doctors could not scientifically establish a causal connection between the increase in injuries and steroid use," says Manfred, "there was a strong consensus that steroid use was a major contributing factor. In this regard, the doctors noted a change in the type of injuries suffered by players, with many of the injuries being associated with a significant increase in muscle mass [which can be attributed to the use of anabolic steroids]."

Manfred's argument focuses solely on the contract between player and owner, labor and management. His figures may or may not be accurate concerning lost workdays and ancillary expenses, including that of bringing up replacement players from the minors. What Manfred never mentions is ownership's contract with the fans, which is most assuredly a matter of trust that begets money, particularly as baseball has learned to market historic record-breaking performances.

Of all baseball's witnesses this morning, Arizona Diamondbacks owner Jerry Colagnelo probably comes closest to speaking to the trust fans place in players. "Based on my experience as an owner of the [National Basketball Association] Phoenix Suns . . . the implementation of a comprehensive mandatory steroid testing program would go far towards addressing this serious problem."

Fehr agrees, but only in part.

"Let me be clear," he says. "The Major League Baseball Players Association neither condones nor supports the use by players, or anyone else, of any unlawful substance—steroids or otherwise. Nor do we support or condone the unlawful use of any legal substance. I cannot put it more plainly."

Equally plain is Fehr's assertion that "the appropriate forum in which to consider these issues is the collective bargaining process, . . . [which] is not likely to take place in public, even before a Senate committee. Accordingly, while I am happy to engage in a discussion of these issues, it should be clear that we are not bargaining here."

Fehr is covering all the bases. He seems at the top of his game. But then he cautions, "While we all agree that this issue is a very serious one, we should take care not to treat unsubstantiated media reports and rumors as if they were proven fact. I trust that you will agree that we must avoid even the possibility of smearing anyone. All who live in the public eye fully understand the damage that unfair accusations can inflict on an individual or group. For this reason, I will not discuss these issues with respect to any particular individual, and I urge the members of the committee to adopt a similar approach."

In other words, Fehr will not touch Curt Schilling's recent observation concerning steroid and HGH (human growth hormone) use: how so many of today's ballplayers "look like Mr. Potato Head."

This strikes me as an open invitation for the commissioner of baseball to counter Fehr's veiled denials and speak up on behalf of the best interests of the game. By job description alone he is obligated to be here and not the corporate VP of labor and human resources in his stead. If nothing else, he owes it to the office.

In the commissioner's absence, however, Fehr politicks to identify a common ground, which the Players Association shares with Major League Baseball, Inc.: "I would . . . like to correct what may be a misimpression," he says. "If one simply were to pay attention to cursory sound bites or sensational magazine covers, one might believe that MLB and the MLBPA have no substance use/abuse program, or that, if one does exist, it makes no reference to steroids. Neither is true. The MLBPA and MLB have long worked with medical professionals to develop the current program, which is directed and administered by physicians appointed by our two organizations. It has a testing component, based upon reasonable cause to believe that a player has engaged in misconduct, or other activity affecting his ability to play."

To underscore his point, Fehr refers to a pamphlet, *Steroids and Nutritional Supplements*, which is "distributed to all players as part of our educational program." However, as he reminds the committee, "this is an issue not so easily disposed of. . . . There are complex public policy issues involved.

"Consider just one example: substances having steroidal properties, e.g., DHEA, or that we believe to be steroids, e.g., androstenedi-one, are fully legal under federal law and are sold over the counter in health food and other stores all across the nation, without even the simple protection of a warning label or an age restriction. As we have suggested in [the pamphlet], it may well be time for the federal government to revisit whether such products should also be covered by Schedule III. We would welcome such a reexamina-tion by the Congress and/or FDA."

It's a brilliant bit of strategy by "the Don," one that even Man-fred can support: shift the onus back to Congress. However, even if Congress and the Food and Drug Administration were to reclassify certain over-the-counter supplements, random testing of players brings with it grave responsibilities, Fehr says, adding that "the MLBPA has always believed that one should not, absent compel-ling safety considerations, invade the privacy of someone without a substantial reason."

As if to ease the mind of the union leader, Colangelo offers: "In the NBA, there was recognition there was a problem. The union agreed to address it. And we did. We have to do the same thing in this sport."

Of course, Colangelo is a relative newcomer to baseball; the bas-ketball union is a weak sister to Fehr's group. In addition, the drug problem the NBA faced did not "pump up" the numbers. Finally, no one present today—as Fehr and Manfred have reminded us—has the authority to do what needs doing. Fehr represents the players, Man-fred the owners, but no one represents the game. The office of the commissioner of baseball was created out of similar circumstances, and the man in office today is being paid more than $3 million to, by his own admission, uphold the game's integrity. He is the one person who must take the initiative here. As they said back in 1920: why not a commissioner? The question goes unanswered—unasked as well by the panel. Management and labor have seamlessly joined one another to render conscience totally irrelevant.

Maybe there has been some progress today, despite the commissioner's absence. If Manfred and Fehr can agree on challenging the United States Senate to "do the right thing" and declare "andro" (which Mark McGwire admitted using during his seventy-homer season in 1998) and similar over-the-counter drugs illegal, then maybe there's still hope for recommitting baseball's conscience to issues of integrity.

Wishful thinking, right? No more so than the final comments of Fehr's formal statement: "Let me address a question that is no doubt on the mind of the Chairman, Senator McCain, and the other members of the Committee, who have for so long been supporters of amateur and professional sports in this country: what message do we send to the kids who are playing ball and may be dreaming of a career in the big leagues? Frankly, it is the same message we send to today's players: Play this great game to the best of your ability, and do so under the rules. Do not jeopardize your health. Do not use illegal drugs. And don't take any substance—even if lawful—except on the advice and recommendation of a knowledgeable physician."

In other words, "Just say no." And just where have those watchwords gotten America and baseball, to date? With the Players Association executive director sounding like he was reading from the commissioner's script, it's worthwhile to recall a moment at the last Senate hearing, in February, when Fehr denied any obligation the players' have to anyone or anything beyond themselves and their union.

Of all three congressional hearings since December 2001, this one calls for the authoritative conscience that ownership imbued the office of the High Commissioner of Baseball with. It's still in the job description. Money counts and money talks, but you know what they say about your health . . . not to mention your integrity or the integrity of what you're selling. Suddenly, this becomes a consumers' rights issue. In 1919 it certainly was. Ask Charles Comiskey.

Commissioner Selig prides himself on being something of an historian, or at least someone who gains insight from history. With so much on the line, with issues of the honesty of the game (and life itself) at stake, the commissioner's absence is incomprehensible. Instead of the perspective that fans deserve and baseball needs, that of a man who knows his baseball history inside and out, who by his own admission acknowledges ownership's failed moments of ethical opportunities fifty years ago, all we get today from base-ball's contingent (*including* the voice of the ballplayers) are lawyerly charades and more posturing and showboat campaigning to gain public favor and congressional absolution.

And here's something else that's troubling. With all this noise about credibility and integrity and players serving as healthy role models, the only significant evidence presented comes from those outside of baseball. Dr. Bernard Greisemer, a pediatrician and sports medicine specialist for twenty-five years, notes that "steroid precursors"—over-the-counter supplements that actually *become* steroids once they're ingested—have the potential to adversely affect "nearly every organ system" in the bodies of young athletes. Greg Schwab, an associate high school principal and former high school football coach, offers the subcommittee his "insights as someone who has experienced steroid use firsthand for two and a half years as a college football player and an aspiring player in the National Football League."

Could Sammy Sosa say, as Frank Shorter (Olympic marathon gold medalist in 1972, bronze medalist in '76, and chair of the U.S. Anti-Doping Agency) testified earlier: "I didn't cheat, and I came in second"? What kind of footnote would Mark McGwire's, Sammy Sosa's, and Barry Bonds' numbers carry were Ford Frick commissioner today?

In retrospect, I remember Brady Anderson hitting fifty home runs for Baltimore a few years back and my comment to a friend: "But Anderson's just not a fifty-homer hitter."

"Of course he is," my friend replied, "you can look it up."

"Right," I said, "and you can look it up that the Reds beat the White Sox in the 1919 World Series."

The Black Sox Scandal of 1919, and Kenesaw Mountain Landis's subsequent appointment and his lifetime expulsion of the eight

"Black Sox" players, is the reason for Major League Rule 21, which concludes with item (g): "RULE TO BE KEPT POSTED. A printed copy of this Rule shall be kept posted in each clubhouse."

As for Items (a) through (f), they run the gamut of shady offenses that could lead to expulsion: "Any player or person connected with a club who shall promise or agree to lose . . . Any player or person connected with a club who shall offer or give any gift or reward to a player or . . . Any player or person connected with a club, who shall give, or offer to give, any gift or reward to an umpire for services rendered, or supposed to be or to have been rendered, in defeating or attempting to defeat a competing club . . . Any player, umpire, or club official or employee, who shall bet, or . . . In case of any physical attack or other violence upon an umpire by a player, or . . . ".

But for this morning's purposes, the most important item is (f): "OTHER MISCONDUCT. Nothing herein contained shall be construed as exclusively defining or otherwise limiting acts, transactions, practices or conduct not to be in the best interests of Baseball; and any and all other acts, transactions, practices or conduct not to be in the best interests of Baseball are prohibited and shall be subject to such penalties, including permanent ineligibility, as the facts in the particular case may warrant."

This very wording empowers the commissioner to enforce what needs enforcing. If steroid use unfairly enhances abilities and performances then it's as much as cheating.

It will be almost eighteen months after this hearing, in the fall of 2003, that Major League Baseball and the players' association will agree to mandatory drug testing. By mutual agreement—because 5 percent to 7 percent of players tested positive for steroids—the plan kicked in. But with little backbone. Counseling, small fines . . . conscience and integrity dumbed-down to merely good intentions. It's the kind of twelve-step plan that Steve Howe could sink his teeth into. What it needed was the imprimatur of the commissioner of baseball, and it needed to address such issues as puffed-up power numbers.

I remember leaving the 2003 hearing genuinely hoping that something good might come of it, that the commissioner might still assert the conscience of his office. I thought that at the very least MLBPA and MLB would drop references to punishment meted out by "league presidents," who no longer exist, in favor of a concise and authoritative warning about steroids and other "performance-enhancing diet supplements" and the severe penalties the commissioner's office would impose on any player whose actions undeniably affect the integrity of the game. I remember thinking about what Fay Vincent said, how "the wonderful thing about [the term *the best interests*] is that it is *not* susceptible to easy definition." That was the commissioner's trump card, and he failed to play it. He failed to even show up to play it.

In the two years since management and labor met to discuss steroid use before the United States Senate the two sides avoided a late-season work stoppage and signed a new collective bargaining agreement. The commissioner announced that the league that won the All-Star Game would have home-field advantage in the World Series. There was talk of reinstituting Pete Rose's eligibility. And Orioles farm hand Steve Bechler, a workhorse pitcher with a live fastball and a good knuckle curve, died in spring training—with traces of steroids in his system.

By spring training 2004, on the heels of the Balco investigation, Major League Baseball CEO Robert DuPuy said at a press conference: "Other than Mark McGwire saying he used andro, we don't have any evidence that any players have used any substances. . . . ,[W]e don't like any of our players' integrity attacked."

Seven months later, on the cusp of the greatest comeback in postseason history and the Red Sox's first World Series championship since 1918, Ken Caminiti, age forty-one, will die of a heart attack in the Bronx. Integrity?

6. Baseball's Other Peculiar Institution

We're shop keepers of the game. We're shop keepers, and we have to preserve that. > **Sal Artiaga,** Philadelphia Phillies director of Latin American operations and former president of the National Association of Professional Baseball Leagues

A lot of very smart people inside baseball will tell you that the office of the commissioner of baseball, as it was conceived by Commissioner Landis and as it has been tweaked over the years, is something of an anachronism, that it has no place within the economic model of today's game, that its voice carries little authority, that its best-interests mission is nebulous, at best. Some of these same folks also want you to know that the economic relationship of the major leagues to the minors is fundamental to the stability and growth of the game and is ultimately, yes, in the game's best (though no less ambiguous) interests.

Ironically, as a case of hypocrisy running headfirst into history, their logic as it supports the latter, the minors, conclusively negates their argument against the former, the office of the commissioner.

Minor league baseball is the game's other peculiar institution. It thrives today as much by good will as by good investment—*good will* as in a collective appreciation of "the best interests of the game" by ownership, labor, and the operating structure of major league ball clubs, particularly in light of the fact that the reserve clause, the bane of ballplayers for over half a century, remains alive in the minor leagues and essential to the future—the best interests—of big league baseball. The same used to be said about the office of the commissioner of baseball. The gambling crackdowns that restored trust among fans and the restructuring of the minor league system during the Landis administration; integration, player benefits, and growth of the minor leagues under Chandler; coastal expansion during the Frick years; the foothold the union took when Kuhn was in office; the licensing and promotional opportunities encouraged by Ueberroth; Pete Rose's baseball ineligibility ruling under Giamatti; Vincent's extension of health benefits and the major league pension plan to former Negro Leagues players—all happened under an independent commissioner and the umbrella of "the best interests of the game."

Those are just some of the details. For nearly seventy-five years, the office of the commissioner of baseball, overseeing the game's best—and, yes, often incalculable—interests, accompanied the financial growth of ownership and players. As steward of the game—*industry* according to management and labor in courts of law and during congressional testimony, anywhere fields of play don't come into play these days—that has spawned new professions and bolstered other industries, the office of the commissioner of baseball's role in creating the American subculture of professional sports, inspired by and modeled after baseball, has been significant. Yet not one of the game's first eight commissioners could have written a definition of the game's "best interests" that any bank would cash. So maybe there's more to this notion of best interests than meets the eye. And maybe, while the value of the game's best interests seems to defy the bottom line, it's time to look at those interests, governed by conscience, as a long-term growth stock. If the game's best interests are the cornerstone of the minor leagues' relationship with the majors, and ultimately major league–caliber baseball, then perhaps those same interests merit rekindling inside the office of the commissioner of baseball, particularly in its present iteration of an owner- (now former owner-) commissioner. At a time when players' association leaders, ownership, and many fans mistake the commissioner's mission as serving only owners, it's important to ask of the game's best interests: why do they apply to the minors and not to the office of the commissioner?

"People don't fully understand how important minor league baseball is in this country," former commissioner Bowie Kuhn told me. "Do something that might have an adverse affect on minor league baseball and major league baseball pales by comparison with the thrust that minor league people go to the Congress. They are *heard.* Congress loves small business."

Kuhn's diminutive notwithstanding, minor league baseball is no longer small business. According to National Association vice president Stan Brand, the major leagues annually spend more than $130 million on "direct player development costs, including minor league salaries, and another $90 million on signing bonuses and scouting." On any given summer evening as many as 180 teams (excluding those without major league affiliation) will be playing minor league baseball in the United States; that's roughly 4,500 ballplayers, each of whom is trying to make the majors.

Big league baseball's formal alliance with the minor leagues, which dates back to 1901, has helped sustain the game's unique position among professional sports in this country. As the graduated system for major league player development, the nineteen minor leagues that comprise the National Association of Professional Baseball Leagues is the worldwide measure of a ballplayer's abilities. Including summer leagues in Mexico, the Dominican Republic, and Venezuela (which also belong to the National Association) and five nonaffiliated independent leagues, there is roughly one minor league "starting nine" for every guy in the big leagues. Getting to the majors takes both talent and persistence; the minor leagues are proof. The recent growth of professional baseball internationally has afforded the minor league game a respectability that has long been taken for granted at home. With the infusion of big league money (something Commissioner Landis never fully appreciated) minor league baseball's popularity over the past fifteen years is unprecedented. In 2004, roughly 40 million people paid to see minor league games, and they sat up close to the field at ticket prices that don't require a second mortgage.

Brand's appreciation of the business side of the minor leagues stems directly from his understanding of its legal affairs, specifically that the minor leagues are the final repository of baseball's most historically controversial covenants: the reserve clause and the antitrust exemption. With major league teams investing millions of dollars in their minor league affiliates, not only are these two legally questionable artifacts flourishing, but they effectively sustain the ongoing development of talent and ensure owners of at least the opportunity—should that talent, in fact, mature—to cash in on their investment. One of Brand's missions is to keep baseball's antitrust exemption alive.

"I hired Stan to bring on board a picture of Washington and the national political scene," National Association president Mike Moore told me. "Stan ran for president against me, is how I met him. I was very, very impressed with him. The day [after] I got elected . . . I hired Stan. A lot of people thought I was crazy. 'Why are you hiring a guy who ran against you?' I said, 'Because this guy brings things to the table that I can't.'

"Most of our concerns in Washington are over the antitrust exemption. And Stan has been very valuable in helping us talk about how we need to organize at the minor league level. Before I hired Stan there really was no organization on the minor league level with a political emphasis on: How do we make the [representatives] and senators understand minor league baseball, and what we're about; and how would the loss of an antitrust exemption, or changes to it, effect us?"

I asked Brand if many members of Congress actually do understand the connection between the antitrust exemption and the reserve clause, particularly as they apply to the business of minor league baseball.

"No," he said, "but they're beginning to. I've educated them in ten years. [Howard] Metzenbaum [the former senator from Ohio] never wanted to hear from me. . . . I ruined his theory, which was that the antitrust exemption makes no sense, that it's obsolete. Why do the major leagues have it when no other sport has it? They have it because of the minor leaguers. . . . The greatest single argument for maintaining the antitrust exemption, as we know it, *is* minor league baseball. They would not exist but for the exemption.

"Reluctantly, I was forced to be part of the [crafting of] the so-called Curt Flood Act of 1998," Brand explained. "I was involved in a bank fraud trial in Riverside, California, during the negotiation of the collective bargaining agreement. I pick up the *Wall Street Journal* and I see that Randy Levine, the owners' negotiator, has put the antitrust thing on the table, essentially to say: as part of the collective bargaining agreement, major league owners and players will jointly lobby to change the antitrust exemption in only one respect, and that is to allow major league players to be like any other professional athlete, to have the ability to sue under the antitrust laws provided they'd be served by it.

"Well, I read that and I went through the roof. . . . [When Utah senator Orrin] Hatch passed the bill with the language approved, I said, 'I'm not agreeing to it, because it doesn't adequately protect us.' We're so intertwined: a [minor league] player who spends one day of service at the major league level is part of the collective bargaining agreement, and you can't just cut the minor–major league cord in half. There are ways in which you have to calibrate an exception so that we don't get hurt on the minor league draft and on the minor league reserve clause, without which we wouldn't exist.

"So, there was a big fight—minor leagues trying to crash the party. I think the owners secretly liked it, because I was such an independent person and had my own standing on Capitol Hill. They could say, 'Well, gee, *we* don't control this guy.'

"I said, 'Look, you can try to pass this but you're going to have to do it over my dead body; and I've got six or seven pretty big-time senators willing to filibuster it in the Senate. I've got 175 votes in the House, which I think I can get to 218; and it's not going to happen unless it's drafted the way it has to be drafted to protect us.'

"So, the Senate people—basically [Vermont's Patrick] Leahy and Hatch—agreed, and we became part of the group that then worked out the current language of the Curt Flood Act. It passed with agreement."

That accord was the defining moment in baseball's labor evolution and brought major league baseball up to speed, in principle—though light-years beyond the bottom line—with the rest of the country. Specific to major league baseball's antitrust exemption, the act states:

> that major league baseball players are covered under the antitrust laws (i.e., that major league baseball players will have the same rights under the antitrust laws as do other professional athletes, e.g., football and basketball players), along with a provision that makes it clear that the passage of this Act does not change the application of the antitrust laws in any other context or with respect to any other person or entity . . . [including] any conduct, acts, practices, or agreements of persons engaging in, conducting or participating in the business of organized professional baseball relating to or affecting employment to play baseball at the minor league level, any organized professional baseball amateur or first-year player draft, or any reserve clause as applied to minor league players.

In short, government saw some virtues in doing things the old-fashioned way: if the minor league system is to remain a viable avenue for player development, an investment in the future quality of major league baseball, then the reserve clause in some form must remain applicable. In effect, the antitrust exemption makes possible the existence of the reserve clause in the minors. Any thinking counter to that application of the exemption is detrimental to the game and its best interests.

"Right now," Brand explained, "when you're drafted out of high school or college you sign a player contract that has, in a sense, a six-year reserve clause, and you're limited to the entry draft. It takes five or six years to develop a major league player. . . . It takes that long to do it. If you took the antitrust exemption away and said you could attack the minor league reserve and draft provisions under a Sherman section 1 illegal restraint-of-trade theory and some court were to say: 'Six years is too long. It's unreasonable, it should be two or three or four years,' major league baseball would lose its economic incentive to underwrite [the minor league] system. That's $130 million a year they pay for that system, exclusive of the signing bonuses. So that's the core incentive they have to support minor league baseball as it exists today. You take that away and all that economic support goes out the window.

"If I'm a major league owner I'm not going to pay a signing bonus and pay the salaries of all these minor league players if in two years or three years the guy's going to be a free agent and go somewhere else.

"I'm not saying that there wouldn't be a minor league system, but it would look vastly different from what it does today. Oneonta, New York; Lowell, Massachusetts; Burlington, Vermont; Bend, Oregon; Odessa, Texas . . . Who knows whether those places would have minor league baseball as we know it? In fact, I know they wouldn't. We would be at risk in probably one hundred venues."

In other words, I suggested to Brand, there's a vestige of the old system that belongs in today's modern structure, a vestige that is totally unique to baseball.

"That's the argument for the exemption," Brand says, "that college football is the minor league for professional football, college basketball the minors for the NBA."

Is Brand willing to define that exemption as being "in the best interests of the game?" He didn't say, though clearly it is. We are not talking about Joe Jackson's reserve clause, and this is not Connie Mack's antitrust exemption. If ownership enjoys a return on its investment then both sides win. As players improve they become more valuable to management, and should they take their skills to the major league level they are very well rewarded, especially compared to those employed in other entertainment industries. With a minimum salary of $200,000 (the annual salary of more than

500 of 832 major leaguers topped $1 million in 2001) and a pension fund actually worth dying for, today's average major leaguer is Scrooge McDuck compared to most actors, say, or musicians. What does your local repertory actor know about signing bonuses? And what kind of incentive clauses are keyboard "side men" pulling in these days? In other words, even players who are bound to their clubs by virtue of the reserve clause are doing awfully well.

Repeal of the exemption, Moore is convinced, "would expose the player draft and the six-year reserve system" that obligates a player to his team. This is a common argument by ownership on behalf of the game's business interests. As far as the *game's* best interests, however, ownership is reluctant to debate the exemption because, as Fay Vincent says, they are "not susceptible to easy definition," and doing so would jeopardize ownership's perceived control of "their" commissioner. Furthermore, the history of players' rights in major league baseball tracks the judicial rulings that, over time, determined that the reserve system was illegal. Just as they willfully suspend disbelief concerning their own affairs, Brand and others deny the commissioner's rights to oversee the best interests of the game. This is a situation that strikes me as remarkably similar to the structure and attitude prior to Landis's appointment, with ownership wanting it both ways, more if they can find any.

Brand calls minor league baseball "a great institution, one of the last community gathering places that exist in America. People don't connect the way they did in the old days," he said. "There's not like a Main Street . . . and minor league parks are like that. It's more like baseball in the 1930s and 1940s than anywhere else."

Stan Brand is one of the sharpest people in baseball, and though we disagree on the scope of the game's best interests and the conscience of the office of the commissioner, I trust his integrity and his commitment to protecting the integrity of the minor league game and its future. But when he waxes romantic about the good old days, when he indulges in a moment of (even well-earned) nostalgia, he sounds very much like baseball's pro-commissioner/best interests faction. In short, very much like me.

"We're the research-and-development arm of Major League Baseball," Brand says. "The principal reason we exist is to create players for the major leagues. The side benefit is that 40 million people come out and watch and buy a lot of hot dogs and hats. . . . It works out pretty well. But sometimes even our owners have to be reminded that it's not necessarily about winning the pennant in the Carolina League, it's about developing major league players.

"I have a litmus test for whether the owners in the minor leagues . . . have the right understanding of what our mission is. I call them up and ask them how they're doing. If they tell me they're in second place and their pitching is bad, then I think these guys don't get it. If they tell me how many hot dogs they sold and what their attendance is for the year then I realize they understand that we are the player development line.

"It's a great thing, in a sense, because winning isn't everything in minor league baseball. It's a throwback. It's a place where, unlike almost anything else in America, winning is secondary. It's learning to play the game."

Winning isn't everything? (What would Landis have said?) A throwback? (What kind of sentimental hooey is this?) Lest I view the landscape he paints as overly pastoral, or worse, quaint, Brand assured me that he doesn't consider himself "a purist at all, not by any stretch; we have skyboxes and all of that stuff, too in the minor leagues."

Light-years from being a purist.

"I like the commissionership as it's presently constructed," Brand admitted, "with an owner who understands—maybe in this case, this particular [former] owner who comes from an old tradition, who [had] been an owner a long time of a small market club."

I took Brand's logic a step further and asked him if he would be in favor of a commissionership that rotated among owners.

"No," he said. "I'm a Tip O'Neill politician: if you get elected and it works, that's good for me. I don't view the commissioner any more as a protector of the public interest. I think that and the tooth fairy are gone."

And the game's best interests? The commissioner's contractual obligation to uphold them?

"Total baloney," he answered. "The best interests of the game is what works for the owners because, in effect, if it works for the owners it works for the fans. . . . Best interests are obsolete. In the modern world . . . the courts won't let you have that kind of power. Fay Vincent wanted to move the Cubs to the Western Division. They sued, and they won. And the judge eviscerated the best interests of baseball and said they didn't do it according to this rule and that rule. After that I thought, well if nobody's going to let us exercise that power then why have it?"

Despite his conviction, which is sincere and which he defends well, Brand's lobbying efforts on behalf of the legality of the reserve clause and the antitrust exemption are based in large part on that very "obsolete" concept. And it's for this reason that I'm convinced that the best interests of the game, its very conscience, are actually alive and well and living in the minor leagues. So too is any hope for salvaging the conscience of the office of the commissioner.

Minor league baseball is as resilient as the cockroach: no matter how many poisons the big leagues invent, the minor league system of baseball in America ultimately thrives. Beyond Commissioner Landis and his benighted view of their importance, the minors, now in their third century, have survived wars, radio, television, cable, and the Internet. Indeed, they have outlived the very expression—the bush leagues—that once defined them. The minors also have held their own against increasingly popular and prosperous collegiate and professional sports, as well as the burgeoning diversions that continually compete for your entertainment dollar and mine.

Minor league ball in the United States is practically a natural resource. The history of the relationship between the majors and minors is a delicate but successful balance of profit and investment that is misunderstood, at best, by the game's big spenders (ownership) and by the players' first line of defense, union leader Donald Fehr. (Except for the time warp and excluding salaries, Fehr has more in common with Kenesaw Mountain Landis than he does with Bud Selig: a distrust of the relationship between the major leagues and the minors.)

During his administration, Commissioner Landis routinely ran into problems with the minor leagues. "Landis lost the first major vote of his tenure," in 1936, writes David Pietrusza, in his biography of the Judge, "when the minors rejected his proposal that all information on sandlot players be filed with himself and the league presidents."

Four years later, sounding like he'd come straight from the union hall and reciting a soliloquy worthy of Fehr himself, Landis told the *New York Times* that he "regarded the farm system as evil; evil not because ownership of several non-competing clubs is bad in itself—although it unquestionably is preferable that every club be independently owned and operated—but evil because such ownerships are operated to control great numbers of players, imperiling their essential rights, if the rules do not prevent such operation, and also because it reduces minor [league] clubs to subservience. . . .

"Instead of being free to advance as rapidly as their ability merits, and to advance to and through any and every club in baseball, players are unjustly restricted to 'grooved' advancement through the one system which controls them and solely as that system may conceive to be in its interests."

Landis's remarks bear clarification, for the times were so different then. When Kenesaw Mountain Landis took his seat as "High Commissioner" of organized baseball—the American and National leagues and their minor league affiliates as we know them today—was less than twenty years old. Over the course of his administration, minor leaguers in the Pacific Coast League often earned more than their major league counterparts. The same was true of the best of the Negro Leagues players. Still, the commissioner's conviction concerning players' rights was always highly suspect, for example, players who "held out" for more money faced suspension, and the game's first commissioner did nothing to modify the reserve clause that similarly "restricted" player advancement. And while Landis dismantled Branch Rickey's St. Louis Cardinals minor league system back in the 1930s, Rickey's vision for player development has served as the model for building a successful big league franchise ever since. For the most part, ownership's attitude concerning the minors was subtle, measured by shades of inference and serving owners' worst selfish and mistaken interests.

On January 28, 1951, for instance, the Associated Press reported: "A big league anti-Chandler faction, determined to carry on its tooth-and-nail fight to oust the commissioner, reportedly has come up with a strong candidate in George Trautman, head of the minor leagues." Trautman, whose term as National Association president coincided with Chandler's tenure as commissioner, was reported to have had "six sure votes" among owners, with more anticipated. Of all the indignities Happy Chandler endured during his final eighteen months in office, this was probably the most offensive. It must have felt like a guerrilla conspiracy: no commissioner loved minor league baseball more than Chandler; and none promoted America's pastime among minor league cities and small towns with his energy, his enthusiasm, or his effectiveness. Not that Trautman wasn't qualified. If anything, he was probably overqualified (after all, the owners eventually chose the listless Ford Frick). In addition to his six years as head of the National Association, Trautman had served as president of the American Association and general manager of the Detroit Tigers. Given their big league conceits, most owners derived untold delight in seeing Chandler and his homespun ways, his old Kentucky tune, and his concerns for players' welfare upstaged by one so far beneath him. In truth, Trautman's nomination doesn't even deserve being called a smoke screen; it was never anything more than an unbridled insult, one of ownership's final digs at a commissioner who remains under appreciated to this day.

The minors are major league baseball's quality-assurance department and, as history would have it, evidence of how integral an independent commissioner is to everyone's success. Not only do the minors shore up an economic structure profitable beyond the wildest dreams of both major league owners and players, but they do so while simultaneously serving the best interests of the game. Today, those best interests, curiously enough, are baseball's strangest bedfellows, the reserve clause and the antitrust exemption, without which the quality of major league play would be questionable at best.

As the major leagues prepared for the 1951 season in search of a new commissioner of baseball to replace Happy Chandler, one owner, anonymously quoted, offered his assessment of the problems facing the game and a redefinition of the role of the office of the commissioner. "Things are different today," he said. "Baseball never had reached the popularity and prosperity it enjoys today. It is big business. Men have tremendous investments in the game. They don't want to trust their investments to an outsider who has no knowledge of the game. What they want is a baseball man who understands their problems and knows how to solve them."

Yet over the course of the next forty-odd years, ownership continued to elect to the office commissioners who accepted the job believing that their primary responsibility was to exercise the very conscience of the game. At times, of course, some of those interests were specific to ownership as opposed to players; sometimes they were coincidental, at other times doctrinaire. Some commissioners were better suited to the task than others, but each recognized the conscience of office. But today, more than fifty years later, ownership's battle cry remains the same: "Things are different!"

And ballplayers, too, have adopted the slogan. Fehr, in his testimony during the February 2002 Senate hearing, challenged Commissioner Selig's "vague reference to a catastrophic impact removal of the [antitrust] exemption would supposedly have on the minor leagues, which has never been clearly articulated. At best this argument sounds like if the majors do not have total monopoly control over the minor leagues, the minors will disappear. Oddly, the minors did quite well in the earlier part of the twentieth century when they operated as more independent forms of entertainment and feeder systems for the majors." But it should be noted that Fehr conveniently forgot the fact that during the time he alludes to the reserve clause *within* the major leagues was virtually carved in stone.

Things are different! each side shouts at one another. Remaining strictly adversarial, both labor and management look to extremes outside the game and beyond its history for solutions. Ownership has persisted in proposing a whimsical economically regulated "competitive balance" structure, contraction, and a self-serving commissionership. Meantime, as the union remains understandably suspect of owners' motives, it runs the risk of following in the footsteps of other "successful" unions, which, by virtue of their growing power, actually destroyed their industries. For at least the short term, and lacking any inspired vision, "there's no hope of any real rapprochement between those two factions," as Fay Vincent suggests.

Baseball, in the person of the commissioner and in the corporate personality of MLB, Inc., continues to argue that the health of major league baseball depends on a competitive balance that will only be achieved by a sharing of the wealth generated by "larger market" teams among their "smaller market" rivals. But their theorem is incomplete. True competitive balance depends on major league teams' ongoing investment in the quality of minor league operations, an investment in the game's best interests.

"I don't subscribe to the argument that if you're not in a big market you can't be competitive," Tal Smith, president of baseball operations for the Houston Astros, told me. "I think the difference is that if things don't work out—if you have injuries, if there's a mistake in judgment, or if a player just doesn't perform the way that he had in the past—that you don't have the ability, like the Yankees may have, to go out and correct that error by buying somebody else. I just think you can work things out. I think that scouting and development is the way for clubs to go. You build greater fan interest, and economically it works. . . .

"Look at the composition of our club [entering the 2002 season]. I'm not saying this is typical, but with the exception of Brad Ausmus, everybody in our regular lineup and four of our five starting pitchers, and our closer, never have played a major league game other than with the Houston Astros. Which is sort of unique today. From our standpoint, I think we've been very, very competitive. We're in the middle of the market, as far as players' salaries, and we've been able to develop a blend of veterans . . . with a lot of young talent. And that's what enables us to compete, and to compete very well, I think. (Well, we haven't fared real well, obviously, in postseason play. But at least we *get* there.)"

It's hard to argue with Smith's take on player development—post-2003 signing of free agents Roger Clemens and Andy Pettitte notwithstanding—as a realistic means of keeping a big league club, regardless of the size of its market, competitive. "The disparity over what is spent on scouting and development isn't all that great between those [teams] at the very top and those at the bottom," says Smith, one of the most respected front office people in baseball and someone who, in the 1980s, was mentioned as a possible successor to Bowie Kuhn as commissioner.

"I think clubs, frankly, make a mistake making [multi-year contract] decisions too early under the guise that it will be cheaper now than it will be later," Smith said. "As we well know, we can all project and have our ideas about future performance, but there are a lot of things that influence that. And I still think that you're better—from a standpoint of the contribution of players, as well as from an economic standpoint—taking it as long as you can, year by year, as opposed to multi-year."

Smith's sense of the importance of player development and a strong minor league system has been fundamental to major league baseball for more than seventy years, particularly after Happy

Chandler entered office in 1945. As Stan Brand eloquently—perhaps unwittingly—expressed, the essence of the minor leagues embodies the best interests of the game, no matter how you define them. The minors grow the game by assuring a quality of play on the major league level—in the game's best interests. They are an investment in a future that falls, if not contractually at least in spirit, within the purview of an independent commissioner. The two are remarkably in sync.

When I asked Mike Moore who he would recommend to replace Commissioner Selig he answered: "You mean if Bud was leaving? Probably Winston Churchill, but he's not alive." Sal Artiaga, director of Latin American operations for the Philadelphia Phillies and the National Association president prior to Moore, offered two bolder nominations: Tal Smith (once again) and Sandy Alderson, formerly of the Oakland Athletics, executive vice president of baseball operations of Major League Baseball, Inc., and currently with the San Diego Padres.

"I'd like to have someone that has a background in the development/procurement area, someone that has run a ball club or has familiarity with that," Artiaga said. "Because, you know what: the responsibilities of that office are *substantial*. They are far, far reaching. You've got the political issues, you've got the antitrust exemption; and then you've got the stability of the franchises, the competitive balance issues, the labor situation, the relationship with the minor leagues, and the ever changing rules on the procurement system—as right now the world draft is being proposed. It's a full plate. So it's imperative, more so today than ever, that you have a commissioner that has a background in what is required."

I like Artiaga's belief in a strong foundation. Reflecting on his years as National Association president, he said, "We were blessed with the fact that, although it was a dying breed, we had people that had historical understanding of issues. . . . Because . . . I wanted to make the minor leagues as attractive as possible to the major leagues, so that I was providing something that they needed.

"The saddest thing I find is that we do very little research in our industry. If you stop and look at different industries, there's a lot of think-tank approach to them. Experimentation. We're looking at different aspects. I'm not talking about reinventing the game; I'm talking about *preserving* the game.

"These are changing times," Artiaga acknowledged, "but we're being reactionary. . . . You have to invest in the development of your product. . . . There have been changes. On the free agent level, we had the era when the draft first started; we had a greater percentage of players being signed from the high school ranks. That, in time, shifted.

"Today, 70 percent of your players come out of the collegiate ranks, 30 percent from the high school ranks. Now you also have 42 percent of the players coming into the game that are foreign players. What have we done about that? How have we adjusted to better serve those needs? And oftentimes, when it's been in the area of Latin Americans, it's been survival systems. Fortunately—and I'm proud that I was one of the ones that started the Dominican Summer League—we've had more than 200 players from the Dominican Summer League reach the big leagues. We have a league in Venezuela, which we started in 1997. . . .

"So, if we're going to invest in those markets, we have to have a system by which when you tender a contract to a player that player has the best possible chance of reaching his aspirations: being a big league player. And that is the same aspiration that the major league club has, too. Otherwise they wouldn't sign him."

The difference between Capitol Hill and Clearwater, Florida, where the Phillies are training and Artiaga holds court, is refreshing beyond weather. Though he never states the words per se, I'm convinced that Artiaga—like many other longtime baseball people—believes the commissioner of baseball is obligated to the game's best interests, as opposed to those exclusive to ownership.

"We have to remember one thing," Artiaga said emphatically, "we're shopkeepers of the game. We're shopkeepers, and we have to preserve that. That is one of the reasons, when I was president of the minor leagues, I focused on the lower levels. I wanted that kid coming out of a great facility in the collegiate ranks to have as good a setting in professional baseball as possible. We were fortunate in that we had a lot of positives come of the PBA. One of those was the facilities standards that was a part of it. The minor leagues now have a great number of new facilities. But I think—although I'm not as close to it as I was before—the economic pinch of the 'have-nots' has already started to reach the minor league operations.

"All I'm saying is this: You have to look at what is the best for the current time. And we can go back to whatever era you want. You can go back to, say, the Pirates [of the 1950s and '60s], when they had Dick Groat and Bill Mazeroski. . . . And you know what, they were competitive. Why? Because they had a good farm system. They had a good development system. . . . Those were the factors in being competitive."

Roland Hemond remembers those Pirates teams. The executive adviser to Chicago White Sox general manager Ken Williams, Hemond began his front-office career in baseball with the Boston Braves in 1951 and has worked under eight of the nine commissioners of baseball. Hemond, too, supports Smith's notion of developing minor league talent and praises the efforts Commissioner Selig has made in this area. "He's made a stamp on quite a few subjects," Hemond says of Commissioner Selig. "The game has grown; . . . the globalization growth of the game is one that he has encouraged. And clubs playing some games in Japan that count in the standings or in Puerto Rico or Mexico, that's creative thinking. . . . He's worked hard to pursue what Bowie Kuhn and Peter Ueberroth cared about, the globalization [of the game], and also cooperating with the Olympic committees. . . . He has been able to convince clubs to cooperate to put out representative teams—mostly minor league players but some of the top prospects—and to participate in those programs, which has helped bring about greater exposure of our game. It was a good cooperative move for the clubs to allow some of the young players to participate."

As Hemond sees it, Commissioner Selig's efforts have been in the tradition of Bowie Kuhn, who "played a big role also in the relationship with the amateur ranks, colleges, youth baseball. . . . But it took continued pursuits along those lines; and it was constant after Bowie and Peter Ueberroth, Fay Vincent and Bud Selig. . . . So they all deserve kudos for that, and they all played a role in the game's growth.

"I find it fascinating. . . . I've been fortunate: When I broke in [major league baseball] only went as far west as St. Louis and now it's encompassing all parts of the country as well as Canada. And the future bodes well for continued growth of our game. Good leadership can help in that regard."

For years, good leadership *has* helped. And what we've learned of late, through the work of Artiaga, Moore, and Brand, among others, is that continued investment in the game *outside* of the majors is essential to the health, the best interests, of major league baseball. And it has been the tradition of the game that leadership in the direction of those interests come from the office of the commissioner. Bowie Kuhn's role in sustaining that leadership is paramount.

"I dreamed—and I believe it was a valid dream—that the international growth of the game would give it the further charge ahead that I wanted the game to have," Kuhn told me. "I wanted baseball to be the best, the most popular, the most beautiful game in the world. (It's the most beautiful game in the world already, but it was the other things I wanted to have happen.) Without international expansion and a gold medal in the Olympics I didn't see that happening.

"I very much believed in the international aspects of the game—when I say international I mean outside of the United States and Canada—so I concentrated a lot of my effort on international expansion, international good will. You found me in the Caribbean all the time. You found me in Venezuela a lot. You found me in Europe . . . the Netherlands, for instance. In England, where people didn't think there was—but there is—baseball. You found me in Italy, going to *professional* baseball games. (A lot of people don't know they exist there, but they do.) And working with the international amateur baseball people, and with the International Olympic Committee, to try and expand baseball. You found me in China, the People's Republic, and you also found me in the other China. We already had a couple of pieces of the communist world—Nicaragua, then under the Sandinistas, and Cuba—on our side. It was probably the best working relationship that had existed between the United States and Cuba for a long time.

"So, the international thing was extremely important to me. Japan was, in many ways, the key. I had great relations with the Japanese, and still do. The day after I left office, on September 30, 1984, I flew to Korea, where I met the Japanese commissioner and the Korean commissioner, who were dear men. [They] understood what the commissioner was meant to be . . . the 'conscience of the game.' I saw all of this as the underpinnings of potentially a great international growth of baseball. Which, after all, had been pretty much an American sport. Except for the odd places where the American military had exported it.

"So, all of that was part of my perception. Getting the gold medal in Barcelona . . . probably nothing in my lifetime, scoreboard boy to post-commissioner, meant more to me than getting that. That was key to international growth."

But where do such concerns rank in terms of the office today? And are Kuhn's views consistent with those of Commissioner Selig?

"I probably will surprise you," Kuhn said, "by telling you it *is* the current view. But it's irrelevant, because I had the time to work on this international issue, because baseball was in a much better balance in my time. The average salary hadn't reached a million dollars. We weren't in a disaster mode. They're in a disaster mode today. And the commissioner, God bless him, he doesn't have time to be running to Tokyo. I went to Tokyo because, I felt not only that it was important but I had time to do it. Baseball prospered in my time. I think it was highly respected. The role of the commissioner was highly respected, even if they took shots at me."

One of the most vocal supporters of Kuhn and his efforts outside of major league baseball is Bob Smith, former secretary of the United States Baseball Federation and for a number of years the head of the International Baseball Federation, the world body for amateur baseball.

"Bowie believed so much in the game and all the aspects of it, and he saw himself as committed to the advancement of the game worldwide," Smith told me. "I just don't think anyone could have worked more closely with the amateur side than Bowie."

But, Smith emphasized, a good measure of Kuhn's "inspiration" came directly out of the very history of the office and of the traditional responsibilities, vis-à-vis the game's best interests, that come with it.

"I'm sure Bowie took his cues from Happy Chandler," Smith offered, in appreciation of the office, its legacy, and of the esteem it claims worldwide.

"Almost without exception—I can't think of anyone I would even name as an exception," Smith said, "who did not respect the office of the commissioner of baseball. For example, think of the Cubans, who you'd think might be an exception, but they were such strong baseball people. . . . They knew Bowie, and I mean they looked up to him.

"We—the amateur baseball world—took a very strong stand when Bowie was under fire. We left no doubt that we wanted him to stay in office. We knew who the opponents were. . . . I wrote letters to every owner. I have a picture taken at our baseball convention of the heads of all baseball organizations signing a letter that we sent to every owner saying: 'We can't speak for what's needed at the professional level, but we can tell you what Bowie Kuhn has done at the amateur level, and he has been the very best and we hope that he continues.'

"I got a letter from George Steinbrenner saying: 'Dear Bob, I appreciate the support that you give to Bowie Kuhn. I happen to be of a different opinion. I feel that after fifteen years'—or whatever it was—'Commissioner Kuhn needs to be replaced. But he has done a lot for baseball.'

"I forwarded a copy on to Bowie, and Bowie's comment was: 'With friends like that you don't need enemies.'

"But we were determined to let the owners know that Bowie was a man who had done tremendous work for us, on our behalf." And on behalf of the health of the game and its future well-being.

Kuhn, of course, was instrumental in getting baseball into the Olympics, first as an exhibition sport and then for medal contention. But, Smith says, "We wouldn't have had Olympic baseball had it not been for Peter O'Malley and Peter Ueberroth. Peter Ueberroth used chits that he had as the head of the Los Angeles Olympic Committee. There were nine sports that wanted to be in as the two demonstration sports. . . . Well, baseball and tennis were chosen because Peter saw to it that we *were* chosen.

"We had to set up a village in the parking lot of—actually down the street from—Dodger Stadium. That went by the wayside. We eventually had our athletes in the village. We went from four teams to six teams to eight teams. We went from not being able to have opening ceremonies to having our own right there on [the field of] Dodger Stadium. From not being able to give medals to being able to give a medal almost exactly like the official one. You wouldn't even have known that we were a demonstration sport . . . except we weren't in the point totals. And it was because Peter Ueberroth helped to make it happen." And that was *before* he actually assumed office.

David Osinsky, who succeeded Smith at the International Baseball Federation and later founded the American Baseball Foundation in Birmingham, Alabama, also acknowledges Ueberroth's part in baseball's international growth. Osinski told me that he sees the office of the commissioner as being essential to the international growth of the game.

"Officials who ran the world body of amateur baseball, officials from all over the world," Osinsky said, "were obviously very cognizant of the thoughts and desires of the commissioner of baseball as it related to international baseball. Meaning, there was a desire to work together for the development of the game. With such commissioners as Bowie Kuhn and Peter Ueberroth and, for a very short period, Bart Giamatti, and to a certain extent with Fay Vincent."

Osinsky's vision for the game, and by extension its commissioner, is imbued with a genuine concern for its long-term health. "I would like to see Major League Baseball take a leadership role in putting the sport at the same level that football [soccer] is globally. Football has its own event, the World Cup, which is arguably the major event every four years in sports. It seems to me that's a goal for baseball, to be at that level. What that means—and as much as I love the Olympic movement, I was part of it for eight years—that baseball has to be bigger than the Olympics. And, of course, it is, in the sense of what it produces as a professional sport. But, it doesn't really have the type of world-level event that rivals the World Cup. So, in some form or another, that ought to be one of the goals of baseball. And major league baseball, theoretically, should be the leader.

"Why is that? Because now more than ever, you have these athletes from other countries, for example, Japan, coming to play baseball in the United States; whereas ten years ago the system did not allow it, or there was a gentleman's agreement. But now they're all coming. And now, even more so, you have everyone looking to Major League Baseball for leadership. In that sense it could be channeled into a very productive effort for the development of the game.

"For example, if you had a world-level tournament it could draw from the best four countries in the world, and that would draw millions and millions of dollars in revenue from those four countries. And if that were the case, then you could actually take a part of that money and earmark it for baseball development back at the grassroots level." (At least part of Osinsky's wish has come true. A sixteen-nation, three-week World Baseball Classic tournament featured the world's best players competing for their countries in

March 2006. On the other hand, the International Olympic Committee decided to drop baseball after the 2008 summer games because of Major League Baseball's drug-testing policy and its refusal to allow players to compete.)

What it all seems to boil down to, once again, is a concern that the institution of baseball preserve the health and the future of the game, as well as having a commissioner in office who has the authority—and the encouragement of ownership—to attend to those interests. Commissioner Selig entered baseball with a passion for those interests, and I believe the passion can be rekindled. Unfortunately, Major League Baseball has applied the what's-good-for-us-is-good-for-baseball rule of thumb to what it's doing with its international efforts. Rather than being driven by growth and good will, in the fashion of commissioners Chandler, Kuhn, and Ueberroth, MLB International is but a marketing tool of the corporation back in New York.

As recently as twenty years ago, owners worked hand in hand with the commissioner to serve the best interests of the game irrespective of caliber of play or professional or amateur status.

"Peter O'Malley was probably equal to any commissioner in what he did," Bob Smith said of the former owner of the Los Angeles Dodgers and his efforts on behalf of the game's best interests. "Because Peter *did* put his money down, and we needed that to become that Olympic sport. Peter O'Malley basically guaranteed the financial success of the games. His staff made it happen: they sold 18,000 tickets to the Olympics, before they even went public, to Dodgers' season ticket holders. We averaged 44,000 people per game for those events. And it was Peter, behind the scenes and putting on staff, who made those games succeed.

"Of course, Peter and Bowie were in the same camp, whether it was the Olympics or anything else. Peter was one of the guys who fought to keep Bowie as commissioner.

"One of Bowie's roles in the 1984 Olympics was to set it up so that the players that we wanted on the U.S.A. team who were drafted [by major league clubs] were kept available to us. Bowie said that any drafted player in that 1984 draft was not to report to the team but was to be available until the Olympics were over. So, for the first time in years, if ever, we had the very best."

Previously, Smith explained, players who were selected for the United States team and drafted by major league teams would be playing minor league ball at the time of international amateur tournaments. "Because of Bowie's action," Smith said, "we knew who we had early on, and who we could count on being there because it was an edict, basically, from the commissioner's office."

Well, *edict*'s a stretch, and I believe most commissioners would have done what Kuhn did at that moment. But all that Kuhn did *before* that moment—the time and the effort and the reason—*that*'s important.

Bob Smith referred to O'Malley, Commissioner Kuhn, and Rod Dedeaux (University of Southern California and 1984 U.S. Olympic baseball coach) as his "kitchen cabinet." What a threesome! Peter O'Malley, the unassuming son of baseball's most brilliant/ hated (pick one, or both) businessman; the commissioner (nee young lawyer Kuhn, who represented Peter's father—if you counseled the National League in the 1950s, you represented Walter O'Malley—in virtually his first job out of law school and his last before becoming commissioner); and the John Wooden of college baseball, a one-for-four lifetime shortstop in two games with the Brooklyn Dodgers in 1935. And all three just worked to keep a guy named Smith and amateur baseball afloat all around the world. No union. No contentious commissioner tilting ever more toward the holdings of MLB, Inc. No hearings.

"Four years later," Smith added, "Ueberroth granted us the same thing, a second time. . . ."

No sooner had Bud Selig replaced Fay Vincent as commissioner than major league owners began to feel a new sense of empowerment—or at least a sniff or two of the power they enjoyed before 1920. How sweet it was! Emphasis on *was*. More than seventy years had passed since owners were the exclusive decision makers.

Having "suffered" under commissioners who saw their primary mission as serving the best interests of the game and preserving it as an institution, owners reasoned that an owner-commissioner would be the strong voice necessary to counter the union's strength. It was an old business (and football) strategy, power versus power, that has never worked all that well in baseball. Thus, the choice of Bud Selig as an owner-commissioner was a response to obvious symptoms rather than to the problem itself, which was not the case when ownership approved the independent commissionership of Kenesaw Mountain Landis. According to their reasoning, because owners selected and paid his salary the commissioner was obligated to work for them alone. Their position was terribly shortsighted. Which is why, as sharp as Stan Brand is, I'm surprised when I hear him argue in favor of the owner-commissioner model—particularly in light of the history of baseball's labor-management relationship and his best-interests argument that major league baseball depends on the minors and particularly when one tracks the paths of the game's antitrust exemption and the reserve clause.

Since the office of the commissioner was created in 1920, ownership and players have each enjoyed one significant victory: management has retained its antitrust exemption; labor has conquered the reserve clause. Meanwhile, neither party seems willing to accept the fact that baseball's antitrust exemption (at the minor league level) and the applicability of the reserve clause (again, at the minor league level) co-exist as essential to the support structure for a major league baseball system in which the average player salary is $2 million and the market price of franchises tops $350 million. And still the relationship between the two groups has remained mostly confrontational, with owners denying that their commissioner's best-interests authority involves anything but the bottom line.

I'm convinced that Brand's argument expresses ownership's aggregate wisdom too—and their frustration—and is the greatest single impediment to the commissioner's ability to look out for the *game's* best interests, which include, by inference, those of owners, players, and fans. Even after a collective bargaining agreement was reached late in the 2002 season, the two sides remained driven by a mutual distrust that is counterproductive to everyone's best interests, including those of fans. It seems clear to everyone *outside* of the game that, in the absence of an independent commissioner, baseball lacks the centralized authority essential to success in the modern business world, particularly an industry that depends so much on "product" development.

I posed a hypothetical to Brand. If you have a commissioner in office, say Fay Vincent, who is constantly under attack, how do you go about strengthening the office so that he isn't constantly under attack? So that he can perform his job in the best interests of the game?

"I think he should be under attack," Brand explained. "He's like the Speaker of the House, he has to keep a political foundation to continue in office. Just like everybody else has to do. I don't believe in czars. I think that he has to have a consensus of support, just like a CEO does, just like a senator does, just like the President of the United States. Why should he be absolved from that check?"

Why indeed? Of course, the Speaker of the House can't threaten outspoken critics with million-dollar fines.

The last I heard, there was a professional baseball team in Parma, Italy, where, in the tradition of the nether reaches of American baseball well into the 1950s, local businesses offer jobs to players and grant them necessary time off to practice and play. It's not hard to picture tonight's starting pitcher racing, half in uniform, from his "day job" to the ball yard on his Vespa. And while a scooter gets, what, seventy-fives miles to the gallon, there's not enough gas in all of Italy to take this guy straight to the majors. Hence our minor leagues. The structure has held for more than one hundred years, an architectural wonder built partly on trust and partly on an appreciation of what's best for baseball as an institution, qualities that have been safeguarded by a strong and independently minded commissioner.

"If you went to a major league stadium today," said Brand, "the number of people who would understand the difference between a minor league–developed player and one coming directly from the college ranks, would be few and far between. But, my take is that whether they understand it or not, they would recognize the quality of play changing. They would understand even further the dilution of pitching . . . that the level of play wasn't what they were used to seeing."

Those thoughts are unsettling, but not at all beyond the realm of possibility. Many baseball insiders, particularly those with an economic or legal background, will argue that any relationship based on best interests for all is flimsy at best. The commissioner should really be a chief executive officer, they say, whose concern is to protect management. Players, they'll insist, have and deserve their own representation, independent of ownership. From a strictly business sense, their argument holds, and there are folks on both sides, players and owners, who support the concept. When you invest as much money as does an owner of a major league ball club, or when you earn as much as today's average ballplayer, you want to be absolutely sure about who's putting what on the bottom line. But this is not the shoe industry.

The Supreme Court and both houses of Congress have consistently gone out of their way to assure the game's public, its participants, and its owners that the commerce of the game is unique within American society. Unfortunately, only the public seems to understand. Despite dozens of hearings, players' union representatives and owners remain in the dark, failing to appreciate government's reluctance to interfere with the way the game governs itself. Similarly, these two groups seem perpetually misguided about the significance of their unusual dispensation and how to make the antitrust exemption and the reserve clause work for everyone's best interests. Is it so absolutely impossible for either side to appreciate that the validity of the former, as it applies to the minor leagues, justifies absence of the latter in the majors? Is it that difficult to recognize that in exchange for a great favor comes a profound responsibility to honor that favor? It shouldn't be. But there's no evidence to the contrary. Instead, both labor and management portray their "industry" not as structurally sound, which it is, but as a house built of cards that could implode any moment. (Of course, given the legalistic hot air inside, the staccato and robotic arguments from both sides, they might be right.) What we're left with is a system crippled from within, one whose two sides can only agree on this: ownership has its commissioner, players their union. Each has what it wants and deserves. And what about the game?

"I don't see any reason why baseball's antitrust exemption should be taken away," Bowie Kuhn offered. "I don't think baseball has functioned in a way that suggests it doesn't warrant that, [though] it's a legal curiosity, for sure. Not one of Oliver Wendell Holmes's better days, to be sure. Was it [Felix] Frankfurter who said that? Somebody said that.

"It was a legal curiosity, but a legal curiosity on which the game, in part, was built."

Accidentally or not—it was accidental!—the National Commission and its owner members hit on a formula that worked when they appointed Judge Kenesaw Mountain Landis High Commissioner of Baseball in 1920. For practically the next twenty-five years owners whined and whinnied while their own all-powerful commissioner cultivated the game's best interests, in part by protecting the independence of minor league ball clubs. If ownership—and now players—want to continue to go back and forth they'll have to swallow some history and allow the principles of trust that apply in the minor leagues to come to bear again on the office of the commissioner of baseball. Commissioner Selig is going to have to borrow some of Commissioner Landis's strategy and some of Commissioner Chandler's good will with respect to protecting and promoting the minor leagues. The growing popularity of minor league ball among fans in recent years, the burgeoning rivalries, the avenues for careers on the field and in the front office—Commissioner Selig has been around long enough to appreciate that the best of the game is grown from within.

7. Pumping Credibility

It's chemical McCarthyism. > Randy Wolf (Philadelphia Phillies pitcher)
March 18, 2005

*House of Representatives Committee on Government Reform hearing,
March 17, 2005 • House of Representatives Committee on Energy and
Commerce, May 18, 2005*

We are here because of steroids. We are here because of cheating
in baseball. We are here because of life and death. If that's not
enough, consider today's date: a congressional hearing on illegal
drug use held on St. Patrick's Day offers nothing if not the promise of at least some serious high drama. This day will fulfill that
pledge, and then some.

Beyond pathos and the empathy for families of athletes dying
young, the day will include a number of those seemingly inevitable, often ironic, allusions that mark historic occasions. And like
the most memorable of moments, there is a rich, substantive plot
and a cast of characters worthy of such an historic juncture. The
presence under subpoena today of former players Mark McGwire
and Jose Canseco, along with five players—Sammy Sosa, Curt
Schilling, Rafael Palmiero, and (via remote from Chicago) Frank
Thomas—in the twilight of Hall of Fame careers inevitably brings
to mind major league baseball's first historic crisis, out of which
the office of the commissioner of baseball was created. Not since
the Black Sox Scandal and the ensuing trial and ultimate expulsion from baseball of Joe Jackson, Buck Weaver, Ed Cicotte, Lefty
Williams, Chick Gandil, Swede Risberg, Happy Felsch, and Fred
McMullin nearly a century ago has baseball seen such spectacle.

As many as 1.6 million households will tune their televisions to C-SPAN or ESPN in a distant attempt to discern the differences between a version of the truth and aversions to the truth. Unlike their forebears, however, today's six are not accused of throwing games and gambling on baseball but of gaining the kind of edge (often unfair) that competitively driven athletes, certainly baseball players, have historically sought.

What the two groups share however, beyond congressional grandstanding that "cheaters" fail as role models for kids, is a matter of full disclosure. Gambling in the 1920s? Steroids seventy-five years later? Everyone knew that gambling on baseball games in the first twenty years of the twentieth century, like the use of steroids today, was common and that management, before Landis's appointment as commissioner, looked the other way. And following baseball's humiliation during and after the lockout and season shutdown of 1994, the home run barrage that ensued helped restore much of the fan support. Indeed, Major League Baseball marketed the phenomenon brilliantly as McGwire, Sosa, and Barry Bonds exceeded the magical home run number of sixty five times in a matter of years. By the time Bonds hit his record seventy-third home run in 2001, McGwire's record of seventy (1998) had barely had time to imprint itself in the minds of fans. Clearly, steroids had served to up the ante for major league home run status. Whereas formerly a thirty home run season would establish a player's slugger credentials, now forty seemed the necessary number, and fifty was now in sight of even players like Brady Anderson (fifty in 1995) who had *averaged* a mere ten home runs over the course of a fifteen-year career. McGwire's admission, in his pursuit of the record, that he had been using the steroid precursor "andro" became something of an imprimatur for the folks who run the game. Since Major League Baseball had not forbade the use of such drugs, the practice would remain within the bounds of acceptability, at least until Congress forced the issue and Major League Baseball was forced to comply. Winning baseball might be 75 percent pitching, but home runs are what pack the stadiums.

Initially, you'll remember, in addition to Canseco and company, the committee had thought to subpoena Barry Bonds and Jason Giambi. But Giambi was excused because of the ongoing BALCO investigation into the illegal distribution of controlled drugs, while Bonds was declared exempt because, in the words of committee spokesperson David Marin, "We want the hearing to be about Major League Baseball and steroids and the impact on young people, not about Barry Bonds." (What was he afraid the committee was going to do, ask for batting tips? relate favorite stories from seasons past?) Then there's the matter of Canseco who, though he claimed in his recent book *Juiced* to have administered steroids to Palmiero while the two were Texas Ranger teammates, decided to plead his fifth-amendment rights.

"Although I have nothing to hide," Canseco would testify, "and although my answers to your questions will be helpful in resolving uncertainties and issues facing this committee, because of my fear of future prosecution for probation violation for other unrelated charges, I cannot be totally candid with this committee. I want to invoke the protections offered to me by the fifth amendment."

Palmiero, too, will be firm in his stand, even invoking the patriotism of his immigrant family in defense of his innocence. "I have *never* used steroids. Period. I do not know how to say it any more clearly than that. *Never*. The reference to me in Mr. Canseco's book is absolutely false. I *am* against the use of steroids, I don't think athletes should use steroids, and I don't think our kids should use them. The point of view is one, unfortunately, that is not shared by our former colleague, Jose Canseco. Mr. Canseco is an unashamed advocate for increased steroid use by all athletes.

"My parents and I came to the United States after fleeing the communist tyranny that still reigns over my homeland of Cuba. We came seeking freedom, knowing that through hard work, discipline, and dedication my family and I could build a bright future in America. Since arriving in this great country I tried to live every day of my life in a manner that I hope typifies the very embodiment of the American dream."

Consider the source, Palmiero seemed to be saying. Four months later, of course, we would reconsider just that as Palmiero's "American dream" turned nightmare after he tested positive for steroid use. Palmiero's forcefully emphatic statement will haunt him for the balance of the season, perhaps his entire career. His volunteerism will also evoke both irony and insincerity: "To the degree that an individual player can be helpful, perhaps as an advocate to young people about the dangers of steroids, I hope you will call on us. I, for one, am ready to heed the call. Mr. Chairman, I think the task force [of players and others looking into steroid use] is a great idea to send the right message to kids about steroids. If it is appropriate, I would like to serve with Mr. Schilling and Mr. Thomas." If it is *appropriate?*

Then there's McGwire's unforgettable performance—which virtually amounted to taking the fifth—of repeatedly choking back tears in pathetic defense of what he will not acknowledge today.

Who here is guilty? And what are they guilty of? If Mark McGwire did, in fact, take steroids to improve his performance during his record-breaking, seventy home run season of 1998, that decision was motivated by the paycheck and an overzealous desire to win. If owners did nothing to put a halt to steroid use, they did it to jump-start the turnstiles following the 1994 lockout and cancellation of over a third of the season and all postseason play. If then-interim commissioner Selig did nothing it was because he was, in mind and action, more owner than commissioner. If Donald Fehr did nothing it was because, rather than acting as a union leader in the best sense of the term (even in the Marvin Miller sense of the term), he seemed more like those invisible agents (none of whom have ever testified before Congress regarding baseball matters) who madly tred water against the deserved indignation of the more than 90 percent of ballplayers who did *not* test positive when Major League Baseball, Inc., and the players' association instituted the game's first drug-testing policy in 2002. All that's missing from today's hearing is the apocryphal story of the young fan pleading to McGwire et al., as he did to Joe Jackson generations ago, "Say it ain't so."

But even before their moments of truth, the testimonies of a Hall of Fame pitcher and the parents of two steroids-related suicides would set such a solemn tone that irony was easy to miss or dismiss.

"Players who break the law and cheat should be severely punished and their records and statistics from when they used steroids should be wiped out," says Senator Jim Bunning, Baseball Hall of Fame inductee in 1996, sounding very much like someone testifying in the Black Sox trial. "If baseball fails to fix this scandal, then there are a lot of things we can do to get their attention. By amending the labor laws, repealing the outdated antitrust exemption (that baseball *alone* enjoys), and shining the spotlight of public scrutiny. The last thing I want the national pastime to be is the subject of a witch hunt. All of the players should be considered innocent until proven guilty. But we can't let anything get swept under the rug either. It's important we hear from the players themselves about the steroid use in baseball. We need to hear the truth. . . . The players and major league baseball must be held accountable for the integrity of the game. After all, it's not *their* game, it's *ours*. They're just enjoying the privilege of playing it for a short time. What I think many of today's players don't understand is that many others came before them and even more will come after them. And all of us have an obligation to protect the integrity. . . .

"Owners? For over a decade they have turned their heads when it came to steroids. They have helped put the game at risk. Not only did they turn a blind eye, they built smaller parks, making it easier to hit home runs. The balls started flying farther. We have to ask why all of these things happened. . . . Baseball has helped to open a Pandora's box, now it has a chance to fix that damage and educate the public on the health effects of steroids. . . . Go ask Henry Aaron, go ask the family of Roger Maris, go ask all of the people that played without enhanced drugs if they would like their records compared with the current records."

Without doubt the most wrenching words of the marathon ten-hour hearing would be delivered by the parents of the late Rob Garibaldi and Taylor Hooton. Both young men were baseball players, Garibaldi with the University of Southern California and Hooton with his high school team. The mother of Garibaldi says her late son told her, "I don't do drugs. I'm a ballplayer. This is what ballplayers do. If Bonds has to do it then I must."

Hooton, according to his father, took his life "two weeks away from beginning his senior year in high school. He was carrying a 3.8 average, made excellent scores on his SAT tests, and he and I were preparing to make college visits. . . . Players that are guilty of taking steroids are not only cheaters, you are cowards. . . . Show our kids that you are man enough to face authority, tell the truth, and face the consequences. Instead, you hide behind the skirts of your union and with the help of management *and* your lawyers you've made every effort to resist facing the public today. What message are you sending our sons and daughters? That you're above the law? That you can continue to deny your behavior and get away with it? That somehow you're not a cheater unless you get caught?

"Your attorneys say they're worried about how your public testimony might play in a court of law, but how do you think your refusals to talk are playing in the court of public opinion? Let me tell you that the national jury of young people have [sic] already judged your actions and have concluded that many of you are guilty of using illegal performance-enhancing drugs. But instead of convicting you they have decided to follow your lead. And in tens of thousands of homes across America our sixteen- and seventeen-year-old children are injecting themselves with anabolic steroids, just like you big leaguers do. Your union leaders want us to be sensitive to your life privacy. Right to privacy? What about our rights as parents? Our rights to expect that the adults that our kids all look up to will be held to a standard that does *not* include behavior that is dangerous, felonious, and is cheating? . . . [And] how about a short message for management; we can't leave them out. Major league baseball and other sports need to take serious steps to stop the use of steroids."

For the remainder of the long and trying day members of Congress and witnesses will express, in the words of McGwire, heartfelt condolences "to every parent whose son or daughter were victims of steroid use." And Robert D. Manfred Jr., executive vice president of Major League Baseball, will add the corporate defense, declaring in his written statement: "In a perfect world, those of us privileged enough to work in Major League Baseball would have been aware of the use of steroids from the minute it became an issue among our players. In a perfect world, the leadership of Major League Baseball would have had the unfettered right to deal with the problem of performance-enhancing substances as soon as we became aware of that problem. Unfortunately, we do not live in a perfect world."

More than eight hours after the hearing began Commissioner Selig delivers a testimony that defends Major League Baseball's drug-testing plan. Unlike Manfred, however, the commissioner offers support to what he calls "our players." "For some time now," he says, "the majority of our great and talented athletes have deeply—and rightly—resented two things. They have resented being put at a competitive disadvantage by their refusal to jeopardize their health and the integrity of the game by using illegal and dangerous substances. And they have deeply—and rightly—resented the fact that they live under a cloud of suspicion that taints their achievements on the field."

Never before has Major League Baseball defended ballplayers in such a fashion. Since the players unionized that job has been left exclusively to the union's executive director. And while Donald Fehr is in the house and eventually testifies on behalf of his constituents, the commissioner's words sound portentous, with the power to carry beyond the day. As if in response to California representative Tom Lantos's comment that he has "a feeling of the theater of the absurd here," the commissioner of baseball seems to be coming to at long last. Before our very eyes, in this most public of forums, the commissioner is beginning to revive the very conscience of the game.

Two months later, following shorter hearings on steroid use in the National Basketball Association and the National Football League, Commissioner Selig will appear before yet another House committee and sound a growing sense of conscience.

"I said this last week at the owners' meetings and I would say it again here today, that this is an integrity issue," the commissioner reports. "Do I believe that our program is working? Yes, I do, I said that . . . but we have issues that now transcend that: we have public confidence; we have integrity; and there should be no doubt left in anyone's mind that we have rid our sport of steroids."

Never has Commissioner Selig sounded so Landislike. It's a new tack the commissioner is taking, one that seems to fit him. For the first time in a while, the commissioner is sounding believable and committed to the "higher standards" to which baseball, as Bowie Kuhn reminded him so many years ago, is held. "I have said that even though I think our program is working, I reiterate again that all of this has brought integrity issues. . . . Anything that impugns our integrity in one form or another we must deal with and deal with directly. . . . The issue is this sport, and all its players who deserve better, and all its clubs that deserve better."

The last thing that anyone anticipated from the steroid hearings of 2005 was the office of the commissioner of baseball and the major leagues' baseball players seeing the world through the same pair of glasses. But when Michigan representative Fred Upton quotes from a letter from the Philadelphia Phillies' first baseman Jim Thome what we may be witnessing is a seismic shift away from Lantos's "theater of the absurd."

"I'm disappointed with major league baseball and the players association," Upton recites from Thome's letter. "We need to prove to the fans that there is no question that baseball should be clean and is clean, and we're not sending the right message with this policy. We're continuing to beat around the bush. Major League Baseball should set a higher standard. Like the Olympic athletes, they're the best of the best, why shouldn't we be accountable for things?"

"Why, indeed?" I think I hear the commissioner asking.

8. One Fan's Modest Proposal

Let it . . . be clear that no individual is superior to the game. > **A. Bartlett Giamatti,** seventh commissioner of baseball

With those words, in the summer of 1989, the commissioner of baseball brought to a close the matter of Pete Rose versus "the best interests of the game." Seventeen years later, Giamatti's pronouncement continues to resonate beyond heartfelt sentiment, truth, even the principals. For it was not just "Charlie Hustle" who wasn't superior; what went for Rose went—and goes—for the commissioner and everyone else in baseball. Indeed, the authority of the late commissioner's sentence owes a great deal to that inclusion. And if that's a fine point, it is not missed by the ninth commissioner of baseball and Giamatti's good friend, Bud Selig. Following the 2003 season and World Series, as Commissioner Selig weighed both the gravity of Rose's offenses and the justice imposed by Giamatti, he found himself looking directly into the conscience of his late friend and of the very credibility of the office he holds. Forget irony. Forget even the coincidental reminder of two commissioners' mutual respect that a request for reinstatement by Rose ought to evoke. When your friend's principles find voice in such high oratory as "the great glory of the game asserts itself, and a resilient institution goes forward," you can't help but call into question your own conscience. I do not envy Selig his decision, but it's one I'm sure he knows that only he, the commissioner of baseball, can make—and *must*, should Rose apply for reinstatement. It is in this light especially that the office becomes most "austere and lonely." Until the steroid hearings of 2005, I wasn't sure this was something the commissioner had experienced—a true baseball moment when no amount of lobbying or corporate advice should sway him. But when the steroid scandal broke and the commissioner publicly defended his obligation to ensure the integrity of the game it seemed that the final draft of the script had been written with no one but Commissioner Selig in mind: a historical drama that offers the potential to inspire the historian in office. I'm betting on "the Commish" to act out of the conscience of his office and restore, more than his own reputation, that of the office and its efficacy.

The office of the commissioner of baseball has come nearly full circle. Like baseball itself, it's all about timing. I don't care what anyone says, as different as the times and particulars are, the demands on the commissioner today are not so different from those that challenged Landis: change the public's perception of the integrity of the game and its operations. It's not a lot to ask. Of course, the institutions that players and owners have created to serve them will continue to do so to the fullest extent of the law. But let's grant the commissioner the power to keep things kosher. Oversight of annual audits, for instance, is a fair start. Let's allow for some checks and balances here. How revolutionary! And wouldn't that just tickle Congress, a genuine effort by baseball to prove it can govern itself?

Though Commissioner Selig disagreed, I still hold that the current steroid controversy is the third-millennium equivalent of the Black Sox Scandal. Fixing a game, let alone a World Series, is practically inconceivable today. There's not enough money in all of Las Vegas to make such propositions enticing to any of today's well-heeled ballplayers. But fix the numbers? That's a different story: a home run title pays off in legal, *contractual* incentives (and think of the endorsements!). Add to the mix the potential for corporate marketing of such feats—70 home runs, 75 . . . everyone gains. True cooperation of labor and management. Now, far be it for me to say that anyone did anything to juice the stats or profit by them; I'm but a lowly fan of the game. Still, as was the case with gambling in 1919, that steroid use has been a popular clubhouse activity recently is common knowledge. (MLB found, in the fall of 2003, that 5 to 7 percent of players tested positive for steroid use, but the number is likely much greater among everyday players, as opposed to pitchers.) Equally troubling is the feeble mandatory-testing solution—they ought to call it the "Steve Howe Act"—agreed to by Major League Baseball and the Major League Baseball Players Association. Their half-hearted commitment to restoring integrity brings to mind Commissioner Kuhn's assessment of the dilemma that owners faced after the 1919 World Series: "The owners weren't willing to crack down on what had to be cracked down on. Everybody knew there was gambling in the game. Would an owner-commissioner crack down on it?" (The answer's in the history—then and through today.)

In addition to steroids, there are too many other matters that either seem to compromise or else call into question the way baseball goes about its business: the legality of then-interim commissioner Selig's loan from a bank in which Twins owner Carl Pohlad had a significant interest; Major League Baseball's unilateral announcement, in 2001, that it would contract two teams; MLB's purchase of the Expos and its refusal to relocate the team to Washington DC until 2005; the sale of the Red Sox to the *second-*highest bidder, among other questionable transfers of ownership. Finally, what is the function of Major League Baseball, Inc? Maybe we need to define, or at least hear explained, the relationship of the commissioner to the corporation. Though it is perfectly logical—legal!—that, just as major league ballplayers have unionized, major league baseball team owners have incorporated to protect their own interests, that corporation's appropriation of the office of the commissioner of baseball is questionable. Does the office even fall within MLB's mandate? And since the MLBPA has historically stated that it, not the office of the commissioner, represents its membership, MLB's assumed oversight of the office goes unchallenged. MLB does not deserve absolution.

The office of the commissioner of baseball was created by owners as a quasi-public institution dedicated to the protection of the best interests of the game. As generations of owners, players, and fans have seen the functions of the office tweaked to fit the changing times—as, indeed, Commissioner Selig himself has emphasized—the essential mission of the commissioner has never been formally rewritten. If the corporation of Major League Baseball and its twenty-nine team owners now believe that the commissioner's responsibilities have changed so radically as to make the office ineffectual, let them abolish—or abandon—the office in favor of a corporate title. Let them call the person in Commissioner Selig's role the Chief Executive Officer of Major League Baseball, Inc., and be done with the sham, already too apparent. (Consider the frequency with which the corporate voice of CEO Robert DuPuy, among others, purportedly speaks "on behalf of" the commissioner, who is, at best, a paper tiger.) Though MLB has all but trashed the office, it's inconceivable that the corporation will do away with it—bad, *bad* public relations—because, whether or not the office has any suasion over either owners or players, the corporation stands only to gain from fans deluding themselves by believing—even wishing—that the office continues to represent the game's best interests, that it's just like the good old days. It's a great diversionary tactic by a corporation that exists, as do most corporations, only to keep itself alive. And *that's* the loophole that could restore baseball's credibility, as well as the office of the commissioner, the conscience of the office, and—as hard as it is to believe—the legacy of Bud Selig.

It's rare that fans, caught up in the moment, are able to objectively assess their current commissioner. That was as true when Landis was in office as it was during Fay Vincent's or Bowie Kuhn's administrations. That's certainly no less the case for Bud Selig. The only two commissioners who left office unscarred are Landis and Giamatti, both of whom died while serving. Commissioner Selig's challenges, given the role of the union, the corporate powers of Major League Baseball, and his own questionable influence as former owner-commissioner are more difficult than those faced by the previous eight commissioners. Still, Bud Selig is the least popular commissioner in memory.

So, why is Selig and not, say, some independent outsider the man to revitalize the office? And just what exactly am I asking of him?

> He is already commissioner.
> No one in baseball knows the game and its history as well as Bud Selig.
> As anyone inside of baseball will tell you, he's the game's consensus builder; though other commissioners often were overly influenced by one or more powerful owners, Selig has sided with all if he's sided with any. And it will be ownership, *not* its corporate identity, that will swing this vote.
> As a fan at heart, he deserves to *exit* the game as he entered the game: as a fan.

Yes, *exit the game.* Commissioner Selig's mission, should he choose both to initiate and accept it, is to chair a committee that would restructure the office of the commissioner of baseball so it represents and is elected by both owners and players, then step aside in favor of the newly elected commissioner. If you think I'm nuts, I probably am, but I'm still right.

A number of people have made persuasive arguments for fixing "what is wrong" with baseball. Bob Costas, for instance, in his book *Fair Ball* logically argues an impressive case for revenue sharing. But he, and others, who tap into such financial answers are looking outside of baseball. Baseball needs to look and think *inside* the game and its history for a moment—think inside the box (as in Minute Maid Park or the Polo Grounds, AT&T Park, or Griffith Stadium) that is as beautifully illogical as baseball itself. Hear me out. Follow the virtual commissioner one last time.

There is a turning point early in the movie *A Beautiful Mind*, when John Nash, played by Russell Crowe, addresses his clubby Princeton fellows in a local beer joint. The subject of the monologue is a group of women who have just entered. As Nash and his cronies simultaneously eye the most attractive blonde, he cautions against a singularly focused assault. With some other-worldly steel drums humming as background, Nash says: "If we all go for the blonde and block each other, not a single one of us is gonna get her. So then we go for her friends. But they will all give us the cold shoulder because nobody likes to be second choice. But what if no one goes for the blonde? We don't get in each other's way [pause] *and* we don't insult the other girls. That's the only way we win. That's the only way we all get laid.

"Adam Smith said the best result comes from everyone in the group doing what's best for himself. Right? That's what he said, correct? Incomplete! Incomplete! Because the best result would come [even longer pause] from everyone in the group doing what's best for himself *and* the group. . . . Governing dynamics, gentlemen. Governing dynamics. Adam Smith."

Cliff Kachline is not Adam Smith, but as a man who has spent a lifetime involved with baseball his argument for a new commissionership is equally persuasive. "I think Bud *is* looking out, in a sense, for the best interests of baseball, but I think there could be other ways that we, the average fan, would be better protected in many things. First of all, the owners used to have complete control over baseball: you either took what they offered to play for them or you didn't play. The judicial branch of baseball was run by owners, the three-man commission. Finally, you got Judge Landis in there who in a sense was an impartial arbitrator. Which worked fairly well for many years. But then you came into the corporate situation, which muddied it. And then followed the unionization, which has been the big issue in recent years.

"I think it's time that baseball's hierarchy is completely changed," Kachline said, "with the owners having one share and the players union having another share. And between them, they suggest a commissioner. . . . Then the owners and the players have an equal voice in the way baseball is run. And if they can agree, fine; if they can't, as in the case of salary arbitration, we get an impartial arbitrator selected by the two parties to name the commissioner."

Kachline's reasoning may sound idealistic, but he's not crazy. In 1996, Senator Jim Bunning, in his Hall of Fame acceptance speech in Cooperstown, spoke out in favor of baseball's hiring "a commissioner by mutual consent" of players and owners. And Bunning is a Kentucky Republican!

None of this is new, of course. But what I've learned is, very much like collective bargaining and the legality of the reserve clause, it's an argument that's not going away. In this regard, Commissioner Selig's take on baseball's business history bears repeating.

"Certainly, the reserve clause should have been modified five or six decades ago," the commissioner told me. "People had to know the reserve clause wasn't going to last."

In defense of my modest proposal I would remind the commissioner how outside the historical norm a permanent (not an interim) owner-commissioner was. Given the commissioner's appreciation of the game, its history, and the obvious stumbling blocks that stymied its growth over the years, shouldn't he have guided his fellow owners toward a more enlightened business model that would serve everyone in the game? Or at least one by which ownership might avoid the very troublesome issues that sparked six congressional hearings within four years? We're not talking about subverting ownership rights but a good-faith effort at improving an ugly situation.

"I think that any time you can get together on anything and create a bridge," former Seattle Mariners catcher Dan Wilson told me, "it can do nothing but benefit the game. . . . I can't *imagine* how the two of us getting together to pick someone to lead would be anything but beneficial."

So, when Stan Brand—and, I think it's fair to infer, ownership, Major League Baseball, and even the players' union in aggregate—argues that a commissioner chosen by owners and players is "inconsistent with the realities of the collective bargaining agreement," he and everyone else in his camp misses the point. Incomplete! Incomplete!

Selecting an independent commissioner of baseball by mutual consent is *not* a collective bargaining issue but a matter of the best interests of the game, a matter of restoring, once again, the office to its rightful place. MLB will still be governed by a CEO; MLBPA will still represent the players. Their rights are inviolate, as has been determined.

"I don't know if it's possible," said Wilson, formerly the Mariners' team union representative. "I think baseball is in a lot of ways gifted by its traditions and how it holds onto its traditions. But sometimes it's cursed by that. . . . Baseball, a lot of times, is slow to change."

Wilson, like many ballplayers today, is better schooled in baseball history than he's given credit for. It's at least conceivable and worth pondering that Commissioner Selig's strength—his grasp of the game's history and its traditions—might also be his weakness. Wilson's smart, but he is *not* virtual commissioner.

As virtual commissioner, I cede collective bargaining to its proper field of play, the courts of law, once and for all. I cede, as well, salary arbitration and all of the other ugly flotsam and jetsam of baseball's business affairs. Good riddance! Major league baseball is not about money—it only depends on it. That's an important distinction, which is born of the spirit that gave credence to Commissioner Giamatti's reasoning—and to much congressional leniency over baseball's business operations over nearly one hundred years. Because "no individual is superior to the game" the rights of *every* individual, including owners—I never thought I'd say this—deserve protection. Think of it: a commissioner with a mandate to pursue a vision beyond the bottom line; a system that equally supports the corporation of ownership and the union of players; an office that, from time to time, actually takes into consideration the interests of the fans.

As virtual commissioner, I call for a two-year study followed by implementation of a reconfigured office of the commissioner and operational model. With Commissioner Selig chairing a committee of former commissioners (Kuhn, Ueberroth, Vincent) along with representatives of Major League Baseball, the players' association, and two independent slots. Immediately, upon assembly of the commission, ownership and players would confirm its trust with baseball's public by initiating a two-year, 6 percent reduction in ticket prices covered by a one-year freeze in player salaries. (I haven't done the math on this one, but it's not like I'm asking for free parking and beer; and I'm not stealing bread from the tables of the next generation of Boones.) In addition, the group would be tasked with:

> developing a method for players and owners to jointly select the commissioner of baseball;
> establishing the scope of the commissioner's responsibilities while protecting rights of owners and players, including collective bargaining;
> determining term length of office;
> defining areas of oversight under the principle of "the best interests of the game."

Commissioner Selig himself supports a more mature relationship between ownership and players. "Absolutely," he told me. "There should be a different kind of relationship some day. . . . You go back to the whole management/player thing. . . . Its tentacles are deep into the turn of the [twentieth] century. This has always been ugly. Should there be more of a mature relationship? Of course. But we have a ways to go."

Well, let's get going!

Fay Vincent agrees and, in offering at least some measure of hope, his position is worth repeating. "It's going to take some very strong leadership . . . but until that happens baseball is going to have this continuing—and other sports are going to have it too—sort of nineteenth-century fight between capital and labor that most other businesses in this country long ago solved. And they solved it by making the workers partners.

"Eventually, they have to come together. They'd have to form a big overall umbrella corporation, where the players own part of it and the teams own part. The players' future would be affected by the value of the franchises. . . . It shouldn't be hard to work that out, mechanically. . . . But, players should own a piece of the future, because otherwise they don't care about it. . . . And that's unhealthy."

Worse than unhealthy, it could be deadly.

No one I talked to could think of anyone inside of baseball who would want the job of commissioner, or even accept it, in its current configuration. Which is argument enough for a drastic change in how the office is constructed and whom the person in office should represent. Granting players a voice in selecting a commissioner is as radical as what owners did decades ago when they collapsed the national commission in favor of a single autocratic leader charged with protecting the game's best interests. But the times—steriods, integrity—demand nothing less. Besides, Congress really wants baseball to rescue its own self this time. As extreme as a totally representative commissionership sounds to some—or all—factions of the major league baseball business equation, there is a great precedent at work here, an advantage that not even the Mountain himself, Judge Landis, was afforded: eighty-five years of a (mostly) impressive history of growth and progress; three ex-commissioners who can bring their joint wisdom and good conscience of the office to the table; and a current commissioner schooled by no fewer than five of his eight predecessors.

Bud Selig could well be remembered as the *other* commissioner who also turned the game around—for the better. It's up to him. And not nearly so far-fetched.

Labor and management partners at last. What a fitting end, what a great all-American story that MLB could sell and market like the next thirty-game winner. Bud Selig, the native Milwaukeean, could leave the office and its conscience in supportive hands and return to what he was born to do: make a winner of the Brewers, the *old* Joe Hardy but the one we all can live with. Baseball saves more than enough of its greatest moments for the least likely of heroes.

A Chronology of the Office of the Commissioner of Baseball, 1920–2005

Kenesaw Mountain Landis, 1920–1944

SEPTEMBER 22, 1920: A Chicago grand jury investigates allegations that eight White Sox players fixed the 1919 World Series. One week later, Sox owner Charles Comiskey suspends Joe Jackson, Eddie Cicotte, Claude Williams, Buck Weaver, Chick Gandel, Oscar Felsch, Swede Risberg, and Fred McMullin.

NOVEMBER 12, 1920: Major league club owners appoint Kenesaw Mountain Landis as baseball's first commissioner.

AUGUST 2, 1921: Ignoring jury's not-guilty verdict, Commissioner Landis bans the Chicago Eight, the Black Sox, for life.

OCTOBER 16, 1921: Commissioner Landis fines and suspends (into the 1922 season) Babe Ruth and others for participating in postseason barnstorming tour.

OCTOBER 16, 1921: Commissioner Landis declares "gentleman's agreements" between major and minor league clubs illegal.

DECEMBER 20, 1921: At winter meetings, Commissioner Landis's vote is the tiebreaker in favor of instituting a seven-game World Series beginning in 1922.

JANUARY 13, 1922: Commissioner Landis denies Buck Weaver's request for reinstatement.

FEBRUARY 4, 1922: Banned from the game for playing against and with ineligible players, Joe Harris is reinstated by Commissioner Landis, who cites the former Cleveland player's being gassed in World War I as the reason Harris did not follow the commissioner's edict.

FEBRUARY 9, 1922: Commissioner Landis fines Giants, Cardinals, and Tigers for violation of contractual and waiver rules.

MAY 29, 1922: Ruling against the Federal League's Baltimore club, the U.S. Supreme Court decides professional baseball is not interstate commerce.

JULY 7, 1922: Commissioner Landis prohibits major league ball clubs from playing in Montreal.

AUGUST 8, 1922: Commissioner Landis bans Giants spitballer Phil Douglas for pitching an offer to the Cardinals to disappear for the remainder of the season, thereby giving St. Louis an edge in the pennant race.

OCTOBER 5, 1922: Despite the sunlight, and in a foreshadowing of the 2002 All-Star Game, umpires call World Series Game 2 on account of darkness after ten innings. Fans are irate, and police escort Commissioner Landis from the stadium. The next day Landis donates game's gate receipts to charity.

MARCH 8, 1923: Landis reinstates former Giants pitcher Rube Benton. Benton, who signs with Reds, had previously acknowledged that he was aware of the 1919 World Series fix.

APRIL 3, 1923: Oscar Felsch and Swede Risberg fail in their attempt to sue baseball for $400,000 in damages and $6,750 in back salary.

APRIL 18, 1923: Yankee Stadium opens, and 74,217 see Babe Ruth hit three-run homer as Yanks beat Boston 4–1.

OCTOBER 1, 1924: Commissioner Landis bans Giants Jimmy O'Connell for life for attempting to bribe Phillies' Heinie Stand in season-ending series.

DECEMBER 16, 1926: Owners vote Commissioner Landis a raise to $65,000 and extend his term in office by seven years.

JANUARY 27, 1927: Commissioner Landis clears Ty Cobb and Tris Speaker of charges that they threw games in 1917 and 1919.

OCTOBER 29, 1929: U.S. stock market crashes, beginning the Great Depression.

JANUARY 20, 1930: Commissioner Landis forbids major leaguers from participating in professional boxing.

APRIL 28, 1930: Western League hosts first night game in organized baseball.

AUGUST 13, 1932: Commissioner Landis rules that Rogers Hornsby did not illegally "borrow" money from Cubs players.

JANUARY 7, 1933: Citing the Depression and a need to cut all salaries in baseball, Commissioner Landis volunteers to accept pay cut from $65,000 to $39,000.

JULY 6, 1933: Babe Ruth's two-run homer leads AL to 4–2 win over NL in the first All-Star Game.

DECEMBER 12, 1933: Owners vote Commissioner Landis a new seven-year contract.

DECEMBER 31, 1933: Twenty-first Amendment to the U.S. Constitution repeals Prohibition.

JANUARY 19, 1934: Commissioner Landis denies Joe Jackson's appeal for reinstatement in baseball.

SEPTEMBER 13, 1934: Commissioner Landis and Ford Motor Company agree on World Series broadcast rights. For $100,000, Ford becomes the first corporation to purchase such rights.

NOVEMBER 8, 1934: Ford Frick appointed president of the NL.

MAY 24, 1935: At Cincinnati's Crosley Field, Reds down Phillies 2–1 in first night game in major leagues.

FEBRUARY 2, 1936: Ty Cobb, Walter Johnson, Christy Mathewson, Babe Ruth, and Honus Wagner are first players inducted into the new Hall of Fame, which will open in Cooperstown, New York, in three years.

JUNE 15, 1938: Reds' Johnny Vander Meer pitches his second consecutive no-hitter, 6–0 versus Brooklyn Dodgers.

JULY 29, 1938: Following a radio interview in which he says his off-season duties as a police officer involve "beating up niggers and then throwing them in jail," Yankees' Jake Powell is suspended by Commissioner Landis for ten games.

JULY 4, 1939: Lou Gehrig announces to more than sixty thousand fans at Yankee Stadium: "Today, I consider myself the luckiest man on the face of the earth." Gehrig's uniform number, 4, is retired, making him the first major leaguer so honored.

JULY 15, 1939: Following disputed home run call, NL president Frick orders two-foot screens installed on all league foul poles.

AUGUST 26, 1939: At Brooklyn's Ebbets Field, Red Barber announces the first televised major league game.

JULY 17, 1941: Joe DiMaggio's fifty-six-game hitting streak comes to an end.

SEPTEMBER 28, 1941: Going 6 for 8 in a doubleheader, Ted Williams finishes the season at .406.

DECEMBER 7, 1941: U.S. enters World War II following Japan's attack on Pearl Harbor.

JANUARY 15, 1942: Despite the war, and citing need for improved morale, President Roosevelt orders baseball not to cancel the upcoming season.

MAY 31, 1942: When Satchel Paige and Negro Leagues' players beat a team of Dizzy Dean's major leaguers, Commissioner Landis prohibits future exhibitions because they outdraw regularly scheduled major league games.

JULY 15, 1942: Responding to an editorial in the *Daily Worker*, Commissioner Landis says that "there is no rule, formal or informal" barring black ballplayers from Organized Baseball.

AUGUST 6, 1942: The *Sporting News* publishes an editorial supporting segregation of the races in professional baseball. Integration, according to the editorial, would damage both the white and black leagues.

NOVEMBER 23, 1943: Commissioner Landis bans Phillies owner William Cox for betting on his own team.

AUGUST 4, 1944: Commissioner Landis creates the forerunner of the Hall of Fame's Committee on Baseball Veterans.

NOVEMBER 25, 1944: At age seventy-eight, Commissioner Landis dies of a heart attack in a Chicago hospital.

Albert B. "Happy" Chandler, 1945–1951

APRIL 24, 1945: Owners elect Albert "Happy" Chandler as second commissioner of baseball.

MAY 8, 1945: V-E Day. War in Europe ends.

SEPTEMBER 2, 1945: V-J Day. War in Pacific ends.

OCTOBER 23, 1945: Jackie Robinson signs with Dodgers organization.

JUNE 14, 1946: Commissioner Chandler bans players who signed with Mexican League.

JULY 8, 1946: In wake of Mexican League signing, and following a failed attempt by Pirates players to unionize, owners agree to $5,000 minimum salary, $25-a-day spring training expenses, 25 percent maximum pay cuts, and a player pension funded by World Series and All-Star Game revenues.

APRIL 9, 1947: Commissioner Chandler suspends Dodgers manager Leo Durocher for the 1947 season for "moral turpitude."

APRIL 15, 1947: Jackie Robinson breaks the "color line," becoming the first black player in modern history to play in the major leagues.

JULY 5, 1947: Larry Doby becomes the first black American Leaguer with Bill Veeck's Cleveland Indians.

JANUARY 29, 1948: Commissioner Chandler levies $500 fines for signing high school ballplayers on Cubs, Phillies, and Yankees.

SEPTEMBER 2, 1948: Declaring Pittsburgh has violated bonus rules, Commissioner Chandler fines Pirates $2,000.

OCTOBER 27, 1948: Commissioner Chandler rules Detroit attempted to "hide" contracts of ten minor leaguers and grants free agency to all ten.

FEBRUARY 9, 1949: Federal court throws Danny Gardella's $300,000 lawsuit against baseball back to lower courts.

APRIL 28, 1949: Pending assault charge by a fan, Commissioner Chandler suspends Giants manager Durocher. Suspension is lifted when Durocher is found innocent.

JUNE 5, 1949: Commissioner Chandler announces lifting of ban on all players who jumped to the Mexican League.

NOVEMBER 1, 1949: Gillette agrees to purchase advertising rights to World Series for $1.37 million, the money being designated for players' pension plan.

JUNE 29, 1950: U.S. enters Korean War.

DECEMBER 11, 1950: Owners vote not to renew Chandler's contract.

JANUARY 29, 1951: In his swan song to baseball, Commissioner Chandler signs $6 million six-year deal for radio and television rights to World Series and All-Star Game.

MAY 4, 1951: Following suit by former Braves pitcher Jim Prendergast that baseball's reserve clause violates antitrust laws, Rep. Emanuel Celler (NY) announces investigation of baseball's antitrust violations.

JUNE 15, 1951: Commissioner Chandler announces resignation effective July 15, 1951.

JULY 9, 1951: Owners and players agree to retain reserve clause.

JULY 30, 1951: Before Celler's congressional committee, Ty Cobb testifies that reserve clause does not violate players' rights.

AUGUST 6, 1951: In testimony before U.S. Senate, former Commissioner Chandler says nothing new: some owners are in baseball only for money.

Ford Frick, 1951–1965

SEPTEMBER 20, 1951: Owners elect NL president Ford Frick commissioner of baseball for seven years at $65,000 per year.

MAY 22, 1952: Celler's committee announces that baseball can govern itself, a tacit approval of baseball's reserve clause.

JULY 30, 1952: Commissioner Frick establishes waiver rule requiring clubs to offer sale of players' contracts to teams within respective leagues before any interleague sales are allowed.

SEPTEMBER 15, 1952: Soviet Union announces that Russians invented baseball, calling all American major leaguers slaves.

JULY 27, 1953: Armistice signed ending Korean War.

NOVEMBER 9, 1953: U.S. Supreme Court upholds lower-court ruling that baseball is a sport, not a business, and thus not subject to antitrust laws.

NOVEMBER 30, 1953: Players refuse to confer with Commissioner Frick because he refuses to allow their attorney to attend.

MAY 17, 1954: In *Brown v. Board of Education* U.S. Supreme Court outlaws racial segregation in public schools.

OCTOBER 8, 1956: In the only perfect game in World Series history, Yankees Don Larsen beats Dodgers 2–0 on 97 pitches.

DECEMBER 11, 1956: Bob Feller named president of newly formed players' association.

DECEMBER 13, 1956: Refusing to accept trade to Giants, Dodgers Jackie Robinson retires.

FEBRUARY 1, 1957: Following approval of new players' pension fund owners again reject players' request to raise minimum salary from $6,000.

FEBRUARY 25, 1957: U.S. Supreme Court denies National Football League's request for antitrust exemption, claiming that baseball is the only sport deserving of such protection.

JULY 8, 1957: Commissioner Frick's contract is extended through 1965.

JULY 18, 1957: In congressional testimony, Kansas City Athletics owner Arnold Johnson perjures himself, denying having ties to the Yankee owners or that he favored New York in trades.

DECEMBER 4, 1957: Owners repeal bonus rule, raise players' minimum salary to $7,000.

JANUARY 30, 1958: Revoking fans' voting "privileges," Commissioner Frick leaves All-Star Game selections to players, managers, and coaches.

APRIL 15, 1958: Before an opening day crowd of 23,448 fans at Seals Stadium (not the Polo Grounds), the San Francisco (not New York) Giants defeat the Los Angeles (not Brooklyn) Dodgers. Giants win first major league game on the West Coast 8–0.

OCTOBER 13, 1958: Twenty-two Milwaukee Braves players are fined $50 each by Commissioner Frick for revealing the amount of their shares of World Series purse.

JULY 21, 1959: Major league baseball's fields are fully integrated when, in the eighth inning, Red Sox manager Mike "Pinky"

Higgins, an erstwhile segregationist, sends Elijah "Pumpsie" Green in as a pinch runner.

JULY 30, 1959: In $1.8 million suit, Portland (Pacific Coast League) becomes second minor league team to sue major leagues for loss of revenue due to televising of major league games.

AUGUST 2, 1960: Making peace with the AL and NL, the phantom Continental League agrees to "disband" when majors agree to take on four Continental League locations. Within months, NL agrees to New York and Houston, the AL to Washington and Los Angeles.

JULY 18, 1961: With expanded schedule to 162 games, Commissioner Frick rules against the record book: Babe Ruth's single-season sixty-homer record will stand unless broken in 154 games or fewer. (All other records are evidently irrelevant to the former ghostwriter of Ruth's autobiography.)

OCTOBER 1, 1961: Yankees Roger Maris hits his sixty-first home run in 162nd game of the season.

JANUARY 8, 1962: Commissioner Frick rules major leagues have not "blacklisted" former Dodgers right fielder Carl Furillo for earlier salary disagreement with Los Angeles owner Walter O'Malley.

JULY 31, 1962: NL owners say no to Frick's proposal for interleague games.

DECEMBER 3, 1962: Former players file suit to be included in increased pension benefits for ballplayers.

NOVEMBER 22, 1963: President John F. Kennedy assassinated in Dallas.

DECEMBER 4, 1964: Owners vote to restore unlimited powers to office of commissioner, agreeing to accept commissioner's judgment of what's "in the best interest of baseball."

DECEMBER 4, 1964: Right to elect All-Star teams returned to fans; three months later, U.S. sends first combat troops to Vietnam.

William "Spike" Eckert, 1965–1968

NOVEMBER 17, 1965: Commissioner Frick retires; retired Air Force Lt. Gen. William Eckert named fourth commissioner of baseball.

MARCH 5, 1966: Players elect steelworkers' union man Marvin Miller executive director of the Major League Players' Association.

APRIL 11, 1966: In Washington DC, first black umpire, Emmett Ashford, makes his debut as Cleveland beats the Senators 5–2.

FEBRUARY 21, 1968: Players and owners reach first Basic Agreement. Basic minimum salary increases $3,000 to $10,000. Per diem and spring training weekly expenses also increase.

APRIL 8, 1968: Rev. Martin Luther King Jr. assassinated; opening day postponed.

MAY 8, 1968: New York senator Robert F. Kennedy assassinated.

SEPTEMBER 14, 1968: Tigers Denny McLain wins thirtieth game. Finishing season with thirty-one wins, he is first thirty-game winner since Cardinals Dizzy Dean in 1934.

FEBRUARY 6, 1968: Commissioner Eckert resigns.

APRIL 8, 1969: New York Mets are the perfect hosts in bowing to Montreal Expos 11–10 at Shea Stadium in major league baseball's first international game.

Bowie Kuhn, 1969–1984

AUGUST 13, 1969: Owners elect Bowie Kuhn as fifth commissioner of baseball.

JANUARY 16, 1970: Refusing to accept trade to Phillies and contending reserve clause violates federal antitrust laws, St. Louis Cardinals' Curt Flood files suit against commissioner of baseball, AL and NL presidents, and all twenty-four owners.

FEBRUARY 19, 1970: Commissioner Kuhn indefinitely suspends Denny McLain on suspicion of bookmaking.

AUGUST 12, 1970: Federal court upholds reserve clause; Curt Flood loses $4.1 million suit.

OCTOBER 3, 1970: Demanding higher salaries, major league umpires go on one-day strike as postseason playoffs begin.

APRIL 6, 1972: First day of historic strike by major league baseball players.

APRIL 15, 1972: Players return, ending strike after more than eighty games are canceled.

JUNE 18, 1972: U.S. Supreme Court upholds lower court ruling in *Flood v. Kuhn et al.*

DECEMBER 31, 1972: Pirates Roberto Clemente is killed in plane crash off the coast of Puerto Rico.

FEBRUARY 25, 1973: New three-year Basic Agreement includes $15,000 minimum salary, salary arbitration, and "10 and 5" rule (players with minimum ten years in majors and last five with present club may veto any attempt by team to trade them).

MARCH 29, 1973: U.S. withdraws last combat troops from Vietnam.

APRIL 6, 1973: With bases loaded, Boston's Luis Tiant walks New York's Ron Blomberg, thus denying major league baseball's first "designated hitter" an official at bat in his first plate appearance.

AUGUST 9, 1974: President Richard M. Nixon resigns from office.

OCTOBER 3, 1974: Citing George Steinbrenner's conviction for illegal contributions to former president Nixon and others, Commissioner Kuhn suspends Yankees owner from baseball for two years.

JULY 16, 1975: Owners extend Commissioner Kuhn's contract for seven years.

FEBRUARY 4, 1976: A federal judge upholds arbitrator's decision declaring Dodgers pitcher Andy Messersmith a free agent.

MARCH 17, 1976: After owners shut down spring training for more than three weeks, Commissioner Kuhn orders training camps open.

JUNE 18, 1976: Commissioner Kuhn declares Oakland A's sale of Vida Blue (to Yankees) and Rollie Fingers and Joe Rudi (to Red Sox) as "not in the best interests of baseball." A's owner Charlie Finley sues Kuhn for $10 million.

JANUARY 2, 1977: Commissioner Kuhn suspends Braves owner Ted Turner for one year for "tampering" in signing free agent Gary Matthews.

APRIL 7, 1978: In second appeal, federal court upholds Commissioner Kuhn's negation of sale of Blue, Fingers, and Rudi.

AUGUST 25, 1978: AL and NL umpires strike. Restraining order brings them back the next day, but amateur and semipro umps work spring training games when major league umpires walk out again two weeks later.

MARCH 9, 1979: Commissioner Kuhn opens all locker rooms to reporters, irrespective of sex.

AUGUST 23, 1979: Commissioner Kuhn charges Ray Kroc with tampering with free-agents-to-be Graig Nettles and Joe Morgan and fines Padres' owner $100,000.

OCTOBER 27, 1979: For accepting position with casino operator Bally, Commissioner Kuhn suspends Hall of Fame center fielder Willie Mays. Three years later, as a lame duck commissioner, Kuhn will also suspend another former center fielder and Hall of Famer, Mickey Mantle, under similar charges.

MAY 23, 1980: Within hours of strike deadline, players and owners sign new Basic Agreement, which increases players' minimum salary to $30,000 and boosts clubs' contributions to the players' pension plan.

JUNE 12, 1981: Players union boss Marvin Miller announces strike, which will extend into August and cause cancellation of more than seven hundred games.

NOVEMBER 1, 1982: Owners' vote not to renew Commissioner Kuhn's contract.

NOVEMBER 22, 1983: Donald Fehr named executive director of Major League Baseball Players Association.

DECEMBER 15, 1983: Commissioner Kuhn suspends for one

season Dodgers pitcher Steve Howe and Royals Willie Wilson, Willie Aikens, and Jerry Martin for conviction for using illegal drugs.

MARCH 3, 1984: Owners elect Peter Ueberroth to five-year term as commissioner, as of October 1.

JULY 26, 1984: For his cocaine possession conviction (11/83), Vida Blue is suspended by Commissioner Kuhn for balance of season.

Peter Ueberroth, 1984–1988

OCTOBER 7, 1984: After less than a week on the job and after four games of NL championship series, Commissioner Ueberroth ends umpires' weeklong strike.

MARCH 18, 1985: Commissioner Ueberroth reinstates baseball eligibility to Mays and Mantle.

AUGUST 6, 1985: First and final day of players' strike.

FEBRUARY 28, 1986: Commissioner Ueberroth brings up twenty-one players on charges of illegal drug use.

JUNE 10, 1986: Yale University president and commissioner-to-be A. Bartlett "Bart" Giamatti named successor to NL president Chub Feeney.

FEBRUARY 25, 1987: With the "collusion era" in gear and a "super station tax" on four clubs worth millions, Commissioner Ueberroth suspends Padres' LaMarr Hoyt for upcoming season for repeated illegal drug charges. Suspension is later reduced to sixty days by arbitrator, but Hoyt will never pitch in the majors again.

APRIL 1, 1987: After testing cocaine-positive, Mets' pitching sensation Dwight Gooden sidesteps suspension by entering drug rehab.

JANUARY 22, 1988: Arbitrator rules in favor of Players Association in lawsuit over collusion.

MARCH 30, 1988: Cocaine troubles earn Reds Eddie Milner a season-long suspension from Commissioner Ueberroth. Three

months later the commissioner will suspend Expos Floyd You-
mans for violation of drug-testing agreement.

AUGUST 31, 1988: Arbitrator again rules in favor of players ("Collusion II"), who contend owners conspired to rig free agent
market between 1986 and 1987 seasons.

SEPTEMBER 8, 1988: Two months after Commissioner Ueberroth announces he will not finish his five-year term of office,
NL President Giamatti named to succeed him.

FEBRUARY 21, 1989: Initial meeting of Commissioner Ueberroth,
Giamatti, and Pete Rose regarding Reds manager's gambling.

A. Bartlett "Bart" Giamatti, April 1, 1989–September 1, 1989

AUGUST 24, 1989: Commissioner Giamatti bans Pete Rose from
baseball for life.

SEPTEMBER 1, 1989: The day after arbitrator rules owners must
pay $10.5 million in damages for collusion against free agents
following 1985 season, Commissioner Giamatti, age fifty-one,
dies of heart attack.

Fay Vincent, 1989–1992

SEPTEMBER 13, 1989: Owners elect Giamatti's deputy commissioner, Fay Vincent, eighth commissioner of baseball.

OCTOBER 17, 1989: Earthquake forces ten-day delay of San Francisco versus Oakland World Series.

MARCH 18, 1990: Thirty-two-day spring training lockout ends as
owners and players sign new Basic Agreement, which includes
$100,000 minimum annual salary.

JULY 30, 1990: Commissioner Vincent orders resignation of Yankees owner George Steinbrenner.

DECEMBER 7, 1990: *New York Times* reports owners to pay $280
million in collusion damages to players.

FEBRUARY 4, 1991: Hall of Fame declares Pete Rose ineligible
for as long as he is banned from baseball.

MARCH 20, 1991: Commissioner Vincent puts Phillies Lenny Dykstra on probation for one year for gambling.

JUNE 15, 1991: Former commissioner Happy Chandler, ninety-two, dies of heart attack at home in Versailles, Kentucky.

SEPTEMBER 4, 1991: Thirty years after breaking Babe Ruth's single-season home run record, Roger Maris's sixty-one is ruled "official" by Commissioner Vincent.

JUNE 24, 1992: Commissioner Vincent bans pitcher Steve Howe from baseball for life for a series of illegal drug charges over a ten-year period.

JULY 23, 1992: Commissioner Vincent's mandatory NL realignment is halted by federal judge.

SEPTEMBER 3, 1992: Owners' vote calls for resignation of Commissioner Vincent.

Alan H. "Bud" Selig, 1992–

SEPTEMBER 9, 1992: Brewers owner Alan H. "Bud" Selig named chair of owners' executive council. The next day he is appointed "acting" commissioner of baseball.

FEBRUARY 11, 1994: Owners vote to amend powers of commissioner and negate his "best interests" authority. Acting Commissioner Selig describes the office as being "strengthened."

MARCH 21, 1994: U.S. senator Howard Metzenbaum (D-OH), in a Florida hearing on baseball's antitrust exemption, says that baseball's new Basic Agreement has "denigrated" the office of the commissioner of baseball.

JUNE 28, 1994: Following failure of second drug test, Mets' Dwight Gooden suspended for sixty days.

AUGUST 12, 1994: Players strike.

SEPTEMBER 14, 1994: Owners vote 26–2 (Baltimore's Peter Angelos and Cincinnati's Marge Schott dissenting) to cancel remainder of season, postseason play, and World Series.

DECEMBER 14, 1994: Players Association files complaint with National Labor Relations Board that owners withheld nearly $8 million due players' pension fund.

JANUARY 1, 1995: Owners lock out all NL and AL umpires.

JANUARY 13, 1995: Acting Commissioner Selig publicly supports use of "replacement" players in upcoming season.

FEBRUARY 17, 1995: Acting Commissioner Selig suspends Tigers manager Sparky Anderson for refusing to manage replacement players.

MARCH 19, 1995: With little hope of resolving strike, owners unanimously vote for Arizona Diamondbacks and Tampa Bay Devil Rays to join the NL and AL, respectively, in '98.

APRIL 2, 1995: Longest strike in sports history to date ends as owners accept players' terms. Season to open April 25.

SEPTEMBER 6, 1995: With his 2,131st consecutive game played, Cal Ripken breaks Lou Gehrig's "Iron Man" record.

SEPTEMBER 29, 1995: Federal appeals court rules owners acted illegally in attempting to eliminate free agency, etc.

JUNE 12, 1996: Owners vote to remove Reds owner Marge Schott from day-to-day team oversight.

OCTOBER 4, 1996: In wake of Roberto Alomar spitting incident, federal judge issues injunction to keep umpires from walking out. Elsewhere, another federal judge dismisses three-year major leaguer (and former Negro Leagues' player) Sam Jethroe's plea for pension benefits. (Current rules grant eligibility after one day of major league play.)

NOVEMBER 27, 1996: Owners approve new collective bargaining agreement, which includes payroll or "luxury" taxes based on amount of team payroll spending.

JANUARY 19, 1997: Owners grant pension benefits to nearly one hundred former Negro Leagues' players and black major leaguers who, because of racial barriers, did not qualify for pension during their careers.

FEBRUARY 28, 1997: Federal judge rules that Bud Selig is *not* commissioner of baseball. Two weeks later owners and players sign new five-year collective bargaining agreement.

JUNE 12, 1997: In first regular season interleague game, San Francisco beats Texas, 4–3, in Arlington, Texas.

NOVEMBER 5, 1997: In the first switch of leagues by a team in modern baseball, Acting Commissioner Selig "realigns" his own Milwaukee Brewers from AL to NL.

JULY 9, 1998: Acting Commissioner Selig named ninth commissioner of baseball.

SEPTEMBER 8, 1998: Mark McGwire breaks Roger Maris's single-season record, hitting sixty-second homer of year in St. Louis off Cubs' Steve Trachsel.

SEPTEMBER 13, 1998: With two homers against Brewers, Cubs Sammy Sosa also surpasses Maris.

SEPTEMBER 27, 1998: Against Expos, in final game of season, McGwire's two home runs give him single-season record of seventy.

SEPTEMBER 18, 1999: In Chicago, Sosa becomes first player to hit sixty home runs in two or more seasons. Two weeks later McGwire will overtake Sosa to finish season with sixty-five to Sammy's sixty-three.

DECEMBER 21, 1999: Commissioner Selig suspends Dodgers' Dominican operations for signing of underage Adrian Beltre.

AUGUST 23, 1999: Commissioner Selig announces that Pete Rose, banned from baseball since 1989, will be invited to World Series if he is elected to the All-Century Team.

SEPTEMBER 15, 1999: Owners agree on merger of AL and NL administrative operations. League presidents Leonard Coleman and Gene Budig will serve as senior advisers to commissioner.

JANUARY 19, 2000: Owners grant Commissioner Selig unlimited powers so that "there is an appropriate level of long-term competitive balance among the clubs."

JANUARY 20, 2000: Owners agree to cede all Internet rights to the commissioner's office, with income divided equally among all thirty clubs.

JANUARY 31, 2000: Commissioner Selig suspends Braves reliever John Rocker until May 1 for racial and ethnic slurs in a *Sports Illustrated* profile.

FEBRUARY 28, 2000: Commissioner Selig suspends Darryl

Strawberry for one year after Yankees OF tests positive for co-caine.

OCTOBER 28, 2001: Commissioner Selig announces the possibility of "contracting" two clubs prior to start of upcoming season.

NOVEMBER 27, 2001: Owner's extend Commissioner Selig's contract through 2006.

APRIL 9, 2002: In his hometown of Milwaukee, Commissioner Selig "calls" All–Star Game at 7–7 tie.

AUGUST 19, 2004: Owners extend Commissioner Selig's contract through 2009.

Also by Larry Moffi
available in a Bison Books
edition:

*Crossing the Line: Black
Major Leaguers, 1947–1949*
(with Jonathan Krondstadt)

Also by the author:

NON-FICTION

*This Side of Cooperstown:
An Oral History of Major
League Baseball in the 1950s*

POETRY

A Citizen's Handbook

A Simple Progression

Homing In

DATE DUE

Demco, Inc. 38-293